SOCIAL PROCESSES AND RELATIONSHIPS:
A FORMAL APPROACH

THE REYNOLDS SERIES IN SOCIOLOGY

Larry T. Reynolds, *Editor*

by **GENERAL HALL, INC.**

Social Processes and Relationships:
A FORMAL APPROACH

Carl J. Couch
University of Iowa

GENERAL HALL, INC.
Publishers
5 Talon Way
Dix Hills, New York 11746

SOCIAL PROCESSES AND RELATIONSHIPS: A FORMAL APPROACH

GENERAL HALL, INC.
5 Talon Way
Dix Hills, New York 11746

Copyright © 1989 by General Hall, Inc.

Publisher: Ravi Mehra
Consulting Editor: Anand Sinha
Composition: *Graphics Division,* General Hall, Inc.

LIBRARY OF CONGRESS CATALOG CARD NUMBER: 87-82055

ISBN: 0-930390-87-3 [paper]
0-930390-88-1 [cloth]

Manufactured in the United States of America

TO THE MEMORY OF MY MOTHER

You have to remember,
they are human too.

Lena H. Couch

My mother was capable of detecting humaneness even in the most base; she insisted upon seeing the best in all. She recognized that human beings often acted meanly toward one another. In her ideal world, that would not occur. When it did occur, and when those who perpetrated acts of meanness were justly cursed, she always attempted to soften the judgment. Throughout our long relationship, she persisted in noting the humane elements and minimizing the evil ones. I am thankful for her long and loving counsel, but I have never been able to adopt her benign standpoint toward all. Even that she could accept — although she obviously wished it were otherwise.

Contents

1 Becoming Social   1

2 Acquiring Temporal Structures   16

3 Touch, Discourse, and Appearance   30

4 Basic Elements of Sociation   47

5 Elementary Forms of Social Action   57

6 Interpersonal Accountability   70

PREFACE

Social forms, not norms, are the primary concern of this book. Many introductory textbooks in the social sciences focus on culture — norms, values and beliefs. Others emphasize what people say and do. Both of these approaches emphasis content. In contrast, this statement draws attention to the formal properties of social encounters and relationships. The objective is to provide students with a frame of thought that they can use to analyze, interpret, and evaluate social encounters and relationships. Each social encounter and each social relationship is unique. Nonetheless, if a formal mode of thought is applied to social activities, it is possible to detect transsituational similarities and systematically note transsituational differences.

The book does not review the current competing theories of social science. Instead social processes and relationships occupy center stage. The phenomena analyzed range in complexity and intensity from ephemeral accommodative encounters to enduring romantic relationships.

The dyad — two individuals capable of independent action but acting interdependently — is the basic unit of analysis. Whenever dyadic activity is produced two individuals simultaneously influence one another. However, when people construct social encounters the reciprocating lines of influence are often highly asymmetrical. When an encounter is contextualized by a tyrannical relationship, the actions of the tyrant usually have greater consequences for the victim than the actions of the victim for the tyrant. Nonetheless, each of them influences the other. In contrast, when an encounter is contextualized by a solidary relationship, the degree of influence of each on the other tends to be symmetrical. Both symmetrical and asymmetrical encounters and relationships are analyzed.

Many textbooks address many of the same phenomena as those examined in this statement. The concepts "the individual" and "society" are two central concepts of many social science textbooks. The paradigm implied by the concepts "the individual" and "society" is fundamentally in error. The individual and society do not interact. Much, but not all, interaction is produced by two individuals reciprocally attending and being responsive to each other. Of course, how a dyad, triad, or larger collectivity interact within each social encounter reflects the symbols, definitions, programs of action, and social linkages that the members who populate an encounter bring to it. Nonetheless most of our social experiences are derived from social encounters wherein two people align their actions to produce social processes. Others may or may not be present. Even when others are present, most of the time we act toward or with one other person. The actions of dyads, not that of individuals or society, are analyzed in this book.

In recent years many students of social life, including microfunctionalists, symbolic interactionists, conversational analysts, and students of interpersonal communication, have come to recognize that face-to-face encounters are the heart and soul of social life. One consequence of that recognition is that most recently developed theories of social conduct concentrate on interpersonal processes. This emphasis stands in sharp contrast to the more traditional theories, which concentrate on culture, values, institutions, norms, and attitudes. The newly emerging theories of human conduct recognize that humans make their culture, as well as being made by it. Hopefully this book demonstrates the utility of analyzing social life from the latter standpoint.

The concepts and principles offered herein are derivatives of an intellectual tradition that reaches beyond the writings of George Herbert Mead and Georg Simmel. But the book is not a reiteration of the ideas of Mead and Simmel. Instead it rests upon research and theorizing that has extended and elaborated that tradition. Instructors who wish to familarize themselves with that research and theorizing might consult *Constructing Social Life* and *Studies in Symbolic Interaction: The Iowa School*. The present book does not presume any prior knowledge on the part of the student. It only presumes an interest in acquiring a greater understanding of social phenomena.

The processes of becoming social are the first topics addressed. The first three chapters discuss processes commonly dealt with under the rubric of socialization. They address how the human infant acquires the abilities to act with others, as well as respond to the actions of others. The transactions produced by children and adults are for the most part asymmetrical; the adult is the dominant member of most encounters between children and adults.

Chapters 4 through 8 attend to forms of social action. These chapters specify the elements of sociation that two people must establish if they are to fit together their individual lines of action to produce units of social action. Each element of sociation is a joint production. An individual may act, but only a dyad can produce social responsiveness, mutually recognized differences, social objectives, agreements, and other elements of sociation.

The discussion of socialization processes and forms of social action proceed from the simple to the complex. For example, a discussion of significant gestures precedes a discussion of significant symbols, not because significant gestures are more important than significant symbols,

but because children must master significant gestures before they can acquire command of significant symbols. In a similar manner, the discussion
of the chase (predator—prey) precedes the discussion of cooperative
behavior. Again, this is not because the chase is the more important form of
social action, but because the chase is a simpler form of social activity than
cooperation.

Chapter 9 is a transition chapter that prepares the student for the
analysis of forms of social relationships discussed in the following chapters.
Issues addressed in chapters 10 through 18 presume a familarity with concepts
introduced in the earlier chapters. Social relationships are more complex
phenomena than are forms of social action. Children are capable of rather
complex forms of social action before they are sophisticated enough to construct social relationships and act within the context provided by social relationships.

The two most basic social relationships, parental and solidary, are
described and analyzed first. The universalism of these two relationships,
all known human societies have them, indicates that they are the fundamental
social relationships. The order of presentation of the other forms of social
relationships is less securely grounded. Instructors may wish to vary the
order of these later topics.

No attempt is made to provide a "causal explanation" of human activity.
Such undertakings are foolhardy and doomed to failure. Exactly how the
belief became established among many social scientists that a scientific explanation, ipso facto, was a causal explanation is an interesting question
but beyond the scope of this preface. But I will observe that the issue is not
what, or what series of whats, cause human behavior; instead the issue is:
How is social life possible? The more specific questions that follow from
that general one are these: How do individuals align their actions to produce social encounters? How are social relationships constructed,
modified, and destroyed? What are the consequences of different forms of
social action? What are the consequences of different forms of social relationships? What alternative forms of social action and social relationships
are possible? What might be the consequences of alternative forms?

Generations before us have contributed to the construction of the social
forms that we currently use and that constrain us. We have little understanding
of the constituent parts of the social forms we use to organize our lives and
others use to organize their (and our) lives. Nor do we, as yet, have much
understanding of the consequences of various social forms. Perhaps if we
change the question from What structures our lives? to How do our lives
become structured? and What are some of the consequences of the structures
we use to organize our lives? we may acquire more insight into the human
condition than we now have. It was to serve that purpose that this textbook
was written.

ACKNOWLEDGMENTS

The theoretical writings of George Herbert Mead and Georg Simmel were given greater substance by several years of empirical research supported by the Center for Research on Interpersonal Behavior (CRIB) at the University of Iowa. Of the many who participated in those studies I am especially appreciative of the contributions of Stan Saxton, Mark Scharlett, Mark Wardell, Steve Norland, Dan Miller, Bob Hintz, Marilyn Leichty, Glenda Sehested, Marion Weiland, Frank Kohout, Steve Buban, Ron Neff, Barbara Sink, Stu Stover, Nawal Lutffyia, Laurel Traynowics, Monica Hardesty, Mike Katovich, Joel Powell, and Mari Molseed. The assessments, suggestions, and encouragements of Richard Travisano, Steve Wieting, Paul Durrenburger, Bob Stewart, Norm Denzin, Peter Hall, David Maines, Emily Paynter, Clark McPhail, and Chuck Tucker were important contributions.

Chapter 1 Becoming Social

Human infants are not social beings. They are the products of social events, but they are not capable of social activity. If they are properly cared for, they may acquire the abilities to participate in social affairs. But that will occur only if other people protect, feed, nurture, and socialize them for the first several years of their lives. Not all infants are given care. A few are abandoned. On occasion, an infant survives as a biological organism but is not given the care necessary to transform her into a competent social being.

All infant mammals depend on others for survival; they must be nursed. The degree and length of the dependency of human infants is greater and more extended than that of any other newborn. Human infants are entirely at the mercy of others for several years. The transformation of a human infant into a competent human being requires that at least one adult treat the infant as a precious object, be sensitive to the requirements for biological survival, and responsive to the infant's behavior.

If others are sensitive to the requirements necessary for biological survival, but are not responsive to the infant's behavior, the infant may survive as a biological organism but will not develop into a human being. The transformation of infants into human beings is not the consequence of either maturation or the infant's environment. Human infants are transformed into competent human beings through a series of extended and complex transactions between the infant and other human beings.

The newborn infant is immobile and cannot act on her environment. Survival depends on others responding to and acting toward the infant. Both maturation and the transactions between the infant and others are necessary for the infant to become a social being.

Some appreciation of the importance of transactions between infants and caregivers for transforming the human organism into a human being can be acquired by imagining the following: Suppose at birth an infant boy was separated from all human contact and arrangements were made to assure his survival. (Given current medical expertise, it is possible to arrange for the necessary intake of food and disposal of waste products in a sterile environment devoid of human contact.) No one touched the infant, appeared before him, manipulated him, responded in any way to his movements, nor talked to him. It is possible that the infant could survive for several years. Presume for the purpose of our imaginary experiment that he did live for

1

several years. Then, perhaps after ten or twelve years, the life- supporting equipment was removed. What would the boy do? Would he seek out food? Would he call for help? Would he walk?

He would, in fact, be a big baby. He would not be able to walk, feed himself, or act with others. Maturation does not automatically produce any of these behaviors. Biological maturation releases constraints, but it does not result in structured behavior.

Infants behave. They respond to internal and external stimuli. But these actions do not provide the foundation for human development. Unless infants are made part of a social context by other human beings, they will never learn to walk, talk, or even feed themselves. These basic activities develop only as the consequence of transactions between infants and others. They do not automatically unfold as the infant matures as a biological organism.

The acquisition of the skills necessary to become a competent social being proceeds through four distinctive stages: (1) acquiring command of significant gestures; (2) mastering significant symbols; (3) becoming a self-conscious person; and (4) becoming conscious of social structures. Movement through each stage provides a necessary foundation for the emergence of the next. For example, the child cannot master significant symbols until she has achieved some sophistication in the use of significant gestures; nor can a child acquire consciousness of social structures until after she has acquired self-consciousness.

Significant Gestures

The first major hurdle toward becoming a social being is overcome when the infant acquires command of significant gestures. The acquisition of significant gestures is not the accomplishment of the infant, nor is it something provided by others. Significant gestures emerge from transactions between the infant and others. Both parties contribute to the accomplishment. Significant gestures are a creation of the infant and at least one other person. It requires a dyad, two interacting individuals, to establish significant gestures; they are not created by an individual. The acquisition of significant gestures depends on the infant's "initiating" action and others responding to the infant's action.

Although immobile, infants can elicit activity from others. Infants sometimes elicit activity toward themselves by responding to internal and external stimuli. These responses are expressive gestures; they reflect feeling states. Or, at least some of the responses are defined as reflecting feeling states by adults charged with the responsibility of protecting and caring for infants. Infants, of course, do not define their expressive gestures as reflecting feeling states. They are not capable of defining them. The most common expressive gesture of infants that elicits action from others toward them is crying. Early crying is not a significant gesture; it is a response to discontent. Crying often is assigned "meaning" by those responsible for caring for infants. Parents commonly respond to the cries of infants by assuming they "want" something. Parents make such assessments as "the baby wants to be fed" to the expressive gesture of crying long before infants can produce a significant gesture.

If the caregiver's responses to an infant's expressive gestures are relatively consistent, the infant acquires the awareness that she can elicit a response from others. An infant who achieves this level of sophistication is participating in a conversation of gestures (Mead 1934). The infant cries and anticipates a response. She acts to elicit a specific activity from another person.

Significant gestures are joint accomplishments. The child initiates a sequence, and the parent attempts to complete the sequence. Significant gestures are established when the action taken by the caregiver modifies the condition that led to the initial act by the infant. The caregiver must locate that part of the infant's environment that stimulated the original act and modify it before the infant can develop a significant gesture.

Parents often have difficulty in completing their "half" of the sequence. Many times, parents act toward the crying infant in an effort to satisfy the child, but are unable to locate what is "causing" the crying. Both infant and parent continue to act; the child continues to cry, and the parent continues to search for the source of the difficulty. Both are frustrated. Sometimes, parents give up the search; other times, the infant "cries herself out."

When the parent is successful in altering the infant's experience, then a third event is produced: The infant discontinues crying. The parent is thereby informed that the child's field of experience has changed; only when the condition that produced the crying in the first place is changed is a foundation for significant gestures provided.

Sequences of this sort require that the child and the parent attend to and act toward a common focus. The infant cries and the parent attempts to modify the infant's field of experience. On this level of interaction there is no sharing of experiences. The experiences of the infant and the parent are different.

The production of the earliest significant gestures requires that the parent subordinate herself to the "demands" of the infant. The parent must attend to the child and act toward whatever stimulated the child. The infant controls the sequence. The construction of the early three-step sequences are usually intertwined with a wide variety of other activities. The parent attempting to modify the experiences of the infant often does a number of different things to the infant that do not significantly modify the infant's experience. In due time, however, most parents learn to locate the source of the difficulty quickly, then parent and child can easily and rapidly produce the sequence of acts that constitute a significant gesture.

The establishment of significant gestures allows infant and parent to link their actions together. When a significant gesture has been established, the infant has taken the first step toward becoming a social being. The infant is no longer merely responding to the environment; nor is the parent simply acting toward the infant. Instead they are fitting together reciprocating acts. The infant who acquires command of significant gestures is no longer merely a precious object, but has completed the first step toward becoming a human being.

The production of significant gestures is not limited to crying. Many different acts can serve as the initiating act for the establishment of a significant gesture. For example, an infant boy sucked his fist. The act was noted by his mother. She assigned the meaning "he wants to be fed" to the infant's fist sucking. In due time, whenever the infant was hungry, he would suck his fist; his mother noting that, would nurse him. The infant never cried to be fed, although on occasion he violently sucked his fist before his mother nursed him.

After a number of sequences initiated by the infant have been produced, then the parent may initiate sequences that become significant gestures. For example, the mother of an infant girl appeared in the visual field of the child and extended her arms as if to pick up the child. But the mother did not pick up the child until she extended her arms toward the mother. Once the infant has learned to respond in a patterned manner to initiations on the part of the parent, then both infant and parent may initiate a sequence that constitutes a significant gesture.

Significant gestures, in contrast to expressive gestures, are not merely acts produced by an infant; they are transactions. Crying and cooing are not originally significant gestures; they are first expressive gestures. Not until an act elicits an anticipated response from another is an expressive gesture transformed into a significant gesture.

As the infant acquires awareness of sequences that constitute significant gestures, it is possible for the infant to respond to and act toward sequences of acts. This level of complexity is present when the child acts and then notes if the anticipated event is forthcoming. If it is not, then the infant reproduces the original act. The child who cries and then stops to listen and then cries again when no one approaches is assessing the significance of her crying. The child is no longer acting solely to elicit a response, but is organizing actions on the basis of the fit between what is anticipated and the responses of others to the action.

Significant gestures are based on the absence, as well as on the presence, of an event. The absence of a desired event (e.g., the parent coming to the infant) is now an event that also has meaning. This level of sophistication involves an infant assessing her own behavior, the behavior of another and the fit between them. The infant who has acquired this ability cannot yet act with others, but can act toward others and respond to the actions others take toward her.

The emergence of significant gestures greatly extends the powers of infant. They learn that they can partially control the future by their own action. They do not understand the processes involved, but they learn that their own actions can significantly modify their world. They learn that by crying they can entice others to take action toward them. The degree of control infants have over their own futures depends upon their parents' responsiveness to them. But, of course, young infants are unaware of that.

As an infant and another establish significant gestures they become socially linked to each other. The earliest significant gestures are limited to the dyad that produces them. When the early significant gestures become stabilized and elaborated infants begin to use them in encounters with others. Then significant gestures are no longer limited to the dyad that originally established them.

Significant Symbols

The line between infancy and childhood is somewhat arbitrary, but then so is the division between day and night. There is always a period of twilight as day becomes night. The transformation from infancy to childhood occurs as the infant acquires command of significant symbols. That transformation does not occur overnight. The emergence of the first significant symbols, like the emergence of the first significant gestures, is a gradual process. And it rests on a foundation provided by the mastery of significant gestures. Children cannot acquire mastery of significant symbols until after they have mastered at least some significant gestures.

Both maturation and the socialization processes that establish significant gestures are necessary before significant symbols can be mastered. Intensive efforts by parents can speed up the acquisition of significant symbols, but significant symbols cannot be mastered until after children have matured sufficiently to have greater control over their behavior than that necessary for the mastery of significant gestures.

Whereas significant gestures arise in the transactions between the infant and a caregiver that are linked to a common focus, the acquisition of symbols requires that common foci be transformed into shared foci. When the relatedness between the infant and the caregiver is limited to significant gestures, the infant produces an act that elicits a response from another that modifies the infant's behavior. Both are acting toward a common focus. When the transactions are limited to this form of interaction, the experiences of the infant and the caregiver are different. There is no sharing of experience.

The emergence of significant symbols requires that the infant and the caregiver *share* experiences. Before an infant and another can share experiences, they must establish a shared focus. A shared focus is established when some event or object is attended to by both the infant and the caregiver, and each is aware that the other is attending to the same event or object. Long before the emergence of significant symbols, the infant can respond differentially toward the environment and call for specific acts from another. Neither of these activities involves sharing experiences with another. When the infant cries or fusses in response to a messy diaper and elicits the response of the parent changing the diaper, there is no sharing of experiences. The experiences of the child and the caregiver are personal, not social.

Nonetheless, transactions of that sort lay the foundation for the establishment of significant symbols. Through a multitude of conversations of gestures, the infant and the caregiver slowly become aware that they are attending to the same events and objects. An essential feature of the emergence of significant symbols is the establishment of co-orientation. Both the infant and the caregiver attend to some event or object and establish mutual awareness of the fact that both of them are attending to the same phenomenon. They become aware that they share experiences.

When child and caregiver relate through significant gestures, the child is aware of her impact on others and the consequences her actions have for subsequent experiences. But the consciousness is that of an individual; it is not a social consciousness. As significant symbols are established, children acquire a social consciousness. They have a consciousness that is partly shared with at least one other person.

Significant symbols are established in two different ways. Sometimes they are established by the caregiver manipulating the child to focus the child's attention on some event or object. The caregiver then produces an act, typically but not necessarily a verbal act, that is linked to the shared focus. When these efforts are first undertaken, the child, of course, does not link the verbal act of the parent to the shared focus. But, if the parent persists and repeats the sequence often enough, the child usually comes to make the same linkages as the parent.

The second general procedure is for the parent to note that the child is attentive to some event or object; the parent then aligns her attentiveness and action with that of the child. For example, the parent may see the child is playing with a ball. The parent then places herself in a parallel fashion with the child toward the ball and utters the word "ball." When such actions are first taken, they are disruptive. The child typically re-allocates attention from the ball to the parent. If the parent is persistent, however, after many trials the child will eventually attend to the ball and simultaneously become aware of the fact that the parent is also attending to the ball.

The emergence of significant symbols requires the establishment of a triangular relation. Child and caregiver must be attentive to each other and to some third object or event. During the early stages of the development of significant symbols, the child has difficulty attending to both the caregiver and a third object. Once children have mastered the ability to attend to both another person and a third object, then additional significant symbols can be acquired quite rapidly.

The establishment of co-orientation toward a shared focus is necessary before a significant symbol can be established. But more is required. A significant symbol is not established until both child and caregiver link an activity, usually a verbal act, to an object or event.

The child has taken the first step toward acquiring command of a significant symbol when the caregiver utters a distinctive sound and the child attends to the object the caregiver has designated. For example, when the caregiver says "dog", the child who looks for the dog has begun to master that symbol. Then co-orientation follows from an act produced by the caregiver. The child truly has command of a significant symbol when she utters a sound toward another person, looks at the other person to note the orientation of the other, and the other person attends to the event or object designated by the child.

Significant symbols are "indicative gestures." They not only call for the attention of another but also indicate to another what the other person should attend to (Denzin 1977a, 96). The earliest significant symbols often are combinations of verbal and nonverbal acts. As the child acquires greater command of speech, nonverbal acts recede to the background, and the child uses only verbal acts to direct the attention of others. The first few significant symbols are shared with only one other person. Usually, only the child and the person who has primary responsibility for the child's care can communicate with each other. No one else "understands" the child.

The earliest symbols also are highly situational. The production of co-orientation between a child just beginning to master a significant symbol and the caregiver is usually contingent on the context. Sometimes the same utterance is used to refer to a variety of objects. For example, a two year old child used the word "baby" to refer to her younger sister, dolls, any small children she observed, and to herself. Yet, in most instances, the utterance "baby" produced co-orientation. The utterances of "baby" were contextualized by the immediate situation and nonverbal activities that usually made the "meaning" of the utterance apparent (Denzin 1977a,61).

Symbolic acts are not limited to verbal acts. They can take a wide variety of forms. Deaf-mutes acquire significant symbols without the benefit of speech. The critical feature of significant symbols is that they elicit co-orientation. They are acts produced with the anticipation of eliciting a specific orientation from another.

When a significant symbol is produced, it simultaneously calls for the attention of another and directs the attention of another. The child who has acquired command of significant symbols is no longer restricted to acting in a particular way and hoping the parent will take the correct action; the child can then take action that will specify the content of the desired action. The child can say "bottle," or some approximation of it, and anticipate receiving the bottle.

The emergence of significant symbols requires the prior establishment of shared foci. When significant symbols are established, children are no longer merely encased within a social environment, they become a part of the social fabric. They can then act with others, as well as respond to and act toward others.

Consciousness of Self

Self-consciousness begins in others. Others are conscious of infants long before infants become aware of themselves. Each infant is assigned a series of identities by others. The infant, of course, has no awareness of these identities. But as the infant acquires mastery of significant symbols and becomes incorporated into the social fabric, she becomes aware of the assigned identities and uses some of them to characterize herself. When that occurs, the child becomes conscious of self; she acquires a self-conception.

Nearly all infants are assigned the categorical identity of male or female at birth. They are also categorized as members of a specific family, or at least the offspring of a specific person. Most infants are also given a number of other categorical identities. These include first child, newest member of the family, citizen of the U.S., first female child, and first grandchild. Most of the time, those who care for the child are in agreement on what categorical identities are to be applied to the child, although on occasion there are disagreements.

The newest member of a family may be categorized as a "spoiled brat" by her older sibling, although that identity may not be spoken out loud when the parents are around. The same child may be categorized as "mother's little darling" by the mother of the child. Whatever the identities assigned to an infant, the categorical identities classify that infant and structure other's behavior toward her.

Each infant is also assigned personal identities. Nearly all are given a personal as well as a family name. Whereas the categorical identities assigned an infant both classify the infant with and separate her from others, personal identities locate the infant as an entity that is distinct in some ways from all other objects. The identity of "baby" is in one sense a personal identity for most children for the first several months of their lives. It is an identity that separates them from all other members of the family. But then, as the child socially matures and becomes aware that others are also called "baby," that identity becomes a categorical identity.

The infant classified as male is acted toward differently than the infant categorized as female. It is not biological maleness or femaleness that structures the actions of others toward infants, but the anticipations and intentions that people have linked to the categorical identities of male and female. In the early months of life infants have no awareness of the identities that separate them from some others and classifies them with others. Nonetheless these early identities are significant. They structure the action of others toward the child and thereby partially determine the child's experiences.

The earliest identities do not directly structure the behavior of the infant. Before identities can be used by a child to structure behavior, the child must become an object unto herself. That is not possible until after the child has acquired command of significant symbols, the ability to differentially identify others, and the ability to adopt the standpoint of others toward herself.

Children differentially respond to others before they are capable of classifying others. Young, presymbolic children frequently reach for their mother and turn to avoid contact with strangers. Rather complex patterns of approach and avoidance are produced by most young children before they master significant symbols. After the ability to respond differentially to others and the ability to use symbols have emerged then the two of them can be linked. The child can then call for the mother while reaching toward her. This development is merely a special extension of acquiring competency in the use of significant symbols. It provides the child with the ability to classify others. The child no longer is merely classified by others, but now classifies others as well.

After the child has acquired the ability to categorize others and recognizes that she is in turn categorized by others, the child can then align herself with another in a parallel fashion, and the two of them can establish the child as their shared focus. When that occurs, the child has become an object unto herself. In the process, the child has become at least vaguely aware of self; the child moves toward self-consciousness and takes an additional step toward becoming incorporated into the social fabric.

To acquire a self-conception it is necessary for one to adopt the standpoint of another and assess oneself from that standpoint. This activity is referred to as reflexive role taking (Mead 1934). It is reflexive role taking that allows human beings to become a series of objects unto themselves. Self-awareness emerges gradually. The child first becomes vaguely aware of self as an object when she recognizes the designation "baby" differentiates her from others.

As children continue to interact, acquire command of more abstract symbols, and learn to adopt the standpoint of many others, they become a multitude of objects unto themselves; they acquire, retain, and discard a series of identities. Some identities are short-lived. A boy may at one moment regard himself as "daddy" and the next moment as superman, followed by taking on the identity of dog. These transitory identities usually do not become central elements of persons' self-conception. On occasion, however, individuals have been known to appropriate such identities as General Custer and wild elephant and insist that others regard the identities as valid. In most instances, the assumption of fantastic identities is short-lived.

Consensual categorical identities are one source of consistency of behavior. For example, in most societies the identities linked to gender are significant and consensual. Most agree that the categories of male and female have significant implications for everyone. Of course, those who advocate a unisexual way of life disagree. Nonetheless, most children are consensually assigned an identity based on gender. Gender-linked identities originally structure the behavior of others toward each child, and in most cases come to be taken for granted by the child. When any identity is taken for granted, it both structures and stabilizes behavior.

The young male who has been consensually identified by others as a "boy" and has accepted that identity as part of his self-conception will resist accepting what he regards as incongruent identities or acting in a manner inconsistent with the identity.

In a similar manner most thirty-year-old adults resist accepting the identity of either a ten-year-old or fifty-year-old and avoid acting in a manner they regard appropriate for ten-year-old or fifty-year-old persons. The cluster of identities that compose the self- conception of each person provides social anchors that give consistency to behavior across social situations.

The earliest identities are derived from the designations and patterns of activity offered by others. But as individuals mature and acquire greater social awareness, most initiate the acquisitions of new and novel identities. Children frequently attempt to appropriate identities ranging from cowgirl to space traveler. Most of them are tentatively taken on and quickly discarded. But some identities are long range goals. Young people enroll in college to acquire the identity of college graduate. Those who are successful acquire a new identity, which becomes part of their self-conception.

As people mature socially, change group affiliations, and move out of and into social relationships, they discard and acquire identities. Some identities are enduring; others are transitory. Identities based on gender endure for the lifetime of most of us, but some have discarded the sexual identity assigned by others. Other identities are very transitory. A young boy may at one moment assume the identity of toughest man on the block only to discard it a moment later to assume the identity of peacemaker between two quarreling friends.

Each identity locates us within a social network. Consensual identities structure both the actions of others toward us and our own actions. Consensual categorical identities are the building blocks of social structures.

Consciousness of Structures

In the process of mastering significant gestures and symbols and acquiring self-consciousness, children and their caregivers establish patterns of reciprocating behavior that link them together. As their social activities become less chaotic and more repetitive, congruent anticipations and intentions become taken for granted. Most children establish a series of patterned contacts with a number of others. The nature of these patterned contacts formed with each adult reflects the conception of the relationship that the adult brings to their relationship, but the child also contributes to the patterned contacts that emerge between self and others. These patterns are not consciously constructed by young children; they have no awareness of relationships or social structures until they become conscious of variation in social linkages between themselves and others.

Parents and caregivers bring conceptions of how children and adults should relate to each other to their encounters with children. These conceptions structure, but do not determine, their behavior toward the child. On many occasions, children do not act as expected and desired by parents and caregivers. Then, usually, the adults attempt to entice or force the child to act as the adult deems appropriate. Usually, but certainly not always, children in due time begin acting in a manner desired by the adults. Then patterned activities between the child and adults usually become stable and taken for granted. These patterned and taken-for-granted reciprocating activities allow the child to acquire consciousness of social structures.

The emergence of consciousness of structures depends on the child's becoming aware of similarities and differences of sets of patterned contacts between different sets of people. Consciousness of a relationship can emerge, for example, when a young boy becomes aware that his relatedness to one of his parents, say, his mother, is similar to that between another child and the other boy's mother, but yet different. The boy is beginning to acquire consciousness of relationships when he says to his mother, "But Tommy's mother lets him bake pies."

The development of consciousness of relationships, like the emergence of significant gestures, significant symbols, and identities, is a gradual process. It begins with a vague awareness that there are patterns in the linkages between persons and matures into an elaborate and refined conception of how pairs of identities are linked to each other. For example, when a little girl first begins to become aware of the general relationships between mother and child, she may conceive of the relationship between her mother and her father as being similar to that between herself and her mother. As the child socially matures, she learns that the identities of mother and father are linked together differently than that of mother and child.

The typical child first acquires consciousness of the relationships within the family. Then, as the child's social world expands, she participates in and becomes aware of other social relationships. Once a certain level of sophistication has been achieved, children conclude that forms of relatedness structure encounters. Children have achieved that level of consciousness when they ask for instructions on how to behave within a specific encounter or indicate reluctance to participate in a given encounter on the grounds that they "don't know what they are supposed to do." They then have consciousness of social structure.

When children become conscious of social structure, they use their conceptions of the structure to organize their own behavior within encounters. Of course, in the early years they still have to be prompted by others. They do not automatically act in a manner consistent with their conception of the structure. Parents rather continually prompt their children on the appropriate behaviors when they enter into encounters for which they do not have a clear conception of the appropriate relationship.

Once children acquire consciousness of family structures they often play with and construct pretend family structures. The following example is taken from Denzin (1977a).

Three three-year-old girls were upstairs in a large dollhouse at a day care center. The following transactions were produced.

Penny: I want to be the baby.
Mary: I'm going to be the mother.
Tina: I want to be the baby, too.
Mary: You be the big baby.
Penny: I have to be the little baby because I have the high chair.

Then a fourth girl joins them. Mary asserts, "She has to be the daddy. Little girl, you have to put your shoes on in the morning."

The situation becomes still more complex when they are joined by a boy. The following occurs.

Mary: Wendall, what do you want to be?
Wendall: I'll be the daddy.
Mary: We'll have two daddys, then. Where do you sit?

These five children used their conception of the family structure to construct a complex set of social relationships. They did not merely act in terms of their conceptions of the relationships, but used their conception to construct a small social system. They then organized their actions within the structure they had constructed. Within this episode, Mary displayed the greatest sophistication; at least she took charge. She used her conception of family relationships to assign others their identities within the structure. "After an opening sequence of position negotiations, the children settled into rather routine conduct in which they revealed their interpretations of mother, father, and baby sitting around a dinner table" (Denzin 1977a, 134).

Conceptions of relationships are seldom, if ever, completely consensual. Children often argue with one another about how two identities are to be linked. In the process of assuming pretend identities and constructing pretend structures, children's consciousness of social structures becomes elaborated and refined. That process continues throughout life. As adults move into new situations and discuss existing relationships, they also expand, refine, and modify their conceptions of relationships.

Agreement on conceptions of relationships is seldom, if ever, complete. Even those who have maintained a relationship for years often have differences of opinion on the specifics of how they are to relate. Nonetheless, people with a consciousness of social structure use their conceptions of various relationships as a framework to organize their conduct with each other. Their conceptions of the relationships not only provide them with guidelines but also provide them with a framework for renegotiating and restructuring of relationships.

The set of conceptions of relationships shared by a community is a source of social stability and regularity for the community. The conceptions of relationships, like all human accomplishments, constantly evolve. Yet they provide a structure and allow for complex forms of social action that would not otherwise be possible.

SUMMARY

If the newborn infant is not encased within a social environment composed of at least one other human being, she will not become a social being. Not all infants who are cared for become social beings. Some die. Being encased in a social environment does not assure social maturity, it only makes it possible. Human life under the best of conditions is problematic. The transformation of a human infant into a social being is always problematic.

When the transformation occurs, however, it proceeds through a series of distinctive stages. The first steps toward becoming a social being occur as the consequence of some of the expressive gestures of infants being noted and assigned significance by others. Then, through a series of repetitive transactions between infant and caregiver, some of the expressive gestures are transformed into significant gestures. The child who acquires command of significant gestures no longer merely responds to stimuli but acts to change her environment. For example, the child who has learned that crying has consequences can then attempt to elicit an alternative environment. Of course, many efforts by infants to entice others to modify their environment are not successful.

But to the extent that the child can act and entice others to act toward or with respect to her, the child has become capable of partially constructing her own world. When infants reach that stage of development, they both respond to and act on their environment. Sometimes they are successful; sometimes they are not.

The emergence of significant symbols is contingent on the prior establishment of a set of significant gestures. Significant symbols rest on a more complex social arrangement then significant gestures. The emergence of significant symbols requires the prior establishment of co-orientation. Both child and caregiver must establish a shared focus and then produce similar, if not identical, acts linked to the shared focus before a significant symbol can be established. A child who has mastery of significant symbols can then direct the attention and behavior of another. When the child says "hold me," she attempts to direct both the attention and the action of another. Reciprocally, as the child acquires mastery of significant symbols, her attention and action can also be directed by others.

In one sense, it is with the mastery of significant symbols that children become truly social. The production of significant symbols both rests on the sharing of experiences and provide a means for sharing additional experiences. As each of us acquired command of significant symbols, we became incorporated within a social world.

The emergence of identities requires the prior establishment of significant symbols. After significant symbols have become established, then children can assume the standpoint of others and become objects unto themselves. They can classify themselves as similar to and different from others. They can then locate themselves as an object among objects. As children are assigned and accept identities, their self-conceptions mature.

The establishment of self-consciousness provides a foundation for children acquiring conceptions of relationships. The first conceptions of relationship are vague, but they become refined as children acquire experiences in a series of relationships. General conceptions of relationships then are employed to structure actions taken toward and with others. Before the emergence of consciousness of structures, the repetitive patterns of activity are taken for granted; they constitute reality. When consciousness of structures emerge, children can negotiate and evaluate their relationships with others.

The earliest conceptions of structures are preceded by participation in and observance of patterned contacts. But after children have acquired command of complex symbol systems and awareness of a variety of identities, then they can acquire awareness of other relationships through symbolic instructions. For example, children can be told about the relationships that prevail between parents and children in other societies and have some understanding of those relationships without becoming a part of those relationships. But the acquisition of consciousness of relationships in this way cannot be acquired until the child has become aware of a variety of social relationships.

Social scientists specialize in the expansion of human consciousness about social structures. By making social arrangements the object of reflective attention, they hope to make all more conscious of social structures and provide the knowledge necessary for the construction of alternative and novel social structures. In that sense, the body of knowledge that constitutes the social sciences is the most abstract form of social consciousness.

Chapter 2   Acquiring Temporal Structures

All human action occurs through time; it has duration. In addition, all human action is temporally structured. At the minimum, human action is informed by a past and is structured by a projected future. Even the simple act of an infant's reaching for a toy has a temporal structure. The infant who sees a toy and then reaches for it projects a future of grasping the toy. From the moment the toy is seen until the infant makes contact with it, or fails to make contact, the baby's action is structured by the anticipation and intention of grasping the toy.

Newborn infants are devoid of temporal structures. They are not "timeful." But as the infant is acted upon, and acts upon, he acquires temporal structures. All temporal structures—anticipations and intentions—are based upon repetitive sequences of experience. An infant who does not have any repetitive sequences of experience cannot acquire the ability to anticipate the future or act with intention.

For example, a simple temporal structure is employed when a young girl uses her sequenced past experiences to extend her arms toward her parent to project a future of being picked up by the parent. In such encounters the infant organizes herself in the ongoing present to achieve a projected future. Other temporal structures are composed of intertwined sequences programmed to achieve several objectives. The young woman who solicits aid from another student so that she is more likely to pass an examination may use a number of past experiences in the immediate present and organize her actions on the basis of multilayered futures. She may be concerned with the future reactions of her parents to her grades, her own evaluation of herself, the successful completion of an undergraduate degree, and opportunities for employment when she graduates from college. All temporal structures rest on sequenced pasts; and all human action is structured by projected futures. When we are incapable of projecting a future, our action becomes chaotic or apathetic.

The infant at birth cannot link the present to the future. The baby can respond to stimuli, but cannot project a future. The newborn infant produces behavior but not action. Through a series of transactions between the infant and the environment, the baby acquires the ability to anticipate and act with intention. As the infant acquires anticipations and intentions, he

16

becomes capable of organizing actions. The infant then uses past experiences to sequence actions.

The original temporal structures are simple and very short. Each infant first becomes capable of short-range anticipations, then becomes capable of acting with intentionality. The infant who becomes capable of projecting a future and organizing himself in an effort to bring that future to fruition is acting with intentionality. The early simple anticipations and intentionalities are extended as the infant continues to be acted on and acts upon his environment.

A major transformation occurs when the child becomes aware of the fact that other people anticipate and intentionally organize their behavior. Still later, children learn to sequence their activity symbolically. Once the ability to sequence events symbolically has been mastered, then children live in a "time factored" world. They project both immediate (proximal) futures and long-range (distal) futures. Projected futures give structure to the activities of both individuals and collectivities.

Anticipations

The ability to anticipate is the first temporal structure acquired by infants. Newborn infants do not anticipate. They respond to stimuli, but they do not anticipate future experiences. Infants acquire the ability to anticipate by being part of an environment that provides them with repetitive sequences of experiences. The acquisition of anticipations is not entirely dependent on the activity of other human beings, but largely so. Transactions between the infant and nonhuman facets of the environment also provide experiences that contribute to the emergence of the ability to anticipate. During the early months of life, however, most of the repetitive sequences of experiences of the infant are provided by other human beings. Repetitive experiences provided by caregivers allow infants to acquire sequenced pasts, which in turn allow them to anticipate futures. The acquisition of anticipations requires that others be at least somewhat consistent in the sequences of actions they take toward the infant.

Repetitive sequences of tactile experiences and biological maturation of the visual and auditory senses allow the infant to acquire anticipations based on different combinations of sensory experiences. Once the infant has acquired the ability to see he can then note the appearance of "something," followed by the tactile experiences associated with being picked up. The infant's anticipations are extended as the infant takes part in sequences of experiences based on various combinations of visual, auditory, and tactile experiences.

In the early months of life infants are largely passive participants in the events that allow them to form anticipations. The immobility of human infants severely restricts their ability to initiate sequences of events. Most of the earliest anticipations flow from the acts others take toward the infant.

Infants continue to respond to their environment as they extend their ability to anticipate. As infants acquire the ability to anticipate, however, their responses become linked to anticipations. Stimuli are not merely responded to, but are both responded to and acted toward. For example, once an infant girl has acquired the ability to anticipate then, when a parent appears in her visual field, she no longer merely responds to the visual stimulus but prepares herself for impending tactile contact. She may delightfully wiggle in anticipation.

The anticipations for the first few months of life are only vaguely formulated and of limited complexity. But repetitive exposure to sequences of experience establish firm anticipations. Infants are exposed to many different sets of sequenced experiences as their caregivers provide them with the necessities of life. As infants take part in these repetitive sequences that involve one of the distance perceptors — sight or sound — and subsequent tactile contact, they acquire the ability to anticipate complex and varied futures.

An infant who upon experiencing the first event of a sequence, responds with a level of excitement greater than previously displayed has become timeful. For example, when the infant girl visually notes the appearance of her mother and then wiggles in anticipation of being picked up, her action has become temporally structured. She is using her past experiences to anticipate a specific future. Her behavior is no longer merely a response to the immediate ongoing present; it is partially structured by an anticipated future.

Of course, not all anticipated futures unfold as expected. Adults as well as children are frequently disappointed when anticipations are not fulfilled. On other occasions, when a dreaded future fails to occur, we are relieved. Nonetheless even when the anticipated futures fail to materialize our action is still structured by our anticipations.

If a human infant is to acquire anticipations of any duration beyond those of the next event or two, it is necessary for those who care for the infant repetitively to produce extended sequences of events toward him. If caregivers behave in a completely chaotic manner toward an infant, he will not acquire temporal structures.

Intentionality

Most, but not all, of the earliest sequenced experiences by infants are initiated by their caregivers. But some are initiated by the infant. The young infant is capable of some actions. For example, infants flex their arms and legs. When they produce these actions they stimulate themselves. Some of these random actions bring them into contact with various parts of their environment, including parts of their own bodies.

Infants do not organize their behavior intentionally at birth. Their actions are, within the limitations of their bodies, chaotic. The range of these activities is very limited, but they do provide sequences of experiences that are linked to the infant's own initiations. For example, the random movement of a baby girl may result in her hand making contact with her mouth. That may stimulate her to suck on her thumb. After this sequence has been accidentally produced a few times, she may then intentionally bring her thumb to her mouth and suck it. When that occurs, the infant is behaving with a modicum of intentionality. The infant intentionally organizes her actions to provide herself with a specific experience.

After infants have acquired the ability to provide themselves with specific anticipated experiences, they no longer simply anticipate a future but now act with intentionality. As with anticipations, the first intentionally organized acts are simple and of short duration. Through maturation and the production of more extended sequences, infants acquire intentionalities of longer duration.

Neither the acquisition of anticipations or intentionalities is dependent on any specific set of experiences. The significant factor for the acquisition of temporal structures is the production of repetitive sequences, not the content of the experience. The infant cared for by sensitive and concerned parents has entirely different experiences than does the abused child. Yet both children acquire the ability to anticipate and to act with intention. As a consequence of their different environments, the infants will relate to their environment in a different fashion, but both, if they survive, will acquire temporal structures that allow them to organize their actions. The content of their experiences are significant in establishing modes of relating to others, but anticipations and intentionalities are generated by both adverse and pleasant sequences or experiences.

The extension of temporal structures and the acquisition of control over one's own actions emerge together. Once children have acquired the ability to act with intentionality, they can then direct their actions toward specific facets of their environment. The acquisition of primitive intentionalities is a necessary prerequisite for giving direction to one's own behavior. As children acquire the ability to direct their behavior toward other objects, they also become capable of extending their temporal structures. As children master the ability to crawl, they initiate complex sequences of action. Severely handicapped children remain dependent on others to acquire extended sequences of experience. In a similar manner, blind and deaf children are highly dependent on others for the extension of their temporal structures.

The acquisition of temporal structures is not dependent on either mobility or any given sensory mode. Nonetheless, the extension of temporal structures depends on the elaboration of repetitive sequences of experiences. Therefore, handicapped children are more dependent on others for the extension of their temporal structures than are nonhandicapped children.

The extension of temporal structures, like the formation of primitive temporal structures, is derived from transactions between the child and the environment. The child produces one-half of the events necessary; the environment, especially other human beings, produces the other half of the events necessary. When the two halves fit together and are repetitively produced, temporal structures become extended. Whereas in the early months of life the infant can anticipate only the next event in a sequence, as the infant socially matures and becomes involved in social activity with others, long-range futures can be projected.

Interpersonal Timing

Interpersonal timing is a facet of all coordinated activity. The earliest timing that involves two people is the child noting the approach of an adult and then projecting a future of affiliation or avoidance. In such instances the child acts with respect to another person and the child's action is temporally structured, but the action is not interpersonally timed.

Before infants can interpersonally time their actions with another, they have to detect the intentions of another. When the infant cries with the intention of eliciting a response from another, the infant is projecting a temporal sequence, but is not timing his behavior with another. The earliest sets of reciprocating acts between an infant and another are produced by an adult noting the intentions of the infant and taking them into account in the organization of his behavior. But the earliest reciprocating acts between child and caregiver are not mutually timed. These reciprocating sequences are produced by the caregiver's timing acts with the acts of the infant, but the infant is not assessing the intentions of the other.

As infants mature and acquire more extended temporal structures, they note that some facets of the environment are more responsive to their initiations than others. In general, caregivers are more responsive to infants' initiations than are the nonhuman facets of the environment. As infants continue to initiate activities with caregivers, they first vaguely become aware that sometimes caregivers are immediately responsive to their initiations and other times caregivers respond only after a delay; further, that there are times the called-for action is never produced. It slowly dawns on infants that the actions of others are not automatic responses to their initiations. Infants thereby learn that others control their own behavior; that the behavior of others is not an automatic response to the infant's actions.

The ability to time action interpersonally slowly emerges as the infant learns to assess the intentions of others. The emergence of that ability depends upon the caregivers sometimes responding more or less immediately to the initiations of the child and other times delaying their responses. As the child acquires the ability to recognize those acts that indicate that while the called-for response will not be immediately produced, it will be produced later, the child becomes capable of assessing the intentions of others. When the child becomes capable of assessing the intentions of others, he then becomes capable of timing actions with the intentions of others, as well as responding to the actions of others.

The child first experiences the responses of caregivers that indicate that the called-for act will not be produced immediately as frustrations. But if a given response to the child's initiations is offered repetitively as an insertion and the called-for activity is subsequently produced, the infant will learn to maintain a state of anticipation despite the fact that the called-for activity is not immediately produced. The child can then time his actions with both the immediate activity of others and the intentions of others. The child can then initiate an act, make an assessment of whether the other intends to produce the called-for reciprocating act immediately or later, and act accordingly. When the child acquires the ability to assess the intentions of others, then the early primitive anticipations based on responding to acts in the immediate situation are extended.

Teasing is one procedure for extending temporal structures based on the assessment of the intentions of others. For example, a mother may approach her little girl and extend her arms as if to pick up the child; then, when the child organizes herself in anticipation of being picked up, the mother may tease the child by withdrawing her arms. Many caregivers entice children to enter into sequences of activity where a specific future is promised and then withdrawn. A major transformation occurs when the child initiates a sequence and then fails to complete the promised act.

The child who becomes capable of assessing the intentions of others not only learns that his experiences are dependent on others willfully relating to him but also that the experiences of others are dependent on the child's willfully relating to them. The child then becomes aware that he can fulfill or deny the anticipations of others. Teasing is a complex form of interpersonal timing that is based on the awareness that others both anticipate and intentionally organize their actions (Couch 1984b, 26).

As children become capable of controlling their own bodies they more actively contribute to the extension of their temporal structures. For example, when a young girl acquires greater mobility by mastering walking, she greatly extends her range of activity and her temporal structures. Her first efforts to master this ability are chaotic. The structure of the first "steps" is provided by her caregivers; they sequence her movements. In order to acquire the ability to walk on her own volition the child must be attentive to the sequences of acts that are necessary to walk successful. But as that ability becomes refined, walking becomes habitual and can be produced without conscious effort.

Much the same thing occurs when military recruits are taught to march in unison. Those with no prior training must be told time and again how to step in unison with others. The acquisition of control of such sequences is in the beginning a very self-conscious activity. It requires the recruits to give close attention to the sequences of acts that constitute "marching." Yet, with extended practice, elaborate marching sequences can be produced in unison. Furthermore, after mastering these elaborate sequences with others, the same sequences can then be produced by the person acting as an individual. A future of "marching" is projected, and the necessary sequence is habitually activated.

The maturation of extended temporal structures is intertwined with the ability to use significant gestures. To engage in a conversation of gestures, the child must be able to both act with intention and anticipate the actions of another. Command of significant gestures and the extension of simple temporal structures are simultaneously elaborated as the child increases the number of significant gestures that he can use.

The acquisition of the simplest significant symbols requires more extended temporal structures than those required for the acquisition of significant gestures. The earliest significant symbols are used to produce coorientation within the immediate ongoing present. The child who has acquired the ability to produce the sound "cat" and consistently link it to a referent can then issue that symbol with the anticipation of eliciting coorientation from another and note the response of the other person to determine if the other intends to attend to the specified object. Significant symbols "touch off" at least a simple sequence of interpersonal timing that results in both the one who issued the symbol and another attending to the same object in the immediate situation.

As the child acquires command of more significant symbols, then he can use significant symbols to specify events and sequences of events. The ability to sequence events symbolically allows the child to attend to and project distal futures, as well as attend to and project proximal futures.

Distal Futures

Before children have command of significant symbols that designate events, they can produce fairly complex units of action both as individuals and units of action that involve them timing their actions with the actions of others. After command of symbols that designate events and sequences of events is acquired, then it is possible for children to establish distal objectives. When the child recognizes that the immediate activity is linked to an objective that will be achieved sometime after the completion of the immediate action, then a distal objective structures the immediate activity. The first distal objectives are rather "immediate." They are the next act to be completed after completion of a simple act of short duration.

Symbolic sequences are first imposed on the child. Young children are introduced to symbolic sequences by being told "to wait." A typical sequence consists of the child calling for something and anticipating that the called for action will be produced immediately, but the parent responds with "in a minute." In these transactions the parent is symbolically sequencing his action, but the child is not. The child is merely frustrated. After experiencing acts of this sort many times, the child acquires the ability to maintain an anticipatory stance in response to "in a minute." When this level of sophistication is achieved, the child is symbolically sequencing behavior on a very simple level.

The child clearly has the ability to sequence behavior symbolically when, in response to another's request, he responds with "in a minute." These primitive symbolic sequences do not extend very far into the future; nor are they very complex. The symbolic sequence merely consists of inserting a period of anticipation between the activity being produced within the ongoing present and some future development. These primitive symbolic sequences do not specify any action to be taken before the projected distal future is to be achieved.

When there is the symbolic specification of two acts to be taken to achieve an objective, the activity is symbolically sequenced. For example, when the child responds to the request, "Let's go," with "Let me finish this" a sequence of activity that consists of only two events is symbolically specified.

The acquisition of the ability to sequence the future symbolically is similar to the acquisition of the categorical attitude. The child has the categorical attitude when he recognizes that everything has a name and asks, "What is that?" The child who has the ability to sequence the future symbolically can then inquire, "When?"

The ability to sequence symbolically allows two persons to project a distal shared future and jointly program the actions to be taken between now and the projected distal future. For example, a mother and her child can then discuss when they will leave to visit a relative and what they must do before they depart. They might, for example, agree that before they leave it is necessary to straighten up the child's room.

Symbols such as first, after, before, and not until temporally link units of action. The production of the second act is made contingent on the production of the first. These simple forms of symbolic sequencing are elaborated, and eventually the child acquires command of symbolic temporal structures that allow for the production of complex programs of social action.

When a parent states to a child, "When I pick up the davenport, you get the ball," the actions of each of them and the fit between the actions of the two of them are symbolically specified. When such efforts are first undertaken, the child usually makes errors in timing. The child fails to understand or responds too quickly or too slowly. With practice, however, most children acquire the ability to sequence symbolically their actions with others. When they acquire this ability, they are then capable of "time-factored" action (Marshack 1972).

Children first learn to sequence their actions symbolically within an immediate situation. After they have acquired that ability, they can then learn to sequence symbolically units of action that include periods of separation. This form of sequencing involves three distinct temporal periods. At time 1, two persons symbolically sequence what each of them are to do at time 2, and they anticipate reconvening at time 3 to complete the act. For example, a father may agree to fix a toy for his son and instruct the child to "get the glue" while the father prepares the toy. The action to be taken at time 2 by each of them is specified at time 1. Their actions during time 2 are structured by the distal future of fixing the toy at time 3.

If they are successful in time factoring their activity, each of them during time 2 will act in a manner that makes the achievement of the distal objective more likely. Of course, they are not always successful. The boy may forget what he is supposed to do at time 2 or cannot complete that phase of the act; or the father may become distracted and fail to complete his half of the time-factored act. Then, either the effort will disintegrate or they will have to reprogram their actions.

Time factoring does not assure that the future will unfold as planned. Students commonly forget to do their homework and reappear at the next class meeting unprepared. Nonetheless, all forms of complex coordinated activity ranging from playing a game of checkers through conducting a religious ritual to space probes are contingent on the ability to time factor. If people are not able to time factor the future, they can produce only very simple forms of social action.

The importance of time factoring is highlighted in team efforts. Before people can play a game of basketball, they have to master complex sets of reciprocating acts that are symbolically sequenced. But a well-trained basketball team can complete extremely complex sequences of action without symbolically sequencing their activities in the immediate situation. For example, one of the guards on the team may hold up one finger. That may set off a complex set of activity by the team. Two players may set a pick for another, while a fourth player fakes an "alley-oop play" to another and then passes the ball to the fifth player.

The activity of the team may not appear to be symbolically sequenced, but it is. Before it is possible for a team to complete such an act, it is necessary that they construct an elaborate shared past in which they have previously performed that sequence of acts. When the act was practiced, it was explicitly time factored by the coach. The coach instructed the players about who was to perform which act.

In a very similar manner, members of a hospital emergency team are capable of producing complex units of action that are not symbolically sequenced within the immediate situation. Again, they are able to do this only if they have previously symbolically sequenced their actions.

After persons have acquired the ability to sequence their actions symbolically and constructed a shared past by acting in unison to acquire specific social objectives, they can then unreflectively produce complex units of time-factored activity. The significance of symbolic sequencing and shared pasts for the smooth production of complex units of time factored activity is indicated by what happens when a stranger, who does not know the symbolic sequences, attempts to become a member of the team. The newcomer will stick out like a sore thumb.

If the stranger has taken part in similar activities with others, then he has a common past. He can use his common past, if it is similar to the pasts of other team members, to time his actions with theirs. On occasion, such persons may fit into the established unit rather easily; more often than not, the absence of a shared past makes it very difficult for newcomers to sequence smoothly actions with the regular members of a team.

After persons have acquired the ability to sequence symbolically their activities with each other, they can be reflective about their past actions. For example, if the guard on the basketball team passes the ball to the center before the center is in position, the play will not be successfully completed. The two of them, or more likely the two of them and the coach, may enter into a discussion about exactly how to time factor their actions.

The production of complex sequences of action requires that those involved have command of complex temporal structures, the ability to sequence symbolically their activities and command of their own bodies. The absence of any of these makes the production of time-factored action impossible.

Elaborate Temporal Structures

Many members of modern societies think of temporal structures as things measured by calendars and clocks. Calendars and clocks are human inventions that greatly extend the ability to time factor the future. They are artifacts used to extend and give greater precision to temporal structures. Calendars and clocks allow for the precise specifications of temporal structures that extend indefinitely into the future and the past. It is not until after children have mastered the simpler forms of of time factoring that they can master the temporal structures reflected in calendars and clocks.

Calendars and clocks are based on celestial events — the revolution of the sun around the earth and the rotation of the earth on its axis. The calendar has an extremely ancient past. The first crude calendars are at least thirty thousand years old (Marschak 1972). Clocks are a relatively recent inventions; the earliest ones were invented about two thousand years ago. The modern calendar and clocks are one of the cornerstones of industrial societies (Couch 1984b). They are used to project distal futures with great precision.

A major facet of socializing young people into modern societies is instructing them to "tell time." In order to tell time they must be able to decipher the information displayed by calendars and clocks and use that information to time factor their actions. Young children are incapable of projecting precise distal futures that endure for weeks, months, or years.

The first distal future mastered by children that extends very far into the future is that of tomorrow. It was probably the first extended distal future that human beings mastered (Marshack 1972; Couch 1984b). They probably then acquired mastery of yesterday and today. Tomorrow, of course, does not have the specificity for young children that it does for adults. Children originally understand tomorrow in much the same way as they manage other insertions, namely, that the action under discussion will not be produced immediately but may be forthcoming sometime in the future.

Citizens of industrial societies take calendars and clocks for granted. But not all human societies have them. The Siriono, a South American hunting and gathering group, did not have a calendar. And, of course, they did not use clocks either. The only symbols they had for specifying extended durations were *tomorrow, yesterday, brother of tomorrow, brother of yesterday,* and *today.* "The year, with its divisions into months or moons', is quite unknown" (Holmberg 1969, 123). The symbol "brother of yesterday" referred to any period before yesterday. It might refer to the day before yesterday or what we would regard as years ago. Holmberg notes that the Siriono had little foresight; they lived day-to-day without any long-range planning. They did not time factor their lives with any precision, nor did their symbolic sequences futures extend very far into the future. To say that we will do it "in the brother of tomorrow" indicated that the activity would not happen tomorrow, but it did not specify it would happen the day after tomorrow.

Most human groups have a calendar of sufficient complexity to program the yearly cycle, although the calendar of some societies is very vague and imprecise. Many primitive calendars consist of noting some major celestial event such as the winter solstice and then keeping track of the sequence of moons that follow each winter solstice. That provides a calendar of sufficient complexity to allow for time factoring hunting game and seeking out other foodstuffs during different seasons. Most agricultural groups have a more precise calendar. But the precise and long-range time factoring based on numerical calendars is not universal; it became common in Western Europe only about two hundred years ago.

The precise time factoring accomplished with clocks is also a relatively recent development. The emergence of timekeeping devices occurred more or less simultaneously with industrialization. Clocks pervade industrial societies. All citizens of industrial societies are socialized into their use. Young children acquire awareness of clocks, seconds, minutes, and hours long before they can use them to time factor their own behavior. And long before children time factor their behavior on the basis of clock time, others time factor their activities for them. For example, the father announces to his five-year-old daughter "It's eight thirty, time for you to leave for school." The child recognized her actions are somehow linked to the clock, but she does not use the clock to time factor her own activity. In contrast, when the parent consults his watch and leaves the house at exactly eight thirty-seven to catch the eight forty-five bus, which will get him to his place of work at nine o'clock, he uses a mechanical device to time factor his activity.

The seconds, minutes, hours, days, weeks, months, years, decades, centuries, and millennia are taken for granted measures of duration for most members of industrial societies. They are used to time factor behavior and coordinate actions with others. They are far more precise than the vague temporal structures used by members of many societies to program their actions. The concept "brother of tomorrow" does not time factor the future with sufficient precision to maintain a modern social structure. One cannot run airlines, city and intercommunity bus lines, nor schools and universities if the only temporal structures are those of brother of yesterday, yesterday, today, tomorrow, and brother of tomorrow. Complex activities like organizing next year's family reunion, a student enrolling in next semester's classes, or a teacher planning next week's class schedule can only be produced by those who have mastered the temporal structures provided by calenders and clocks.

Summary

Sequenced pasts provide human beings with the ability to anticipate and act with intentionality. When infants acquire the ability to act with intentionality — to project a future and organize themselves to bring the projected future to fruition — they have acquired a will. They are no longer merely organisms that respond to an environment, but are capable of acting on their environment. Willful behavior is temporally structured behavior.

The first temporal structures are of short duration. But as infants and children interact with others, their temporal structures become more precise and extended. The earliest temporal structures are individualistic; they are not shared with others. After children acquire the ability to assess the anticipations and intentions of others, they become capable of interpersonal timing. When children acquire the ability to time their actions interpersonally, they can then act *with* others. It is by acting with others that we acquire shared pasts. After children have acquired shared pasts, they can project shared futures as well as personal futures.

Shared pasts emerge by acting in unison with others. Once individuals have acquired shared pasts, they can use them to produce complex units of coordinate action with others without explicitly programming future courses of action.

Learning to manage insertions and assess the intentions of others extend the temporal structures of children. Then children acquire the ability to project distal futures as well as proximal futures. Through the application of symbols to sequences of actions, human beings become capable of symbolically sequencing the future. When children become capable of symbolically sequencing the future, they can then time factor the future. They can specify which action will be taken first, second, third, etc., and organize themselves to achieve distal objectives. Symbolic sequencing also allows people to time factor the past. After acquiring mastery of time factoring, the past as well as the future can be sequenced and given reflective attention.

Symbolic sequences temporally order events, but they do not establish duration. Awareness of duration requires the comparison of two sequences of events. The awareness that one sequence of events endures longer than another is the most primitive measurement of duration. Concepts like a day, a week, a moon, and a year allow for the specification of extended units of duration. One of the distinctive features of industrial societies is the precise specification of extended units of duration by calendars and clocks.

Calendars and clocks are artifacts we use to program precisely complex and long-range distal futures. We use them to temporally structure our lives. Without them modern societies would not be possible. They allow us to precisely time-factor the future and the past. Calendars and clocks both constrain and free human beings. To create and maintain complex social structures it is necessary for human beings to subordinate themselves to the complex and precise time-factored sequences. These timekeeping procedures allow for complex human endeavors that otherwise would not be possible. Without our precise calendars and clocks, we would have neither international wars nor space probes.

Temporal structures have a relationship to human action that is analogous to the relationship between the backbone of a vertebrate animal and locomotion. Temporal structures are an absolute necessity for the production of orderly human action; a backbone is necessary if a vertebrate animal is to locomote from one location to another. If the backbone of a mammal is turned into jelly, the organism will remain, but the animal will be incapable of moving with direction. In a similar manner, if an individual or group loses its temporal structures, the person or group will remain, but will be incapable of organized action.

Chapter **3** Touch, Discourse, and Appearance

Human beings acquire sensations from their contact with other human beings and their environment primarily through the sensory modalities of tactile contact, vision, and hearing. Our senses of smell and taste also provide us with sensations. But most of the experiences we use to organize our actions with respect to and with others are acquired via touch, vision, and hearing. The sense of smell is of some significance. We avoid people who stink; if the television advertisements are to be believed, we chase after those who smell nice. Nonetheless, for the most part we respond to others, share sensations with others, and acquire information about others through touch, vision, and hearing.

As we act and are acted upon, we have a host of sensations that stem from our tactile, visual, and auditory contact with the external world. We are not conscious of most of these sensations. For example, if we are engrossed in what we are reading, we might remain unaware of a drop in the room temperature until we become chilly. Men have been wounded in violent conflict and not become aware of the damage to their bodies until after they have withdrawn from the conflict.

We are incapable of continually attending to all the sensations that stem from our sensory contacts with the external world. We are only aware of a small part of the host of sensations we have at any given moment. The reader of this material probably was not conscious of the sensations provided by the contact between her footwear and her feet until this moment. If she directs her attention to that contact, however, she becomes conscious of it. Our sensations are partially a consequence of what we direct our attention toward.

We all exercise some control over our experiences, but no one has complete control over her own experiences. The nature and intensity of our sensations is always partially determined by external factors, including the activities of other people, that impinge on us. Some external stimuli provide us with pleasant sensations; others with painful ones. In general, we seek out stimuli that provide pleasant sensations and avoid those that are painful.

In addition to our external senses and visceral sense, each of us has a proprioceptive nerve system that provides us with kinetic sensations. Kinetic sensations allow us to determine our bodily movements independent of our

30

external senses. When we move an arm, we feel it move. Those blessed with vision can see the arm move at the same time they have the kinetic sensation of its moving.

In our transactions with other people and with other facets of our environment, the sets of sensations derived from our external sensorium, our visceral sense, and our kinetic sense become linked to each other. These linkages give us control over both our experiences and our movements. Although we never acquire complete control over either our experiences or our actions, as we socially and biologically mature we acquire greater control. But, even then, some of our experiences remain accidental, and other experiences are the consequences of the actions of others over whom we have no control. Still other experiences are the consequences of a combination of our actions and external impingements.

The experiences of infants are highly contingent upon the actions of others; and children have more accidents than adults (Although even the most competent adults have accidents). As children acquire control over their movements and the ability to anticipate events, the early, diffuse sensations are transformed into focused experiences. The acquisition of control over movements and the ability to anticipate events transforms the infant from a sensate organism that merely responds to stimuli to a being capable of exercising control over her own experiences.

The world is an incredibly dangerous place for the unprotected infant (Leichty 1975). Most infants learn to subordinate their tactile contacts to visual and auditory experiences within a protected environment. An infant who is not afforded protection from life- threatening features of the environment is unlikely to survive into childhood. Infants learn to anticipate unpleasant and threatening tactile contacts by sight and sound. As children forge these linkages, the early, diffuse sensations are transformed into structured experiences.

The linkage of kinetic sensations with other stimuli is intertwined with acquiring the ability to anticipate pleasant and stressful experiences. The acquisition of command over one's own movements is based on linking kinetic sensations with sensations derived through the external sensorium. After these linkages have been made, the child can intentionally make and break contact with various facets of the external world; the child can intensify and lessen contacts with other human beings.

Linkages that provide the foundation for control over one's own movement are forged early in life. They become so taken for granted that adults are no longer conscious of them. They have become habitual. Some regard the linkages as inborn, but the linkages between kinetic sensations, on the one hand, and visceral and external sensations, on the other, are not inborn.

Several studies have demonstrated that these linkages are acquired. One of the more informative sets of studies that demonstrated the acquired nature of these linkages reversed visual stimuli. Individuals were equipped with eyeglasses or prisms that reversed all visual stimuli. What was seen as *up* became seen as *down;* what was seen as *to the left* became seen as *to the right.* When people first put on the prisms it was very difficult for them to act. They became disoriented; many suffered headaches. Nonetheless, if they continually wore the reverse-lens glasses and acted toward their environment, they soon learned to manage themselves quite well. After several days, a person who was capable of driving an automobile could drive an automobile when wearing lenses that reversed images.

The linkages forged between external, visceral, and kinetic sensations allow human beings to organize their action toward their environment. One of the most significant dimensions of their environment is composed of other human beings. And human beings constantly use the information acquired through the external senses to organize their action toward, away from, for, against, and with other human beings. We use the information acquired through our external senses to establish, maintain, modify, and break contact with other people. As children become incorporated into the social fabric, they become capable of sharing sensations with other people, establishing co-orientations, identifying others, and identifying themselves. When people share sensations, they communicate in the universe of touch; when they establish shared foci by performing a specific discrete act, they communicate in the universe of discourse; and when they mutually identify others and self by appearance, they communicate in the universe of appearance.

Sensory Contacts

Whenever people make sensory contact, they provide each other with sensations. The more intense visceral sensations are based on tactile contact. When two individuals make visual or auditory contact, however, they also provide each other with visceral sensations. Usually when contact is limited to vision or sound, the visceral sensations are of slight intensity, but on occasion sights and sounds provide intense visceral sensations.

The relative immobility of infants restricts their ability to make, modify, intensify, and break sensory contact with others. The young girl in the crib may call for her parent to pick her up. When the baby cries, she intensifies her contact with another, but if the parent refuses to look at her or pick her up, her contact with her parent is limited to the auditory mode.

When both parties are capable of movement, intensity of contact is a mutual construction. Each person can then act to make, modify, or break contact. This is so, even though the contact is between two people with different abilities. The more powerful person exercises more control over whether or not contact will be made and the nature of the contact once contact has been established, but if both have control over their actions, the less powerful can exercise some control over the nature of the contact. Among mobile persons, the intensity of their contact is more or less in a constant state of flux. At one moment, the child and parent snuggle together; the next moment, one of them moves to free herself of tactile contact with the other.

Sensory contact is sometimes established accidentally; at other times, one person initiates contact; and sometimes it is mutually initiated. On occasion, we literally bump into one another. In general ,however, as we acquire control over our own movements, we use our distance perceptors, especially sight and sound, to note each other and then act to intensify or lessen our contact.

We can see and hear another person without being seen or heard; reciprocally, others can see and hear us without our seeing or hearing them. In contrast, when we make tactile contact, whether accidentally or intentionally, nearly always we simultaneously become part of each other's perceptual field. To touch is to be touched (Leichty 1975).

Through the sense of sight we more or less constantly monitor our environment. We note others entering and leaving our perceptual field and their general line of activity. We use the information acquired to control the intensity of our contact with those we note. Sometimes we visually note the approach of other people and then cross the street to avoid them. Other times, we catch sight a loved one and rush to greet her.

Sensory contact based on vision is often established sequentially. One person notes another; then the second person notes the first person. Visual contact, however, like tactile contact, is sometimes established by two people simultaneously becoming aware of each other. When two people make eye contact, they simultaneously acquire information about each other and display themselves to each other. When eye contact is established, it "serves not only for me to know the other but also enables him to know me" (Simmel 1981, 98). Eye contact is an intense form of contact. In some ways it is more intense than tactile contact. Eye contact is seldom maintained for more than a moment or two and then only in very special circumstances. We often avert our gaze to lessen the intensity of contact.

On occasion, we hear another person before we see him. Nearly always, when social contact is established via sound, it is sequential; we seldom hear another person at the same time she hears us. Both of our distance perceptors — sight and sound — provide us with information that we use to lessen or intensify our contact with others. Sometimes we hide when we hear someone approaching.

When contact is originally established in the tactile mode, it is usually unintentional. Then we usually withdraw and attempt to lessen the intensity of the contact. On occasion, for example as when we are packed in like sardines on a crowded bus, it is difficult to break tactile contact. In general, however, when we make tactile contact with strangers, we break it if possible. If it is not possible to break it, we attempt to minimize the level of tactile contact although occasionally individuals have been known to take advantage of crowded situations and maintain greater tactile contact with another person than the situation required.

The visceral sensations elicited by tactile contact may be mild, but in a sense tactile contact is always an "intrusion." Young children are relatively insensitive to the experiences of others that stem from the tactile contacts they initiate. As children become aware of the consequences of tactile contact for the experiences of others, they learn to control their "intrusions."

Whenever people establish sensory contact, they become vulnerable to each other. If the contact is limited to the visual and auditory mode, the degree of vulnerability usually is slight although both sights and sounds occasionally can be very offensive. In contrast, whenever we have tactile contact with another person, each party is vulnerable to the other. Tactile contact inherently carries with it the risk of great stress. Of course, tactile contact can also be the source of great pleasure.

Whenever people make sensory contact through any of the sensory modalities, they have an impact on each other's visceral experiences. The experiences of the two of them may be much the same or very different. When two lovers reunite and greet each other with kisses and hugs, they have similar pleasant experiences. In contrast, when an enemy sneaks up on us and delivers a dastardly blow to the side of the head, the experiences of victim and attacker are vastly different.

On a more mundane level, a handshake may elicit highly similar experiences or vastly different ones. A firm handshake may be pleasant to both parties; but if one suffers from arthritis, the handshake may be pleasant for one and painful for the other.

When contact is limited to vision, it always (with the exception of identical twins framed by the same context) provides the two people involved with somewhat different experiences. When you and I meet, I see you and you see me. People share visual experiences only when they establish a shared focus.

Auditory contact elicits both similar and differentiated experiences. When I speak in your hearing, both of us hear the sound. Nonetheless, the sharing is not complete. The experience of the speaker is somewhat different from that of the listener. When people sing in unison, however, they can have very similar visceral experiences. Auditory contact is somewhat distinct from visual and tactile contact. It often provides both the hearer and the speaker with almost identical experiences. Good storytellers can elicit excitement, happiness, and dread from both themselves and their audience.

Touch

A distinctive feature of human beings is the extent to which they can share experiences. Other animals have common experiences at the same moment. For example, when a hunter frightens a herd of deer, all the deer probably have much the same experiences, but they are only slightly, if at all, conscious of one another's experiences. To share experiences it is necessary for two people to become aware that they have much the same sensations at the same time. Children are able to share visceral sensations at a very early age.

Infants experience complex and intense sensations long before they enter the universe of touch. They are pleasantly stimulated, suffer deprivations, become anxious, are fearful or angry before they become aware that they have experiences similar to those of others. Entry into the universe of touch requires that children first become aware of the sensations of others. They move into the universe of touch as they become aware of the fact that they and another person have similar sensations whenever they are part of a specific context.

Before children can enter the universe of touch, they must learn that expressive gestures reflect internal sensations. Children produce expressive gestures before they acquire command of significant gestures. Expressive gestures reflect internal sensations. They become significant gestures when the child becomes aware that her action may elicit a response from another person. After that linkage has been made, a given gesture can be both an expression of an internal sensation and a call for attention. The child who cries out in pain displays an expressive gesture; however, the child may then cry both to express distress and issue a call for attention.

As children acquire the ability to issue a gesture that is both expressive and significant, they also note the expressive gestures of other people. It seems that children learn to recognize that the expressive gestures of crying and laughing reflect the internal sensations of others early in life. They can then infer the feelings of other people. Children enter the universe of touch as they acquire the ability to infer the internal sensations of others. Only then can they intentionally act to elicit specific sensations from others.

Caregivers employ auditory, visual, and tactile contacts to entice children to enter into the universe of touch. The earliest and most intense forms of shared visceral sensations are derived from shared tactile experiences. For example, when a mother places her baby in the bath, both visually note the water and may more or less simultaneously make tactile contact with the water. At the same time, the mother is holding the child in her arms and perhaps speaking to the child. If the water is chilly, the baby is likely to begin crying; the mother then makes a brrr sound, quivers, and withdraws the infant from the water. The differences between the sensations of mother and infant are likely to be greater than the similarities. If the mother is successful in getting the child to become aware of the similarities in their visceral experiences, the child takes a step toward entering the universe of touch.

Some parents go to great lengths to share visceral sensations with their children. In some families, whenever the child laughs, the parent too. Other parents are relatively indifferent to sharing visceral sensations with their children.

It is not necessary for people to have tactile contact to elicit shared sensations. Sensations may also be shared via voice. Parents frequently note their child approaching something the parents regard as disgusting and attempt to discourage the child from handling the object by uttering "Icky" in a distressful tone of voice. In the early years these efforts usually do not elicit shared sensations. It seems that visceral sensations are more successfully shared between children and their parents when there is tactile contact between them. If child and parent have established what the parent regards as a disgusting object as their shared focus, while the parent is holding the child and the parent makes sounds of disgust and quivers, the child is more likely to share feelings with the parent than if the only contact between the parent and child is via voice.

Nonetheless, many sensations are shared as the consequence of vocal activity. "Speech nearly always reflects a visceral element" (Leichty 1975, 76). When a mother sings a nonsense lullaby or pleasantly coos while holding the child in her lap, she provides her child and herself with shared auditory experiences that are usually pleasing to both.

Entry into the universe of touch is not always the consequence of parents attempting to share experiences with their children. Children, especially those who have extensive and pleasing tactile contact with their parents, frequently respond to external experiences in much the same way their parents do, even if the parents do not deliberately attempt to elicit shared sensations. For example, a friend of mine is deathly afraid of large dogs. She did not want her daughter to suffer from the same fear. When she and her daughter were near a large dog, my friend attempted to act in a calm and nonfearful manner. Despite her efforts, by the time the daughter was three years old the daughter was also deathly afraid of large dogs. Apparently my friend communicated her fear of large dogs to her daughter despite her intentions not to do so.

Entry into the universe of touch is not the automatic result of biological maturation. It is a social accomplishment. Some children become capable of sharing many sensations with others early in life; others participate only minimally in the universe of touch. Early involvement in the universe of touch seems to be largely a consequence of the nature and intensity of contact between children and their caregivers.

Once children have learned that they share visceral sensations, they can empathize with others. After children have become capable of empathizing with others, they can then intentionally act toward others to elicit specific feelings in others. For example, once the little girl has learned that her father is pleased whenever she hugs him, then she can hug him to please him.

When we can determine what pleases or distresses someone, then whenever we establish contact with them, we can attempt to provide them with either pleasant or distressful experiences. But people also learn to mask their visceral sensations. "'Coolness' is a demeanor adopted to inhibit others from effectively manipulating our feelings. A placid demeanor is cultivated among nearly all, if not all, traditional ruling elites" (Leichty 1975, 77). People who are are capable of masking their visceral sensations are less vulnerable to others.

Interaction in the universe of touch varies from the most intense tactile contacts that elicit intense emotions to mildly satisfying or mildly dissatisfying transactions. For example, two children on a thrilling ride together on the Ferris wheel at a carnival share intense sensations.

The universe of touch tends to be a present-centered activity. When intense sensations are elicited, those involved focus their attention on the here and now; little attention is given to either the distal past or the distal future. When emotions are linked to temporal structures, however, the universe of touch can extend into the distal past and distal future. When our attention is directed to past events experienced with delight, we reexperience the original sensations. When it is directed to past events that were painful, embarrassing, or shameful, we reexperience much the same stress we previously experienced. Reciprocally, we sometimes delightfully anticipate future developments; other times, we are infused with dread and anxiety about the future.

Discourse

Discourse has an auditory base, but not all auditory acts are discourse; nor is all discourse expressed auditorily. The auditory acts of cooing, babbling, and crying by infants are expressive acts; they are not discourse. Many auditory acts are inherently pleasant or stressful to the person who produces them. The humming and solitary singing of adults is a pleasant form of self-stimulation; violent crying is stressful. The wild shriek of surprise is auditory, but not discourse. These acts are expressions of feelings; they are in the universe of touch. The words on this page are discourse displayed visually. Deaf people enter the world of discourse through sign language.

Most, but not all, discourse is discrete vocalization that establishes co-orientation. The auditory acts of children are largely expressive for the first couple of years. As children socially mature, they acquire the ability to use their vocal powers to establish co-orientation. The expressive dimensions of speech acts recede into the background, and the instrumental dimensions of speech acts move into the foreground as the child acquires greater control over vocalizations. When children begin uttering sounds with the intention of establishing co-orientation, they move into the universe of discourse. The first such acts are largely expressive; the child wiggles, flails her arms, and utters sounds. The parent sometimes is able to determine what the child wants done. Parents frequently call for their children to "tell them" what they want before the child acquires the ability to establish shared foci by producing discrete vocal acts.

Early discourse acts establish co-orientation only in the immediate situation. They are instrumental acts that allow the child to establish shared foci by vocalizations, and they usually call for another person to perform a specific act. For example, when the child says, "Mil," it may indicate that the mother is to give the child a drink of milk.

As children acquire greater control over their vocalizations and as their temporal structures become extended, they can produce vocalizations that establish objects as shared foci that are not part of the immediate situation. The first expression of this ability seems to appear in the form of the child calling for something to be made part of the immediate situation that is not now present. When the little girl calls for her mother to produce the doll that the child cannot find, discourse is used to direct attention to an object that is not part of the immediate situation. Discourse is no longer limited to the immediate present.

One important function of discourse is that it allows for time factoring. Children share feelings long before they can symbolically sequence either the future or the past. To construct the simple social program of "tomorrow we will go to the zoo" requires communication in discourse. Discourse allows for far more refined and complex communication than is possible in the universe of touch. Discourse provides us with the means for specifying with precision the relations between sets of objects, the specification of complex sequences of events, and even more complex interrelations between events and objects. It allows us to specify that before we go out to eat, it is necessary to call Uncle George, put the cat out, and comb our hair. These simple and mundane activities cannot be programmed in touch.

Nearly all speech acts contain elements of the universe of touch. The little boy who delightfully shouts, "Look at the elephants! Look at the elephants!" displays his feelings as well as calls for another to attend to the elephants. When an adult relates an exciting personal venture, variations in tone, rhythm, and intensity of feeling expressed tend to elicit the same visceral sensations from listeners as the teller experiences. The spoken word nearly always communicates in the universe of touch as well as in the universe of discourse. Sometimes the spoken word is very exciting; at other times it is boring.

The universe of discourse allows human beings to construct, retain, modify, and share complex bodies of information. If human beings were restricted to communicating via touch and appearance, they would be capable of constructing far more complex forms of action than that possible by other animals. But they would not be able to construct the complex sets of social relationships we take for granted. For instance, the complex social programming required for running a city bus line could never be accomplished without discourse. It is discourse that allows for the construction of social structures.

After we learn to read and write, we translate discourse into the visual mode, but it remains discourse; writing does not communicate in the universe of appearance, but photographs do. Discourse, even in the written mode, can elicit shared feelings. And, of course, many features of appearance can also be put into discourse. Nonetheless, the old cliche "A picture is worth a thousand words" has some validity. Not all aspects of appearance can be readily translated into discourse.

Appearance

Children visually monitor their environment and organize their actions in the light of the information they acquire, are provided with "an appearance," and appear before others long before they enter the universe of appearance. Early in life, infants learn to anticipate on the basis of the appearance of others; they learn that certain actions will be taken toward them by their mothers and that other actions will be taken toward them by older siblings. They also learn that they can anticipate future developments on the basis of the facial gestures and expressive sounds of their caregivers. They learn that if mother approaches singing, with a smile on her face, she is likely to behave differently than if she approaches in silence and with a frown on her face.

Almost from the beginning, infants have appearances foisted on them. Little boys are dressed in blue and little girls in pink. These appearances structure the actions of others toward them, but they do not originally structure the actions of infants. Nonetheless, the appearances provided for infants by others are significant. To the extent that others use the appearances of the infant to organize their actions toward the infant, the appearances of the infant have consequences for the patterns of behavior established by infants and children.

Another step into the universe of appearance is taken when the child becomes capable of adopting the standpoint of others and becomes an object unto herself. For example, a little girl moves into this level as she learns to attach labels to herself, to designate herself. She thereby has acquired an identity. The first identity acquired is a personal or unique identity. She recognizes that she is something different from others; she is a baby, and others are Mommy and Daddy. When she learns that she shares the identity of baby with others, she has acquired a categorical identity as well as a personal identity. Then she learns that other people, in addition to her mother and father, are mommies and daddies. Also she learns that the categorical identities of baby and mother are linked to each other differently than are the categorical identities of baby and father. When the child has achieved this level of sophistication, she can then self consciously act toward herself with the intention of appearing before others to display a specific identity. From that time on, when the child makes social contact, she does not merely have contact with others; she also situates herself in relation to others.

The universe of appearance has both stable and dynamic dimensions. Those features of appearance that remain more or less constant across situations, such as sex, age, and physical features, constitute the stable dimensions of the universe of appearance. Those that regularly vary, such as direction of eye gaze, smiles, and grooming, make up the more dynamic dimensions of the universe of appearance. We use the information we acquire visually to categorize others, formulate anticipations and organize our actions toward others.

When people situate themselves via appearance, usually a series of identities are offered. For example, one is not merely a professor but a male, six feet tall, sixty years old, white haired, and fat. Some of these identities may be rendered more or less irrelevant as one of the identities is made especially relevant. Often, the level of agreement on which identities are relevant is almost total; other times, there are disagreements on which identities are relevant.

After children have entered the universe of appearance, they are aware that, nearly always, whenever they establish social contact, they at the same time are a "what" or a series of "whats" to others. Exceptions include when contact is made in the dark or via the telephone.

Many identities presented in appearance become so taken for granted that people are not aware that they are presenting themselves as a distinctive object. Identities that remain relatively constant—size, age, gender, and physical appearance—become part of our taken-for-granted social reality. They structure both our behavior and the behavior of others toward us. But even the most taken-for-granted identities were at one time problematic. Nearly all take it for granted that they will clothe themselves before they appear in public. Yet very young children do not always clothe themselves before leaving the house. Usually, when children run out of the house in the nude, their caregivers firmly inform them that they are not to appear on the streets naked.

The presentation of some identities in appearance is a very self conscious activity. For instance, the woman who complains that she has "nothing to wear" to a social function usually has a closet full of clothes. It is not that she has nothing to wear in the literal sense of the phrase but that she does not have clothes that will allow her to present the identity she wishes to present for the occasion.

When we are self-conscious about our appearance, we are "onstage"; we adopt the standpoint of others toward ourselves and assess our appearance from the standpoint of others. Some professors, for example, would not be caught dead in front of a class without a suit and tie; others dress casually. Whenever we self-consciously select clothes to wear, decide to shave or not shave, comb or not comb our hair before we appear, we adopt the standpoint of an audience—the audience may be one person or a multitude—and act toward ourselves from the standpoint of the audience. When we give conscious attention to our appearance, "we dress toward' or address some audience whose validating responses are essential to the establishment of our self" (Stone 1981b, 193).

When we exercise control over our appearance and have the identity we wish to project validated, it is a source of pride, poise, and confidence. In the words of one respondent, "When I get the dress I feel right in, I feel like a million dollars. It makes an altogether different person out of me" (Stone 1981b, 194). Conversely, when we present an appearance that renders problematic an identity that is important to us, it can be the source of great embarrassment and loss of poise (Gross and Stone 1964). For instance, the professor who has been holding forth with great enthusiasm in front of a large class may note snickers from the class and that several students are glancing at his crotch. If he looks down and notices that his fly is unzipped, he may become so embarrassed that it is only with great difficulty that he continues the lecture.

Those who regularly encounter strangers in their work are usually self-conscious about their appearance. Salespeople, judges, police, and doormen self-consciously clothe themselves to announce their identities clearly. They manage their appearance to elicit particular responses from others.

The establishment of particular identities and the eliciting of specific responses from others through appearance is not limited to clothing, grooming, and personal demeanor. Offices are decorated to present, or at least enhance the presentation of, some identities. The judge not only appears in a robe but in addition sits behind an imposing desk and is framed by props that enhance a special position. Those who work in government offices, have a command position in the military, are business executives, or offer professional services usually self-consciously arrange their offices with the intention of eliciting deference from others.

People do not always have control over their appearance. For example, the handsome young man, dressed fit to kill and having dinner in the most expensive restaurant in town but with a spot of gravy on his beard, does not have complete control over his appearance—although he might think he has. His friends are likely to direct his attention to the spot of gravy so that he can present the identity he wishes; but strangers may simply note the gravy spot in passing and smile.

Our appearances are not incidental and shallow dimensions of our lives. Even those who belittle the importance of appearance are concerned with some facets of their appearance. They merely reject some dimensions of appearance that others think are important.

Whenever we appear before others, we announce our identities. The woman with uncombed hair, in dirty jeans and with her shirttail hanging out, shopping in the supermarket, makes a statement about herself as surely as does the woman who appears at the supermarket dressed as if she were going to a cocktail party. Each time we appear before others, we present ourselves; we thereby imply pasts and futures. The identities announced in appearance allow others to situate us within the macrostructure. The person dressed in a police uniform announces to all that she has been employed by the community to perform certain tasks; she has certain responsibilities and prerogatives that have been authorized by the community.

Just as it is possible to lie in discourse and to mask one's feelings, it is possible to announce false identities in appearance. Con artists, for example, specialize in announcing false identities in both appearance and discourse. Their success hinges upon the effective presentation of false identities.

The universe of appearance allows us to locate ourselves and each other within our social structure. If every time two people made contact it was necessary for them to become situated by announcing their identities in discourse, becoming situated would consume far more time and effort than it does. In contrast, the universe of appearance allows us to establish consensual categorical identities the moment copresence is established. Two of the common procedures for activating categorical identities via communication in appearance are uniforms and insignia. Visual symbols of that sort announce identities as soon as contact is made.

Interrelations

In most encounters we simultaneously communicate with each other in all three universes. Many encounters are contextualized by identities that are announced and validated in appearance. Almost from the moment of contact, each person informs the other of her feelings. Then, through discourse, each provides the other with additional information. Far more occurs in most encounters than merely a series of turn-taking vocalizations.

When people engage in face-to-face interaction by tone of voice, facial expressions, and maintaining physical distance or coming nearer, they indicate to each other their attraction to or repulsion from each other while they address a host of topics by speaking about them. Most face-to-face encounters are originally contextualized by identities announced via appearance. Most of these identities are taken for granted; they are not given conscious attention. When the taken-for-granted world of the universe of appearance is violated, then we become very conscious of the significance of appearance. For example, if we are discussing the good fortunes of the local athletic team with a woman acquaintance at the local tavern and she begins disrobing in the middle of our conversation, most of us would have difficulty continuing the conversation as if nothing out of the ordinary was occurring.

The significance of discourse activity often is contingent on the communicative acts in touch and appearance that accompany the discourse. Consider the following transaction: One man, who had acted as a representative for two others in a confrontation with an opposing group, was relating his encounter with the opposition to the other two in a boastful tone of voice. He claimed he had frightened the person he had met with. He was interrupted by one of the other two with, "Right, Jack! Right!" The statement was delivered in a mild shout with biting sarcasm. The name of the one who was bragging was not Jack. He stopped in midsentence and a bewildered look spread across his face. Had the statement been directed at someone whose name was Jack and been delivered with a tone of voice indicating pleased enthusiasm, the impact of the statement would have been entirely different. The discourse content of the two statements would be exactly the same, but the consequences would be different.

The significance of discourse acts also is often contingent on what has been previously or is simultaneously being communicated in appearance. Most encounters are contextualized by categorical identities that remain constant during the encounter. For example, when a woman approaches the service desk of a local department store, she and the clerk establish the categorical identities of clerk and customer as soon as they establish copresence; and those identities usually frame their subsequent transactions. If, however, during the subsequent transactions the clerk and customer uncover the fact that they both are newcomers to the community and that both previously lived in the same city, the significance of their categorical identities of clerk and customer is likely to recede to the background as other identities are established in discourse.

The presentation of categorical identities in appearance is one way of achieving stability in social structures. People who routinely interact with strangers usually don uniforms, badges, and other devices to announce their categorical identities in appearance to all. These announcements in appearance not only allow for quick and easy identification but also are a source of social order. Physicians, nurses, and other employees of hospitals usually announce their categorical identities in each encounter with new patients in appearance.

As social encounters unfold, people change their postures, shift their gaze, come closer to each other or withdraw from each other, change their facial expressions, gesture with their hands, and sometimes touch each other. They also converse with each other in discourse. Sometimes they laugh, squeal with delight, grunt, and whine. Through these and assorted other activities they indicate their attraction to or repulsion from each other, as well as discuss a host of topics. There is far more to face-to-face interaction than what is contained in discourse. Those with affection for each other often lean into and touch each other as they converse. Strangers usually maintain their distance as they converse.

In general, when people interact in face-to-face encounters, they indicate the nature of their relatedness in the universe of touch and appearance, while they attend to other issues in the universe of discourse. Some children snuggle up against their parents while the parent is instructing them; other parents and children seldom touch each other when the parent is instructing the child. Some children and their parents routinely become intertwined like baboons when they do things together; others act like robots.

The sounds, facial expressions, and other movements of young children directly reflect their internal sensations. As they become more sophisticated, however, they learn to control the public display of their emotions. Individuals frequently display a sweet smile when they are upset; other times, individuals indicate they are angry when they do not feel angry. Control over the display of one's emotions can be achieved only after the individual has learned to adopt the standpoint of others toward herself. Before people can intentionally attempt to deceive others by masking their internal feelings, they have to have entered the universe of appearance. Young children usually are rather incompetent liars.

Just as we are not always in control of our actions, we often are not able to control the display of our internal feelings. For instance, the man who has internalized the belief that homosexual behavior is vile has difficulty controlling his expressive behavior when he observes two male homosexuals kissing and fondling. When we experience intense emotions, we usually have difficulty in controlling our expressive acts. Often, when intense emotions are aroused, our actions tend to become responses to the immediate situation; they are not structured by a distal future.

Summary

Infants first come into contact with the external world through the tactile mode. Then they acquire the ability to differentiate sights and sounds. They link the sights and sounds to tactile experience and visceral sensations. As these linkages are forged, the infant acquires the ability to anticipate tactile contact and visceral sensations. As the child acquires the ability to anticipate, the original diffuse sensations are transformed into experiences. In the process the child acquires some ability to control her own experiences. During the same period, the child establishes linkages between kinetic experiences and experiences derived via the external sensory modes. External, visceral, and kinetic experiences become complexly intertwined. These intertwinings become taken for granted and provide the child with the ability to structure actions.

The emergence of structured sensations in conjunction with the emergence of greater mobility provide children with the ability to initiate, modify, and break social contacts. In the early years of life children have little control over either the establishment or breaking of social contact. They are at the mercy of others for the social contacts they establish. But as they socially mature, they acquire greater ability to make and break social contacts. The ability to break contact is as critical as the ability to make contact; both give the individual autonomy (Leichty 1975, 67).

Early social contact provides the child and caregivers with differentiated experiences. When the child cries for and receives attention, the child has one set of experiences and the caregivers a different set of experiences. As children acquire the ability to establish shared foci, they become capable of sharing experiences with others. Children begin to enter the universe of touch by becoming aware that they have the same internal experiences as another person. They become full-fledged participants in the universe of discourse when they can establish shared foci without reference to an object in the immediate environment. They begin to enter the universe of appearance when they can differentiate others on the basis of their appearance and link anticipations to appearances. They have become full-fledged participants in the universe of appearance when they self consciously attend to their own appearance with the intention of eliciting a particular response from an audience.

Entry into these three universes is complexly intertwined. Children become participants in the universe of touch before they enter either the universe of discourse or appearance. Entry into the universe of appearance appears to be contingent on prior mastery of enough discourse symbols to allow the child to become an object unto herself. The capacity to participate in each of these universes continues to expand as each person enters into new social worlds.

It is by sharing sensations that human beings become embedded with each other. The universe of discourse, especially when supplemented with the written word, allows us to accumulate and retain large bodies of information. By becoming competent in the universe of appearance people quickly and effectively socially situate themselves. The universe of touch allows us to empathize with each other; the universe of discourse allows us to program complex shared futures; and the universe of appearance allows us to locate ourselves and each other within the social structure.

Chapter 4 Basic Elements of Sociation

Through our sensory modalities, primarily those of tactility, sight, and sound, we establish contact with each other. Through the universes of communication — touch, discourse, and appearance — we share sensations, share information, and mutually identify ourselves. Our sensorium and communicative abilities allow us to relate to each other in a multitude of ways. We appear before each other, identify ourselves and each other, speak to each other, caress each other, and punch each other. Each time we become involved with another, elements of *sociation* are produced. Sometimes, the interconnection between people is limited to a single basic element of sociation; other times, the involvement is composed of complex clusters of several elements of sociation.

Each element of sociation is a joint accomplishment. An individual can initiate an element of sociation, but unless a second person responds to the first person's initiation, an element of sociation is not produced. Most connections between people are initiated by one person; but sometimes elements of sociation are established by two persons simultaneously noting and acting toward each other. When we and another person have a shared past, we often produce composite clusters of elements of sociation the moment we make contact with each other.

Some of our associations with others, especially strangers, are of minimal intensity and duration. Others are intense and enduring. At one extreme, two strangers may merely note each other in passing. At the other extreme are the complex clusters of elements of sociation established when a married couple reconvene after an extended separation.

Infants are surrounded by others; others act toward them, do things for them, and provide them with a host of sensations. But young infants cannot establish elements of sociation; they are conscious neither of others nor themselves. The establishment of all elements of sociation requires two persons who are conscious of the presence of the other and conscious of the fact that they constitute part of the perceptual field of the other. Both consciousness of the other and self-consciousness are necessary precursors for the production of elements of sociation. After consciousness of other and self have been acquired, people can produce elements of sociation whenever they enter each other's perceptual fields.

47

The acquisition of the ability to establish elements of sociation proceeds from first mastering the simplest elements to the mastery of more complex elements. In a similar manner, the establishment of complex composite social connections between adults also proceeds in an orderly sequence. Persons with common or shared pasts, however, can simultaneously establish several elements of sociation the moment they make social contact.

The six primitive elements of sociation are (1) copresence; (2) reciprocal attentiveness; (3) social responsiveness; (4) functional identities; (5) shared focus; and (6) social objective. If it is impossible to establish copresence, none of the other elements of sociation can be established. Social responsiveness cannot be produced until after reciprocal attentiveness has been established; and functional identities cannot be activated until after people have become socially responsive. And a shared focus must be established before a social objective can be produced.

Copresence

Copresence is established when two people are aware that they constitute part of the other's perceptual field. We continually enter into and leave the perceptual field of others. Sometimes we are aware of our presence in the perceptual field of others, and sometimes we are not. If another attends to us, but we are unaware of their attention, copresence is not established. Or, reciprocally if we note the presence of another, but the other is unaware of our presence, copresence is not established. Copresence is established when people are mutually aware that they are part of each other's perceptual field. For example, when a young boy sneaks up behind his mother without his mother's noting his approach, they are not copresent. As soon as the child shouts, "Boo!" copresence is established.

It is not until children acquire consciousness of being an object in the perceptual field of others that they can establish copresence. Infants have extensive social contact with others before they acquire consciousness of copresence. After children have become conscious of the fact that they enter and leave the perceptual field of others, they can act to establish, maintain, modify, or destroy copresence.

When consciousness of copresence has emerged, the distinction between private and public becomes viable. Then children become aware that when they enter the presence of another person, they and their actions may be noted by others, and others may act toward them. After consciousness of copresence has emerged, children can act to keep their actions private or make them public. Then children sometimes hide some of their actions from others.

Each time a person enters the presence of another, he surrenders a degree of privacy. Whenever we are in the presence of another, our actions become part of the public domain. At least one other person has the opportunity to acquire information about us. Sometimes others spy on us. When we subsequently learn that another person has spied on us, we usually feel the other person has taken advantage of us. The victims of spies have control of their privacy taken from them.

Copresence can be established visually, auditorily, tactilely, or through some combination of these three sensory modes. When copresence is established visually, the identity of each, at least to a minimal extent, is known by the other. If they subsequently make contact with each other, one or both may recognize the other as the same person they saw earlier. When copresence is established only in the auditory mode, it is often difficult to identify the other. Of course, when auditory copresence is established between persons with a shared past, then each can identify the other on the basis of voice recognition. When an unknown person calls us on the telephone and harasses us, however, it is impossible subsequently to identify the caller. Identities can, of course, be offered in discourse. When we make telephonic contact with a stranger, we often provide our identity via voice — "This is Carl Couch of the sociology department." When copresence is limited to the tactile mode, it is almost impossible to identify the other.

The establishment and maintenance of copresence may be very supportive or very threatening. Young children frequently look around to see if a parent is nearby. If they note that the parent has disappeared, they may become distraught and cry. Those who have mutual affection for each other usually enjoy each other's presence even when each is involved in a personal activity. For example, a husband and wife may feel more comfortable when each is doing homework for their respective jobs when they are in each other's presence than when alone.

Of course, the opposite is also sometimes the case. We often isolate ourselves so that we do not have to concern ourselves with the fact that another might intrude on us while we do our work or enjoy ourselves. Whenever we are copresent, we are aware that the other may act toward us. And whenever another acts toward us, we lose a degree of autonomy. At the minimum, we have to ignore the other's actions.

Reciprocal Attentiveness

Copresence may be established unintentionally, but the establishment of reciprocal attentiveness requires at least a minimal degree of intentional activity. Two strangers who enter the same elevator are copresent. They are aware that they are part of another's perceptual field. But they may not direct their attention to each other; or only one person may attend to the other, while the second person is "lost in thought" or focuses attention on the floor indicator.

If one person focuses attention on another, unilateral attentiveness is established, but not reciprocal attentiveness. The element of reciprocal attentiveness is not established unless both parties direct their attention to the other. Spies and eavesdroppers avoid reciprocal attentiveness; they attempt to maintain unilateral attentiveness. Reciprocal attentiveness is established when each party monitors the other, acquires information about the other, and both are aware that they are the recipient of the other's attention.

Reciprocal attentiveness may be very fleeting and incidental. For example, two shoppers at a mall may indifferently glance at each other as they almost bump into one another rounding a corner, with each proceeding on without giving the other a second thought. Or reciprocal attentiveness may be fleeting but intense. Two strollers on a dark street in a dangerous part of the city may unexpectedly enter each other's perceptual field. Both might be frightened and intensely monitor each other until copresence is broken. Each is likely to give the other as wide a berth as possible as both continue on their separate ways.

In a similar manner, two solitary pheasant hunters walking across the prairie a half mile removed from each other may note each other. They may continue on their separate ways as they watch each other out of the corner of their eyes. If that occurs, for a short time they have been reciprocally attentive. They have entered each other's perceptual field and directed their attention to each other.

In some encounters, people are engrossed with each other. Their attention is riveted on one another as they gaze into each other's eyes and closely attend to what each says. Young children and their parents sometimes cling to each other's hands when they are in danger of being separated at a crowded shopping mall. People who cling to each other often are visually and auditorily attentive to external events while maintaining reciprocal attentiveness through touch.

Reciprocal attentiveness is not necessarily symmetrical. Young children are sometimes very attentive to a parent, while the parent gives them only incidental attention from time to time. Conversely, sometimes, as when children undertake something the parent regards as dangerous, the parent is very attentive to the child, and the child is indifferent to the parent's attentiveness. Sometimes reciprocal attentiveness is symmetrical, and sometimes it is asymmetrical.

Whether reciprocal attentiveness is symmetrical or asymmetrical, it creates and maintains a social bondedness. The experiences of both parties are partially determined by the activities of the other; and both parties acquire information about the other that they may use in the organization of their behavior.

Reciprocal attentiveness underlies all social action from the simplest to the most complex forms. If people cannot attend to each other, they cannot act toward, for, against, or with each other. In some encounters reciprocal attentiveness is sustained and intense; in others it is intermittent and incidental. When two people who are very fearful of each other establish copresence, they carefully and intensely note each other's action. When the encounter is of little significance and routine, they often only indifferently make note of each other.

Whenever two strangers attempt to coordinate their activities to accomplish a novel objective that is significant to both of them, it is necessary for them to monitor each other's actions carefully to achieve the objective. For example, when two mountain climbers who have never climbed with each other before attempt to scale a mountain for the first time, they are very attentive to each other. In contrast, when two people with an extensive shared past work in unison on a routine task, usually all that is necessary is for each of them to note each other's activity from time to time. For example, after a priest and an altar boy have performed Mass together hundreds of times, all that is necessary is for each of them to now and then note the other's activity. The reciprocal attentiveness in such encounters is often so habitual that those involved are not even conscious that they are attentive to each other.

Often when people establish reciprocal attentiveness, they acknowledge each other. But sometimes they merely note that they are the recipients of attention from the other, but do not acknowledge the other's attention. When each acknowledges the attention of the other, they become socially responsive. It sometimes occurs that one person acknowledges the attention of the other without the other reciprocating in kind. Then only unilateral responsiveness is established.

Social Responsiveness

When friends or acquaintances establish copresence, they usually acknowledge each other. The acknowledgment often consists of simple reciprocating acts. Each smiles, waves, or nods to the other. They may also speak to one another. When strangers establish copresence, they usually allocate some attention to each other, although often it is only a minimal level of attentiveness. Often they do not acknowledge each other's attention. Depending on the nature of the copresence, they may acknowledge each other's attention or may actively avoid acknowledging each other's attention by pretending the other is not there.

When people reciprocally acknowledge each other they move from merely attending to each other to being socially responsive. The level of social responsiveness ranges from curt exchanges of head nods to screams of delight by dear friends who reunite after a long period of separation.

Social responsiveness cannot be produced until after reciprocal attentiveness is established. But the establishment of reciprocal attentiveness does not assure that people will be socially responsive. Two people may note each other, but be indifferent to each other's presence and pass by without either person's responding to the other's presence. And, of course, one person may be responsive while the other is indifferent. Social responsiveness is established when both use the information they obtain in the organization of their actions.

There are two basic forms of social responsiveness: bilateral responsiveness and mutual responsiveness. People are bilaterally responsive when they indicate that they have noted the presence of the other and modify their own actions on the basis of the other's presence or activity, but only to act with respect to the other. People are mutually responsive when they indicate they have noted the presence of the other and act to inform the other that they either acknowledge a shared past between them and/or indicate a willingness to act with the other.

For example, when two people who know each other but dislike each other establish reciprocal attentiveness, they may snub each other. In such cases, at least a minimal level of bilateral responsiveness is established. Each acts with respect to the other, but each indicates an intention not to act with the other. In a similar manner, when two strangers note each other's approach as they meet in a hallway, each may modify his line of action to avoid bumping into the other. When that occurs, they are bilaterally responsive.

When two friends meet in the hallway — perhaps each is on the way to his office — they are likely to be mutually responsive. When they exchange greetings and smiles, they indicate that they have a shared past that both acknowledge. Friends and acquaintances are often both bilaterally and mutually responsive. They are bilaterally responsive as they modify their actions to pass by each other and mutually responsive when they exchange smiles.

Whenever people are mutually responsive, there is at least a minimal merger of self and other. Each indicates that he is implicated with the other and/or is willing to become implicated with the other. Each indicates the other is worthy of a response, and a degree of autonomy is surrendered. When people are mutually responsive, they indicate to each other that they are willing to associate with the other.

Whenever people are socially responsive, either bilaterally or mutually, they indicate the other is of some significance. Even when two people snub one another, each indicates the other person has been noted and is of some significance, even though only negatively so. When people are mutually responsive, they have a more intense association than when they merely note each other.

Functional Identities

Reciprocal attentiveness and social responsiveness are present-centered activities. Functional identities are future-centered. Functional identities are established when each person displays his intentions and has those intentions noted by another. The display and detection of intentions are necessary for the production of complex forms of social action. When persons do not display their intentions, or if one fails to detect the displayed intentions of the other, coordinated action is impossible. Without the display and detection of each other's intentions, persons may act toward or with respect to each other, but they cannot act with each other. Functional identities are established when "both parties mutually impute to self and other sequences of forthcoming behavior" (Scheff 1970, 203).

The functional identities displayed may be either congruent or incongruent. Congruent functional identities are established when each person notes and accepts the intentions of the other. Incongruent functional identities are established when the intentions of the other are noted but are ignored or rejected. For example, the little boy attempting to sneak out of the house and has his intentions noted by his parent is projecting a line of action incongruent with the action preferred by the parent. If the child is quick enough, he might escape despite being detected, but his intentions are incompatible with the intentions of his parent. They have incongruent functional identities.

Functional identities may be parallel or differentiated. For instance, when two persons attempt to free a vehicle stuck in the mud by pushing in unison, they establish parallel and congruent functional identities. They may attempt to free the vehicle by one pushing and the other driving, then they establish differential congruent identities. The projection of similar lines of forthcoming action may result in the production of incongruent functional identities. For example, when two persons, on approaching a narrow doorway, both pause and wait for the other to proceed, they display parallel intentions, but their intentions are incongruent. To become congruent one must indicate that the other should proceed, and the other must detect and accept the line of action projected by the first person.

Incongruent functional identities are sometimes established when two people inform each other that neither will subordinate himself to the other. Each indicates that he intends to retain his autonomy. That condition, of course, is often a prelude to either disassociation or conflict. In contrast, when congruent functional identities are established, then each informs the other that not only will they be responsive to each other in the ongoing present, but in addition they will mutually subordinate themselves to each other's forthcoming lines of action. They indicate that they will coordinate their future actions to accomplish either compatible personal objectives or a social objective.

Congruent functional identities establish mutually acceptable intentions. But the establishment of mutually acceptable intentions does not assure the successful completion of the projected activity. One or both may not be capable of carrying out their intentions. Furthermore, intentions are often blocked by unexpected external events that cannot be controlled by either of them.

Shared Foci

Persons establish a shared focus when both become aware that the other is attending to the same event or object. Two persons may have a common focus without its being a shared focus. For example, students in a classroom may be attentive to the teacher without being attentive to each other. A shared focus is established when they attend to each other and both indicate that each has noted a given event. For instance, the teacher may make a mistake. One student may note the mistake and make eye contact with another. But if the other was daydreaming and did not note the mistake, no shared focus is established. If each indicates that he noted the mistake, then they have a shared focus.

A shared focus may be anything. It can be one person's clothing, a television show, or a third person. The critical feature of a shared focus is that each is attentive to some third object and that mutual awareness of that condition is established between them.

A shared focus may be established simultaneously with reciprocal attentiveness, or it may not be established until congruent functional identities have been established. For example, when two students in a classroom make eye contact and smile in unison immediately after a joke has been offered by the instructor, they simultaneously establish reciprocal attentiveness and a shared focus.

On other occasions, a shared focus is established when each detects the line of action projected by the other. For example, two persons may independently of each other hear a cry for help and take action to render assistance. When they near the source of the cry, they may note that both of them are going to the aid of the same person. In such instances, a shared focus is established simultaneously with congruent functional identities.

When a shared focus is established, it broadens the relatedness. Two people with a shared focus are interconnected through their shared focus in addition to being reciprocally attentive and socially responsive. Then, if they link congruent functional identities to the shared focus, they indicate they will continue, for at least a moment or two, to act with each other.

Social Objectives

When persons link congruent functional identities to a shared focus, they establish a social objective. They establish mutual intentions that they, as a unit, will accomplish something — an objective — by coordinating their actions toward the shared focus. When a social objective is present, persons indicate to each other that they have a shared future. The duration of the shared future may be very short, or it may endure for a lengthy period.

When two persons act in unison to achieve a social objective, they must maintain reciprocal attentiveness, mutual responsiveness, and link congruent functional identities to a shared focus. Persons may act toward and with respect to one another without a social objective, but to act in unison requires a social objective. A social objective must be established before cooperative action can unfold. The presence of a social objective, of course, does not assure that cooperation will be achieved. One or both may be incompetent, or external factors may intrude and prevent the achievement of the objective.

Summary

Children acquire the ability to produce elements of sociation in a sequential manner. They become capable of establishing reciprocal attentiveness before they are socially responsive; and they are socially responsive before they can produce congruent functional identities. In a similar manner, they are capable of establishing shared foci before they are able to project social objectives. It is not until after they have acquired the ability to produce these basic elements of sociation that they are able to act *with* others.

Socialized persons with common or shared pasts can produce complex clusters of elements of sociation in an instant. But when persons with neither a common nor shared past establish copresence in a nonroutine situation, take each other into account, and act in unison, these basic elements of sociation are usually produced in a sequential manner. The sequence is the same as the sequence children go through in becoming competent interactors. After establishing copresence, strangers in a nonroutine situation first produce reciprocal attentiveness, then become socially responsive, and then produce functional identities. A shared focus is produced before a social objective is formulated. Although often a social objective is formulated almost the instant a shared focus is established.

Two people may produce a shared focus at the same moment they become reciprocally attentive. For example, two copresent persons may here a loud noise and then make eye contact. In such encounters they recognize that both of them have a shared focus the moment they make eye contact. In other instances a shared focus may not be produced until after they have established functional identities. For example, two people may independently of each other act to aid a fallen child and not note each other's presence until they have both began going to the aid of the child. In such an encounter a shared focus and social objective are established the moment they become aware of each other.

When two people with a shared past make contact, all of these elements of sociation and perhaps several additional elements can be established the instant copresence is achieved. Then elements of sociation are produced vertically or hierarchically instead of sequentially. The ability of human beings to use their common and shared pasts allows them to construct complex sets of elements of sociation instantaneously.

With the exception of copresence, the production of all the other elements of sociation is a social accomplishment. One person may enter into the perceptual field of another and thereby establish copresence. In order to transform copresence into reciprocal attentiveness, however, each must attend to the other. If one of the persons is entranced with something else, he may not allocate any attention to the other. Of course, the one who has entered the other's perceptual field can then take action "demanding" attention. Young children often enter the perceptual field of their parents without the parents immediately allocating attention to them. Children may scream for attention and thereby command the attention of the parents, but they are not always successful in getting it.

Elements of sociation are dyadic phenomena; it requires two persons willfully relating to each other to produce them. If one person refuses to allocate any attention to the other, reciprocal attentiveness will not be established. In short, it takes two people to establish elements of sociation and coordinated activity, but one person can prevent the establish of any element of sociation. A degree of mutual consent underlies each element of sociation. For example, even when one person beats another, if the victim can focus attention on something else, no elements of sociation are established.

Chapter 5 Elementary Forms of Social Action

Human beings sometimes help one another, other times they compete, occasionally they do violence to one another, and they often cooperate. Some of the actions they take toward, for, and with each other are of short duration and simple; other instances of social action endure for extended periods and are composites of two or more forms of social action. For example, individuals frequently accommodate to each other while they compete with each other. The production of social action requires two people to establish elements of sociation. When two people produce simple units of social action, only a few elements of sociation are established. When they produce complex units of social action, several elements of sociation are established.

The elements of sociation can be combined in several different ways to produce many different kinds of social action. Eight elementary forms of social action commonly produced are (1) autocratic action; (2) the chase; (3) conflict; (4) social competition; (5) social panic; (6) accommodation; (7) mutuality; and (8) cooperation. Many encounters contain complex intertwinings of two or more of these eight elementary forms. People often simultaneously compete and cooperate with each other. A friendly game of cards contains features of both cooperation and competition. In this chapter, however, each of these eight forms is examined in pure form.

The production of all units of social action requires that at least two persons establish copresence and produce one or more additional elements of sociation. Social action is a dyadic phenomenon. Individuals can seek out each other to initiate social action, but social activity cannot occur until two or more persons have established copresence. Once copresence is created, then additional elements of sociation can be established. In many social encounters, individuals act with respect to more than one other person. When that occurs, others are sometimes taken into account in a global manner, as when the speaker scans the audience. At the conclusion of the speech, the audience may applaud. Then the speaker is the recipient of acts from a multitude of others. In such encounters, the speaker is one half of the dyad and the audience is the other half. In other situations, as at a meeting of a small group of friends, each may take turns speaking. Even then, the interaction tends to be dyadic. One party speaks at a time, while the others listen.

Not all human behavior is social action. Human beings spend a considerable amount of their time alone. An explanation of the action taken by an individual who is alone would require an examination of that person's social past and what the individual intends to do with others in the future. For example, to explain the phenomenon of a young man spending hours alone practicing shooting baskets necessitates giving attention to his social past with others that were focused on the game of basketball and his intentions of becoming a star player. Nonetheless, the actions of a single person practicing in a gymnasium is not itself social activity. To explain the actions of solitary individuals it is necessary to analyze their social pasts and how they link themselves to the social world that encompasses them, but the actions of an individual separated from all others is not social action.

Autocratic Activity

Autocratic activity occurs when one person acts toward another and treats the other person as an object. Strictly speaking, it is not a form of social action. One person attends to another, is unilaterally responsive to another, and intentionally organizes actions toward the other. The target is not aware of the person acting toward her. Only the intentionality of the autocrat structures the action. The target of an autocratic act may be intentionally organizing her action, but not toward the autocrat. The activity of the target may require the autocrat to modify her intentions, but the target is unaware of the consequences of her actions for the autocrat. For example, the target of a hired assassin may unexpectedly take a vacation and thereby prevent the assassin from accomplishing her objective. The activity of the target may keep the autocrat from achieving her objective, but the activity was not intentionally organized to do so.

Autocratic actions may be either tyrannical or parental. Tyrannical action, whether an instance of a parent forcing a child to take a bath or an assassin killing a political figure, is organized to control the life of another. Parental action, whether in the form of a parent grabbing a child to prevent the child from falling or a nurse putting a blanket over a sleeping patient, is organized to benefit the other.

All early infant care is autocratic action. The survival of human infants requires that others give extensive attention to their welfare. The infant must be treated as an object; most are treated as precious objects. Severely injured and ill persons also are often treated as precious objects.

Tyrants adversely impinge on others. The tyrant is unconcerned with the welfare of the other. The tyrant organizes actions toward others on the basis of her personal objectives; the interests of the other are only of consequence when they interfere with the tyrant's achieving her objective. The initiator of tyrannical activity attends and responds to the other, but only for purposes of acting upon the other person.

Parental activity attempts to facilitate the well-being of another. It is a necessary form of activity to transform the human infant into an autonomous person. Tyrannical action is to some degree destructive of others. At the minimum it deflects the intended action of another. For example, when a little girl sticks her foot out to trip another child walking by, the intended action of the target is deflected.

The Chase

The chase is truly social action. The production of a chase requires two organisms capable of autonomous action to be reciprocally attentive and bilaterally responsive. In addition, they project incongruent functional identities. The prototype of the chase is a predator attempting to capture prey, while the prey attempts to escape. When a predator stalks a prey, the predator is acting autocratically. Only after the prey becomes aware that it is the focus of attention for the predator and organizes itself to escape the clutches of the predator and the predator notes the prey's effort to escape do they produce social action. Once the predator is spotted, both have taken the other into account; the chase is on.

Predator and prey are reciprocally attentive and bilaterally responsive to each other. Both attend to the other, and each organizes actions in part on the basis of the information obtained about the other's behavior. Each intentionally organizes behavior with respect to the other, and each projects a future. The predator projects a future of capture; the prey, one of escape. The chase is primarily a future-centered activity; the behavior of each is structured by the futures projected, but the futures projected are incongruent.

While the chase is future centered, the parties to a chase are highly attentive and responsive to each other. They focus their attention on each other and respond rapidly to each other's actions. They also continually assess and reassess each other's intentions.

The incongruent futures of the predator and prey in combination with the high level of bilateral responsiveness make this form of social activity highly unpredictable. It is an exciting form of social action for both participants and observers. The intriguing quality of this form of social action is indicated by the popularity of stories, movies, and television shows that have the chase as a major theme. Detective stories are convoluted chases. Even when the outcome of a chase has only minimal consequences, it tends to generate excitement. A game of tag can be very exciting.

Most chases are of short duration. For example, when a parent appears with her young daughter's pajamas in hand to ready her for bed, the child may attempt to escape, with the parent playfully chasing her for a moment or two. On occasion, however, chases endure for some time. Police detectives sometimes chase after a criminal suspect for months and years. Some chases are playful; others are deadly serious. Some parents and children regularly construct a playful chase whenever the parent attempts to ready the child for bed. When the police seek out escaped convicts, the chase is deadly serious for the police, the escaped convicts, and those living in the area.

During a chase one party is, for the moment at least, mutually recognized as more powerful than the other. Both the parent and the child who construct a chase recognize the parent as the more powerful party. The chase, like autocratic action, is an asymmetrical form of social action. Both autocratic action and the chase are asymmetrical, however, they are different. The target of autocratic action is merely an object; in chases, the prey is both an object and a subject. The prey notes the action of the predator and intentionally organizes her action with respect to the predator.

Chases end either with the capture of the prey or when the prey avoids the clutches of the predator and destroys copresence. When escaped convicts are captured, they are treated as objects. They are handcuffed and confined in prison. They are stripped of their ability to flee, bringing the chases to an end. Other times, the prey escapes and the predator cannot locate them. Then, after a passage of time, which may only a few seconds or several years, the predator gives up the chase.

Conflict

Sometimes the targets of a chase fight. That usually occurs only when they are cornered. Then they organize themselves, not to terminate copresence, but to act upon the other. The young boy who has been caught after a short chase by his parent may beat upon and scream at his parent. He then organizes himself to impinge adversely on his parent; he and his parent have transformed their predator-prey relation into one of combatants. The child's chances of success in the ensuing conflict are not great, but for the moment at least he attempts to answer adverse impingement with adverse impingement. In contrast to autocratic activity and the chase, conflict is symmetrical. Each combatant presumes she is capable of acting on the other. In many instances, each presumes she is more powerful than the other.

Intensity of conflict varies from an exchange of verbal insults between children to deadly combat between warriors. In all instances of conflict the participants are reciprocally attentive, socially responsive, and project parallel but incongruent identities. Conflict is enjoined when each acknowledges the other and acts upon the other. Combatants establish a degree of mutual responsiveness when they act toward each other. At the minimum they inform each other that they will fight. Once conflict is under way, then each often becomes only bilaterally responsive as each notes and responds to the other solely for the purpose of avoiding impingements and to organize herself to impinge effectively upon the other.

As with the chase, the action of combatants is structured by incongruent functional identities. But combatants project similar forthcoming action — each indicates a willingness to act toward the other to subdue or destroy the other. Combatants project identical futures, yet the futures are incongruent. Success by one means failure of the other. The futures projected in the chase are differentiated — one projects a future of escape and the other a future of capture.

The adverse impingement that is an integral part of conflict makes conflict a short-lived form of social action. Only when the combatants have extensive resources, as when two nations with equal protective and destructive powers confront each other, or when the conflict is constrained by "agreed-to rules," as in professional boxing matches, is prolonged conflict possible.

Conflict may be structured by a distal future. One or both parties may project a distal future of establishing a relationship wherein the other is the subordinate. When that is the case, the proximal future of subduing the other is encased within the distal future of achieving a stable dominant — submissive relationship. But conflict with any degree of intensity between parties who are relatively equal tends to become present-centered activity. To be an effective combatant when the other has equal resources, it is necessary for each combatant to be very attentive and responsive to the actions of the other within the immediate situation. If one combatant in a conflict between equals allocates some attention to the distal future, it places her at a disadvantage. Consequently, conflict between equals tends to escalate as combatants are very attentive and responsive to the immediately unfolding events.

Each combatant organizes herself primarily either to subdue the other or to drive the other from the scene. If the latter alternative occurs, then conflict may transform into a chase. The outcomes of conflictual encounters thus are subordination of one party by the other, flight, unilateral destruction, or mutual destruction. Combatants only in a limited sense act with each other; they act primarily upon one another. They attempt to interfere with each other and deflect one another's projected future. Conflict usually is chaotic. Neither combatants nor observers can predict with any certainty the outcome.

The actions of each are structured by her projected future. But each attempts to prevent the other from achieving the objective projected and deflects the actions of the other. It is usually an intense form of social action. Combatants are usually engrossed in their conflict and are relatively unaware of anything else.

Social Competition

A competitive encounter is established when two or more persons are aware of each other striving for an objective and the success of one renders the success of the other(s) less likely. A race is the prototype of social competition. People compete for many different things. Children sometimes compete with each other for the attention of their parents. Athletes compete with the opposing team and with their fellow team members for recognition. Competitors recognize that not all can be equally successful.

Competitors monitor each other, use the information acquired to organize their own behavior, and are aware that other competitors are doing the same. They have a shared focus and project parallel but incongruent identities. They are bilaterally responsive. They act with respect to one another, but they do not act toward each other nor do they merge their individual lines of action into a unified course of social action. Each competitor retains her autonomy. Competitors note the actions of the other(s) and use the information acquired to structure their own action. But they neither infringe on others nor are they infringed on by others.

Competition is a future-centered activity. The primary focus of attention is the future, the winning of the contest. The bilateral responsiveness of competitors is subordinated to and structured by their parallel but incongruent personal objectives. During competition, others are attended to, but primarily to note how they are doing. Each racer, for example, notes the relative location of others in relation to the finish line. But competitors do not act toward others, they only act with respect to each other. Of course, on occasion persons who have located themselves as competitors do act upon other competitors to increase their likelihood of success. When that occurs, however, they are no longer acting as competitors, but either autocratically to deflect the other or making a bid to transform their competition into conflict.

Competition, like conflict, rests on the presumption of equality. Each competitor presumes that she has a chance of success. Like conflict, the outcome of competitive encounters tends to be unpredictable. But in contrast to conflict, the behavior of competitors is highly predictable. Parallel personal objectives structure the behavior of competitors. As long as each allows the other to exercise autonomy, each of them pursues much the same course of action as they strive for success. Surprises occur, but generally speaking, the action follows a predictable course.

The intensity of the relatedness between competitors is far less then that established between combatants. Each competitor may give only incidental attention to others as she organizes herself almost solely on the basis of her relationship to the prize, while giving incidental attention to her fellow competitors.

Social Panic

Social panic prevails when a plurality of persons have a common focus that is defined as an uncontrollable threat, are attentive to each other, bilaterally responsive, and all attempt to avoid the threat by flight. The flight may be physical or social relocation of self. Those fleeing from a fire physically relocate themselves; when panic hits Wall Street and investors sell their stock to avoid further loses, they socially relocate themselves.

Social panic is in one sense the converse of social competition. Panicers act away from a shared focus, while competitors act toward a shared focus. Panic differs from the chase and conflict by the presence of a shared focus. It thereby is a somewhat more structured form of activity than the chase or conflict.

In pure panic, those involved are only bilaterally responsive to each other; they note the presence and activity of others only for the purpose of more effectively organizing their action to separate themselves from the threat. Others are noted, not to act toward them or with them, but to avoid them. Successful flight not only removes one from the threat but often destroys copresence.

Each participant in panic projects the same line of forthcoming behavior—flight. The functional identities may be congruent or incongruent. If the flight of one has no consequences for the flight of others, their functional identities are congruent. If the flight of one inhibits or interferes with the flight of others, their functional identities are incongruent. They then impinge on each other, and the action is likely to become chaotic. As long as panicers do not impinge on each other, however, their behavior retains the structure provided by their personal objectives.

Panic is a past- and present-centered activity. Futures are projected, but they are derivatives of the immediate past or the ongoing present. Yet the reciprocal attentiveness and bilateral responsiveness that prevail in panics are subordinated to the future of escape that is projected by all. In contrast to combatants, predators, and preys, who are highly responsive to each other in the ongoing present, competitors and panicers may be only incidentally responsive to each other. Others are of secondary concern. Successful panicers not only remove themselves from the threat but also disassociate themselves from each other. Most panics are of short duration.

Accommodation

Not all social contact is intentional; people often unintentionally enter one another's perceptual field. Many urban residents establish contact with a host of strangers each day. Travelers endure extended periods of copresence with others in subways, at bus stops, and on airplanes. When strangers make unintended contact both usually act to minimize their infringement on each other; they minimize their level of copresence; they thereby accommodate to each other.

Autocratic action and chases usually begin by one party intentionally seeking to establish contact with the other. These two forms of social action are initiated by unilateral intentionality. Combatants and competitors usually, but not always, convene as the consequence of bilateral intentionality. Both parties to conflictual and competitive encounters anticipate contact. In contrast, the contact that frames most accommodative encounters is unintentional. Neither party is normally interested in acting toward or with the other.

When people accidentally establish contact and neither is interested in becoming involved with the other, they act to minimize their level of copresence. The other is noted but usually not acknowledged. Each acts to minimize the level of social bondedness between them, not to enhance it. Each is attentive and responsive to the other, and each projects the functional identity of avoidance. Each displays the intentions of allowing the other as much autonomy as possible given the constraints of the immediate situation. For example, when three or four strangers are waiting at the same bus stop, they often avoid eye contact and maintain some physical distance. Then, if they board a crowded bus and have to stand next to one another, usually they will still attempt to minimize their infringement on each other.

When people accommodate to each other, they project personal objectives that are common and congruent; they act in a parallel manner, not with each other, but with respect to each other. When people accommodate to one another, they are not always successful. Bus riders sometimes become momentarily entangled despite their efforts to minimize involvement with each other.

Most accommodative encounters are constructed by strangers. We avoid becoming implicated with others we know little about and have no interest in knowing. But accommodative encounters are not limited to strangers. Friends frequently establish copresence unintentionally. When that occurs, they are often both bilaterally and mutually responsive to each other. They are bilaterally responsive to avoid becoming entangled with each other in the immediate situation and are mutually responsive as they acknowledge each other with smiles, nods, and hand waves.

When an accommodative encounter is successfully completed, each party provides the other with as much freedom as possible; accommodative encounters facilitate personal autonomy. When persons unintentionally find themselves entering each other's territory and accommodate to each other they act with respect to one another, but not toward or with each other. Social accommodative encounters are frequent occurrences in urban centers; without them, life in large urban centers would be impossible. But accommodative encounters are not limited to the urban scene. They can be found almost anywhere a plurality of persons convenes. Two lone hunters on the prairie, upon noting each other's presence, are likely to give each other a wide berth.

The social action of accommodators is coordinated, but only to minimize or dissolve copresence, not to intensify it. Yet it is a rather complex form of social action. Each must monitor and be responsive to the other. In addition, each must project a forthcoming line of action that is detected and accepted by the other. The complexity of this form of social action is suggested by the difficulty people often have in accommodating to each other. We have all witnessed strollers on a downtown street do little dances in their attempts to avoid becoming entangled with each other when they meet.

Mutuality

Examples of mutuality range from reciprocating flirtatious glances, through the playful teasing of a parent and child, to the intense lovemaking of reunited lovers. In mutual encounters both parties willfully relate to each other and offer or hint at pleasurable excitation. Mutuality is frequently sexual or has sexual overtones, but it is not limited to sexual activity. Nor are all instances of sexual activity mutuality. For example, rape is an autocratic act. When rape is committed, the victim is treated as an object.

In sharp contrast to social accommodation where people indicate they are not interested in each other as persons, those who construct a mutual encounter at least hint that they are interested in becoming implicated with each other. The future projected is one of involvement, not avoidance. The involvement can be as minimal as two strangers winking at each other, or as enduring as a love relationship.

To open a mutual encounter persons are not merely reciprocally attentive, they also reciprocally acknowledge each other. They at least suggest an interest in becoming implicated with each other, if only for a few seconds. They mutually inform each other that the other is an object of interest and that perhaps the activities of the other will be incorporated into the subsequent activity of self. They are mutually responsive. The intensity of the relatedness between them is greater than that of predator and prey, competitors, panicers, and accommodators. If one person refuses mutual responsiveness, no mutuality is produced, only a snub. To construct a mutual encounter each must indicate a willingness to make herself available to the other as a subject as well as an object. Each responds to the other to achieve personal objectives and fulfill the objectives of the other. Mutuality is self- and other-centered. The interests of the other are acknowledged. Each at least implies the interests of self are contingent on the other and congruent with the interests of the other. Each invites pleasureable stimulation from the other, but not adverse impingement.

The congruent functional identities established in mutual encounters are of a somewhat different order than the functional identities established in other forms of social action. Each projects forthcoming action toward the other, but the specific content of the behavior has a degree of uncertainty. The pleasurable excitation that pervades mutuality stems in part from an inability to anticipate the forthcoming behavior of the other with complete accuracy. If the future can be completely anticipated, excitation moves toward boredom. The continuation of a mutual encounter requires that each provides the other with pleasant surprises.

The coordination of action that is present in mutual encounters is achieved by each being highly attentive and responsive to the other in the ongoing present. Mutuality is a present-centered activity; it is only minimally structured by projected futures. Rapid-fire mutual responsiveness is the hallmark of intensely satisfying mutual encounters.

Mutuality has many formal properties similar to those of conflict. In both, the participants are highly attentive and available to each other and concentrate on the present. Nonetheless, the content of the transactions are entirely different. Combatants attempt to impinge adversely on each other. In mutual encounters, each excites the other but does not adversely impinge on the other. Yet the high level of availability that prevails in some mutual encounters makes each party vulnerable to adverse impingements. The high level of vulnerability, combined with an interest in providing the other intense pleasureable stimulation intended to produce excitation, can result in adverse impingement. This feature of mutuality sometimes has the consequence of transforming mutual encounters into conflict or disaffiliation.

Satisfactory mutual encounters implicate people with each other. Some are the foundation for enduring relationships. Selves are established, modified, and expanded in satisfying mutual relations. Of course, unsatisfactory mutual encounters can be destructive. Nonetheless, mutuality is a form of social action that is one of the foundation stones of human existence.

Cooperation

The completion of a cooperative act requires the establishment of all the basic elements of sociation. When people cooperate, they are reciprocally attentive, mutually responsive, establish congruent identities, establish a shared focus, and move toward the accomplishment of a social objective. Cooperative action is future- centered; it is primarily structured by the social objective, by what interactors are attempting to accomplish. None of the other elementary forms of social action contains a social objective. Competition and panic are structured by a shared focus and parallel personal objectives, but not by a shared objective. When people cooperate, they act in unison to achieve a mutually recognized objective.

The completion of a cooperative act requires congruent functional identities. The lines of action projected by each person are linked to a shared focus and are fitted together so that two or more can act in unison to achieve a social objective. The projected lines of action may be either parallel or differentiated, but they must be congruent. To sing together requires that all establish a given song as their shared focus and then to produce parallel activity—they must sing together. Of course, congruency is always a matter of degree. Some may be out of tune and others may lag behind. To complete a conversation interactors produce differentiated acts. One speaks, the other listens. Usually they take turns. They may interrupt and thereby create a degree of incongruency. But the completion of a conversation requires a degree of congruency.

The complexity and duration of cooperative acts are limited by the duration and complexity of the futures projected and detected. The limited temporal span of young children restricts the complexity of their cooperative action. Adults can produce cooperative acts that extend over years. Further, their cooperation is not limited to the immediate situation. The parents of a family may agree that they will separate and that during the intervening period one will migrate to a foreign country to make money and then send for the remainder of the family, while the other remains behind to care for the children. Then, years later, the family may be reconvened.

When people cooperate, they share experiences. The sharing need not be total or even very extensive, but at the minimum they share the experience of acting in a coordinated manner to achieve an objective. When they achieve an objective, they then share the experience of having accomplished something together.

Cooperative action, like all action, is always somewhat problematic. Sometimes cooperative efforts disintegrate because of the incompetence of one or both actors; other times, because one or both are distracted; and, as is always the case, external impingement can prevent the completion of the projected activity. Nonetheless, cooperative action is the foundation of human existence. Other forms of social action occur with varying degrees of frequency in all human societies, but cooperative action is necessary for the survival of human beings as a species.

Summary

All forms of social action require the exercise of will. Even autocratic action requires that one person willfully relate to another. In the other forms of social action, two parties exercise their will to either associate or disassociate. All forms of social action also require that each give some attention to the intentions of the other and that each organizes herself in part on the basis of the intentions of the other. The exception is autocratic action where only one party assesses the intentions of the other.

The elements of sociation that constitute these eight elementary forms of social action are produced sequentially. Social responsiveness, whether in the form of bilateral or mutual responsiveness, cannot be produced until after reciprocal attentiveness is established. In a similar manner, it is impossible to act toward a social objective until after a shared focus has been established. When people have an extensive shared past, however, then the elements of sociation that compose these forms of social action can be established vertically, instead of sequentially.

One of the distinctive features of human beings is the complexity of the shared pasts they can construct. When two friends have a shared past of having a beer together every Friday afternoon establish copresence by one walking into the office of the other on Friday at four o'clock, they can immediately begin moving toward the local tavern. On the basis of their shared past they can establish all the elements of sociation necessary for cooperation in an instant. Two strangers, of course, could not produce a unit of cooperative action in this manner.

The eight elementary forms of social action can be combined in a variety of ways to produce composite forms of social action. For example, chess is a highly constrained form of conflict. The objective of both players is to remove the pieces of the other player from the board. The conflict is subordinated to the social objective of completing a game of chess, the rules of the game, and proper etiquette constrains the behavior of both players. If one player rejects the objective of completing the game, their encounter will be transformed. They may conflict or simply disaffiliate. It is a rather common occurrence for personal objectives to become paramount when people are cooperating. Then the cooperative encounter may be terminated before it is completed. Aborted cooperative acts are common.

Human beings are capable of producing far more complex forms of social action than these eight elementary forms. But these eight forms of social action underlie the construction of the more complex forms of social action and the establishment of complex and enduring social relationships.

Chapter 6 Interpersonal Accountability

As people come in contact and act with each other, they anticipate each other's actions and intentionally organize their actions toward each other. In many instances they correctly anticipate each other's actions and act as they intend. Often, however, we inaccurately anticipate the actions of others; sometimes we fail to act as we intend. Consequently, sometimes our actions have unintended consequences. We do not always have ourselves under control, and sometimes we intrude on others. When that occurs, our actions sometimes have undesired consequences for others. We then are accountable.

Each person is potentially accountable every time he establishes social contact. Each shopper at a sale, each bus rider, each neighbor is implicitly accountable for any of his actions that infringe on other bargain seekers, bus riders, or neighbors. We almost routinely unintentionally infringe on and disturb others, and are almost routinely infringed on and disturbed by others in our daily lives. When responsible people infringe on others and are aware of their infringement, they make themselves accountable. Not all infringements are followed by an accounting. For example, a bully attempting to pick a fight, thieves, and spoiled brats do not make themselves accountable. Others sometimes attempt to make irresponsible persons accountable, but they are not always successful.

Nonetheless, accountability is a pervasive feature of social life. Interpersonal accountability rests on the presumption that each person is responsible for the consequences of his action, even if the consequences were not intended, and that the welfare of others is partially our responsibility. Responsible people offer an account when they recognize that their actions had undesired consequences. Accounts are offered to preserve social order and personal integrity.

Accounts are always a social act within a social act. They are framed by mutual recognition that the intended future did not unfold as anticipated; something went amiss. Accounts are also always contextualized by at least one party recognizing or presuming some act of commission or omission created stress; often both parties recognize one or both were distressed. The recognized stress that touches off accountings may be as mild as two strangers accidentally touching each other while riding an

70

elevator or as great as one person accidentally killing the loved one of another person.

If the stress is minimal, an account may be completed by two simple reciprocating acts. Other accounts are composed of a series of complex and convoluted reciprocating acts. Not all accounts are completed. Some disintegrate or transform into other forms of social action. And, on occasion, one party may abort the process.

Interpersonal accounts are often contextualized by a failure of one person to accommodate to another. When one person intrudes on another, as soon as the intrusion is recognized by the intruder, he is likely to offer an account. Accounts do not automatically flow from intrusions. Sometimes intruders leave the scene without acknowledging that anything out of the ordinary occurred, without offering an account.

Accounts are often touched off when some act inhibits or blocks the achievement of a social objective. Acts that interfere with the achievement of social objectives are called disjunctive acts. Disjunctive acts do not automatically lead to accounting. The disjunctive act may be ignored or overlooked.

Accounts are produced when all has not flowed as smoothly as it might have. Some act or set of acts are identified as disruptive, as disturbing the anticipated course of events. Furthermore, those involved presume the disruption was unintended. Some event at least slightly surprising and unpleasant has occurred, and one or both parties think some sort of corrective action is required.

For example, when a customer of a fast-food restaurant notes that he has been shortchanged, he is a little surprised and mildly distressed. When the clerk is made aware of the goof, he is usually mildly embarrassed. Most clerks will accept responsibility for the mistake and take corrective action. Many disruptions are very mild; often only a minimal amount of corrective action is required.

Of course, some disruptions are very stressful. When the disruptive act is the source of considerable stress, then extensive corrective action may flow from the situation. For example, when a patron of an expensive restaurant violently bumps into a waiter carrying a large tray of dinners, and the food and plates crash onto diners seated at a table, considerable stress is created. The patron, unless he is completely insensitive, who bumped into the waiter, is usually at least a little distressed. The waiter is likely to be angry and confused. And the customers with food in their laps are likely to be very upset. Extensive corrective action is usually required before social order is restored. The unhappy victims are likely to call for more than a mere apology. They may call for restitution; they are likely to demand that someone pay the cleaning bill. They may call for sanctioning either the waiter or the clumsy patron or both.

Whatever the level of distress, whenever unanticipated disruptive events occur that stem from the actions of human beings, those involved usually attempt to determine who was responsible, whether the consequences were intentional, and how to correct the situation. When extreme distress is linked to the disruptive acts of others, more than an account is often called for. If the victims of the disruption are equal to or more powerful than the perpetrator, they are likely to call for sanctioning the perpetrator. If the victims have little power and cannot effectively demand sanctions, they may flee the scene. When young children are violently impinged on by a bully, no account is likely to be offered unless an adult steps into the situation and demands an account from the bully.

Interpersonal accountability presumes a degree of equality. Masters are not accountable to slaves; slaves are very accountable to masters. Friends are equally accountable to each other. And, of course, the powerful do sometimes make themselves accountable to the weak. All accounting rests on a recognition that our acts sometimes have consequences for the welfare of others and that each of us is at least partially responsible for the welfare of others.

Elements of Sociation

A completed account includes six distinctive elements of sociation: (1) mutual recognition of a disruptive act; (2) mutual recognition of undesired consequences for at least one party; (3) mutual recognition of responsibility for the act; (4) establishment of consensus on the nonintentionality of the consequences; (5) offering and honoring an account; and (6) closing off the accounting. Accounting, like all forms of social action, can be produced sequentially or hierarchically. Also like all forms of social action, it is joined activity. An interpersonal account cannot be completed by one person, although in many instances one person provides most of the content of the act while the other merely indicates acceptance of the content. Sometimes accounting is initiated by the perpetrator of the disruptive act; other times, by the victim; and sometimes they simultaneously begin the process.

When a disruptive act occurs within an encounter between strangers in a novel context, then the elements of sociation that constitute an account usually are produced sequentially. First they will recognize that a disruptive act has occurred and that it had undesired consequences. Usually, but not always, it is apparent to both parties which of them was responsible for the act leading to the undesired consequences. Then, if the process is to be completed, they have to agree that the consequences were not intended and one or both can offer an apology or excuse. That will usually close off the accounting process.

In contrast, people with an extended shared past often complete accounts hierarchically. Several of the elements of sociation can be produced simultaneously. As soon as they mutually recognize a disruptive act has occurred, one may apologize and the other may accept the apology before it is completed. Strangers with common pasts in routine encounters can also complete an account hierarchically. When two strangers bump into each other, they often immediately mutually recognize that the intrusion was not intended. Then, as is the case for those with a shared past, an apology can be offered and accepted more or less simultaneously.

Accounting occurs so frequently in our daily lives that we often fail to appreciate its complexity. Some appreciation of its complexity can be acquired by observing parents attempting to transform their young children into responsible persons. Young children literally have to be led through the process several times before they become interpersonally accountable.

Disruptive Acts

Any human act can be disruptive. What is a disruptive act cannot be specified by the content of the act. The critical feature of all disruptive acts is how the act fits in with the context, intentions, and ongoing activity. A caress may be welcomed in some contexts; in other contexts, it may be the source of considerable stress.

Whatever the act, it must be mutually recognized as disruptive and become the shared focus. Whatever was the focus prior to the disruption is momentarily pushed aside, and the disruptive act is made the shared focus. Young children often are unaware of their infringements; they often intrude on others with no awareness that they are disturbing others. The impact of their behavior on others often has to be spelled out for them in detail before they recognize that their actions sometimes infringes on others. Even then, they are often slow to acknowledge that they have interfered with others. Adults almost routinely inform young children that they are responsible for disturbances.

In contrast, adults frequently establish a disruptive act as their shared focus without speaking of the act. As soon as one infringes on another, they often immediately mutually recognize what act is the source of the disruption. Of course, adults are not always aware of infringing on others. It is not unknown for one person to step on the toe of another without being aware of it. In such cases, the victim is likely to speak of the infringement. However the disruptive act is established as a shared focus, it must then be agreed that it is disruptive before the accounting process can proceed.

People often have differences of opinion over whether or not a given activity is disruptive. For example, when one roommate turns on the radio, the other may define the radio as a distraction. He may indicate that the noise is disturbing him and call for corrective action. The one who wishes to listen to the radio may deny that the music is a disturbance. He might even insist that background music is conducive to studying. In such a situation the two may become embroiled in conflict, but unless both agree that a given event is disruptive, the accounting process will not be completed.

Undesired Consequences

Usually, as soon as a disruptive act is established as the shared focus, it is mutually recognized that it had undesired consequences for at least one of them. But that is not always the case. To return to our roommates and their radio, both might agree that the music is disruptive. Nonetheless the one who turned on the radio might argue that it is more desirable to listen to music than it is to study assignments. The studying, not the radio, causes stress.

Children and parents often differ about the desirability of consequences. When a child distracts the mother in deep thought and commands her attention the child may regard the consequences as desirable even if the mother becomes angry. Children frequently claim that their actions had no undesirable consequences, while parents offer an alternative assessment of the situation.

Responsibility

After it is agreed that an undesirable event has occurred, then one or both may attempt to locate what is responsible for undesired consequences. What or who is responsible can be located almost anywhere. Often it is quickly agreed that the disruption flowed from an act committed by one of the parties. Other times, it is agreed that the disruption was created by some external factor. For example, a child may knock a glass from the table with the parent demanding who knocked the glass over. The child may attempt to blame it on the family dog.

On some occasions there are strong differences of opinion on who or what is responsible for disruptions. When a softball team fails to execute a double play, for example, the second baseman may blame the shortstop for being too slow in covering second base, or the shortstop may blame the second baseman for throwing the ball too quickly. Or they might agree that the source of their difficulty is the rough surface of the playing field. If the latter definition is accepted then of course there is no need to offer an account.

Intentionality

Usually, when consensus is established that one party was responsible for the disruption, that person indicates that he did not intend to be disruptive. Sometimes the victim refuses to accept that definition of the situation. If the victim claims the act was intentional, they are likely to argue over the intentionality of the act. The accounting process may then be transformed into a situation where the victim attempts to extract retribution or apply sanctions. In other instances, they may disaffiliate. When parties to a disrupted encounter disaffiliate without resolving the intentionality of the act, each party usually feels resentful toward the other.

Offering and Honoring Accounts

Once one of the parties has been mutually recognized as the perpetrator of the disturbance, the stage is set for that person to offer an account. An account may be simply, "I'm sorry," or it may be an elaborate explanation. The elaborateness of an account usually, but not always, reflects the severity of the disruption. Mild intrusions can usually be patched over with a brief apology.

When the disruption has only minimal consequences, sometimes both parties offer an account; each insists on taking responsibility and at the same time indicates that the disruption was not intentional.

This step is not completed until the second party indicates acceptance of the account. When one offers an account and the other either ignores it or rejects it, both are aware that the damage has not been repaired. When a victim refuses to honor an account, something more is required before social order is restored. On occasion, when an account is not honored, the one offering the account will call the other into account for not honoring the account. Then we have an accounting within an accounting.

Closing Off

Once an account is honored, that usually concludes the accounting process. Order has been restored, or at least acceptance of the situation. No further corrective action is called for; those involved can now turn their attention back to their original objective. The disrupted order has been attended to and either the preexisting social order restored or a new one constituted. In contrast, when the flow of interaction has been disrupted by a disjunctive act and neither party assumes responsibility alienation or conflict is a likely consequence.

Intrusions

Intrusive accounts take several different forms, but all are touched off by and linked to the mutual recognition that one or both intruded on the other. An account is likely to be offered when two people bump into each other. They may complete the accounting by making eye contact, followed by slight head nods, and both proceeding on their way. In this situation, at least one person has intruded on another; the intrusion and the undesired consequences are mutually recognized; responsibility for, but nonintentionality of, the intrusion are also mutually established; an account is offered and accepted; and each goes his own way.

Not all intrusions are recognized, and often there are differences of opinion on what constitutes an intrusion. What one person regards as a routine act another might regard as a severe infringement. That was the case in the following situation (Moser 1982).

In a large indoor swimming pool one young man was swimming laps. A second was practicing diving. As the swimmer approached the end of the pool where the diver was practicing, the diver dove and missed the swimmer by inches, not more than a foot, and he may have brushed the swimmer. The swimmer stopped. When the diver surfaced, the swimmer shouted, "Hey! Hey, you! What the hell do you think you're doing?! You almost landed on top of me." As the diver climbed out of the pool and headed toward the diving board without looking at the swimmer, he retorted, "Don't worry. I didn't even come close. Anyway I have as much right to the deep end as you do." He began climbing up the ladder. The swimmer went to the other end of the pool and asked the lifeguard to intervene.

The swimmer thought the diver had intruded on him. The diver might agree that a disruptive act had occurred, but he obviously did not agree that he was the intruder. He apparently believed that the swimmer was as responsible for the intrusion as he was. These two people did not agree on who was responsible for the intrusion. The accounting process was aborted. The swimmer called for a third party to intervene. The third party did. He informed the diver that it was the diver's responsibility to avoid swimmers. The failure of the two to complete the accounting process was followed by one of them effectively calling for a third party to sanction the other. It seems likely that both swimmer and diver felt resentful toward each other. They did not reconstruct a social order. Instead, a third party imposed an order.

The following incident was observed at the same pool (Moser 1982): Two young women were swimming laps—one using the crawl stroke, the other the back stroke. They brushed against each other once, with both continuing on. Then they collided. Both stopped and stood up, about three feet apart. The backstroker, in a rather harsh tone, inquired, "Can't you be more careful? That's the second time you've run into me." The crawlstroker looked at the backstroker and noted that she was pregnant. She responded in a demure tone, "I'm very sorry." The pregnant woman said, "OK" and nodded. She then suggested, "Why don't you swim in your own lane over there, please?" The harsh tone was no longer present. The other nodded and quietly said, "OK".

An account was successfully completed. The pregnancy of the back-stroker seemed to have been a major factor in structuring the content of the accounting process. The process need not have taken the form it did. The crawlstroker might have insisted she had as much right to the center of the pool as the backstroker and that the backstroker was equally responsible for the collision, but she did not. She accepted responsibility, offered an apology, and made the necessary adjustment to prevent future intrusions.

It seems the residue of emotions flowing from this encounter would be different from that of the encounter between the two men. The two women, on their own, constructed a social order that was at least minimally satisfactory to both.

In the following encounter between two brothers—one seven and the other nine years old—there is strong difference of opinion on the intentionality of the intrusion. The nine-year-old was proudly showing his grandfather his toy train arrangement. The younger brother entered the room and called out to his grandfather. He stepped on one of the plywood pieces to which the tracks were attached. Some of the tracks became disconnected, and a train overturned. The older brother shouted, "Johnny! Look at what you did!" Johnny stepped back and said, "I didn't mean it." The older brother retorted, "You did too!" and approached his brother with a raised fist. The grandfather intervened. He asked the younger brother to apologize, and enticed the older brother to accept the apology.

The brothers had consensus on both the fact that an intrusion had occurred and that the younger was responsible for it. They did not establish consensus on the intentionality of the action. The older brother maintained that the act was intentional, and he was willing to impose sanctions. The grandfather guided the two through the accounting process, and no sanction was applied—although it is likely that the older brother still thought his brother deserved a punch or two.

Young children frequently have difficulty in establishing consensus on the intentionality of action. The inability to resolve intentionality is not restricted to young children, however. Adults, communities, and nations often become embroiled in major hassles over intentionality. For example, in 1958 the USSR shot down a US airplane flying over its territory. American officials acknowledged that an intrusive act had occurred and that the United States was responsible for the intrusion. At first the spokespersons for the United States claimed that the intrusion was not intentional; that the plane was observing weather patterns and had become lost. The USSR failed to accept that explanation. When it became known that the pilot has survived and was a captive, then the United States admitted the intrusion was intentional and offered an account. An account, which not surprisingly, was not honored.

Unintentional minor intrusions are rather routine events in the day-to-day world. When those involved are responsible adults, an accounting sequence is usually produced with ease. If the intrusion has only minimal consequences, social order usually is quickly reestablished. On occasion, however, the accounting process is not successfully completed. Then there is usually a residue of ill will.

Some intrusions are of such magnitude that it is impossible to reestablish social order by an account. Then flight, mutual avoidance, or conflict follow intrusions. Social order dissolves.

Disjunctions

Disjunctive accounts are encased by a social objective and an act judged to interfere with the achievement of the social objective. "Untoward acts" touch off disjunctive accounting. These acts are untoward, not in the sense that they are sins or crimes, but that they inhibit movement toward social objectives or are thought to threaten a relationship. Disjunctive acts range from minor goofs ups to stressful catastrophes.

Many cooperative acts are routine and are completed with dispatch. Others are problematic. Disjunctive acts are relatively uncommon when the act is routine, but even in the most ordinary situation, disjunctive events appear. When movement toward a social objective is delayed by human error, an account is likely to be offered by the one responsible for the difficulty. If an account is not offered, it is likely that one will be called for. And if the called-for account is not forthcoming, then the situation may transform into conflict. If an account is not provided when one person thinks it should be, some resentment is usually generated. The completion of the accounting process does not assure the reestablishment of cooperative and smooth relations, but that is the objective.

Consider the following example: Five family members were playing a game of Monopoly when one of them, while reaching for the dice, caught his sleeve on the edge of the board. The tokens, cards, and houses were scattered about. All reacted. The guilty party said, "I'm sorry," and displayed a contrite demeanor. Two or three of the other players mumbled, "That's OK" All turned to restoring order. They queried each other about the location of their tokens. The responsible one reiterated, "I'm sorry. My sweater just got caught." He appeared crestfallen. The mother said, "That's OK, just don't get so rambunctious." The son gave his mother a resentful glance and stated, "I said I didn't mean it." The mother responded, "OK" and turned away. The game resumed.

The accounting process was not as smoothly completed as it might have been. All the elements of the accounting process were constructed, but a minor sanction was also offered. The one responsible for the disjunctive act was slightly resentful of the sanction. The reluctance of the other to accept the account demonstrates that an account does not always completely erase the consequences of a disjunctive act.

In this case, the participants did become reengaged in their game. No lasting damage was inflicted. The game was completed, and the existing relationships among the players were sustained. Had the account been rejected and/or the guilty party severely sanctioned, the game probably would not have been completed; and the relationships of the players might have been at least mildly disturbed.

On occasion, the untoward act destroys the possibility of accomplishing the objective. The following transactions were observed in a videogame arcade (Byrne 1982): Two boys, about twelve and fourteen years old, were playing together. The older boy assumed command of the situation. Their objective was to "destroy" as many of the "invaders" as possible. The older boy instructed the younger, "Hey, don't push any controls; stay in temporary safety." The younger boy continued to play and said, "Anyway, I can get this one." They both continued to play for a few moments, then their men ran into each other, causing the loss of the older boy's man. Immediately the younger boy said, "Oh! I'm sorry! I didn't mean to. I forgot. Was that your last man? You can play mine!" The older boy glared at the younger boy. Then, in a sarcastic voice, stated, "That's OK, you didn't know any better", and walked away.

Within this encounter, as soon as the untoward event of the two "men" running into each other occurred, there was mutual recognition of an untoward event. Further, consensus was immediately established that the younger boy was responsible for the untoward event—although, from an outsider's point of view, one might argue that the two of them were equally responsible for the untoward event. Their men had collided while both were attempting to shoot down the same invader. When the younger boy began his apology, however, he thereby designated himself as responsible for the untoward event. That he had violated the strictures of the older boy to maintain his man in a position of safety contextualized the collision and implicitly made him responsible for the untoward act. The discourse content of the older boy's response indicates the account was honored. But the sarcastic tone and his walking away indicates that the account was not accepted. Disaffiliation was the result.

In this instance, the intentionality of the untoward act is surrounded with a degree of ambiguity. It is certain that the younger boy did not intentionally run his man into the older boy's man. Yet the younger boy had been explicitly instructed not to enter the field of combat, but had rejoined the fray. The enticement of the opportunity to destroy invaders was not resisted. His account that he forgot seems to rest on shaky grounds. At least the older boy doubted the validity of the account.

Untoward acts may be acts of ommission as well as acts of commission. In the following situation a mother and her nine-year-old son, on the initiative of the son, were making candy. The mother was working at the sink with her back to the stove. A kettle boiled over. The mother called out, "Matthew, where are you? The kettle is boiling over." The son came running into the kitchen and began stirring the contents of the kettle.

Mother: Are you going to watch that stuff or not?
Son: Yeah, I was just in getting my glove.
Mother: Well, you're not going to play baseball now. You've got to watch that stuff so it doesn't boil over. (Stated forcefully.)
Son: I know, I know.

In this instance, the mother called attention to the untoward event, which was quickly acknowledged by the son. He acted to remedy the situation. The mother called him to task with, "Are you going to watch that stuff or not?" The son provided an account of having been momentarily distracted by another interest. That account was rejected by the mother when she reminded her son of his obligation. The son explicitly acknowledged his obligation, but did not offer an apology. This particular accounting sequence was left dangling.

The central issue in this encounter was responsibility. The mother informed her son that he was responsible for watching the boiling kettle and that any untoward developments were his responsibility. He implicitly accepted the responsibility but indicated that in this instance his distraction freed him of his immediate responsibility. That definition of the situation was rejected by the mother.

It is through a multitude of encounters of this sort that children are transformed into responsible adults. Infants and young children are not responsible. They do not have awareness of the consequences of their actions and nonactions for others. Only by being made accountable can they achieve awareness of how their actions infringe on, interfere with, and disturb others. Those children not held accountable for their infringements are more likely to become irresponsible persons than are those who are.

FUTURE ORIENTED ACCOUNTS

To construct a future-oriented account, a forthcoming act is made the shared focus, and concern is expressed about the reaction of another to the forthcoming act. These accounts are referred to by Lutfiyya and Miller (1986) as bank accounts. They are typically produced when it is anticipated that another might be offended by the forthcoming act. A pre-apology is offered that is directed toward preserving the relationship in case the other is offended.

In the following situation two young men were attempting to repair a car door that had been twisted in an accident. Despite their efforts, the door would not close smoothly. One stated, "I'm going to hit the hinge a good one. OK?" He stood posed with a hammer. The other nodded and said, "OK" The first then reaffirmed his bank account with, "I'm not guaranteeing success," and looked at the second young man. He retorted, "I said OK" Whereupon the hinge was dealt a healthy blow.

The social objective of repairing the car door contextualized the accounting. The first young man recognized that the action he was proposing might further damage the door. He also recognized that the other might be offended by failure. A bank account was completed when the second young man assured the first that it was acceptable to take the proposed action and that he recognized it might fail. Bank accounts take the same form and attempt to achieve the same objectives as past-oriented accounts. They differ from past-oriented accounts only by making probably forthcoming events the shared focus, instead of an event that has already occurred.

Summary

Children cannot initiate an accounting until after they have acquired the ability to assess the consequences of their activity from the point of view of another. Before a child can be called into account, it is necessary for the child to understand the linkages between his actions and the experiences of others. Until that linkage is forged, children cannot effectively be made responsible. Of course, an adult can issue a call for an account to a young child who cannot make that linkage, but the call for an account is not an effective one until the child understands that his actions have consequences for the experiences of others and can make the distinction between intentional and nonintentional consequences.

Young children without command of a symbol system that allows them to establish co-orientation toward past events infringe on others and are infringed on, but they are not accountable, nor can they call others into account. The production of accounts requires the prior production of shared understanding of the consequences of both intended and unintended acts. Only then can children become responsible interactors. The acquisition of the ability to produce accounts provides people with a means for maintaining social order despite the fact they have committed a disruptive act.

Children first acquire awareness of the consequences of their actions for others by adults' identifying specific acts of the children and their consequences for others. Children thereby learn that what is a satisfactory experience for them is sometimes a distressing one for others. Children presumed incapable of assessing the consequences of their actions for others are relieved of responsibility. Parents commonly offer the account for their young children that "He did not know any better."

If children are never required to assess their own actions from the standpoint of others, they can never become responsible persons. In order for children to become responsible persons they must adopt the standpoint of others toward their own acts, understand the consequences of their acts for others, and respect the integrity of others. Responsibility does not automatically emerge.

When young children are first subjected to such statements as "Look what you did," it only creates confusion. But as children acquire the ability to co-orient toward their own past actions and link those to the experiences of others, they can become responsible persons.

Those who are never or seldom required to assess the consequences of their actions from the point of view of others have high likelihood of becoming spoiled brats. It is through adopting the standpoint of others toward their own acts that children become full-fledged members of the social order. Children are capable of quite complex social action long before they become responsible. And the acquisition of responsibility is a long, drawn-out affair. Nonetheless, as each child learns to adopt the standpoint of others and then assesses his and others' action from the standpoint of others, he becomes less self-centered.

In day-to-day encounters between adults, each makes the presumption that the other is a responsible person. If an intrusive or disjunctive act is committed, it is presumed that the other will render himself accountable. This presumption is not always fulfilled. Then others may issue a call for an account, which may or may not be acknowledged. Or, if the other presumes that the intruder is unaware of the disruptive behavior, the act itself may be pointed out with the anticipation that the person will then make himself accountable. Again, on occasion an account is not produced. The failure to acknowledge an intrusive or untoward act usually creates still greater disruptiveness.

Accounts can do more than patch up disturbed social encounters but sometimes they fail to accomplish that. Accounting is primarily past-oriented and "nonproductive" activity. Persons discontinue their movement, at least momentarily, toward objectives when they turn their attention to messed up transactions in the past. Accounting is only nonproductive in the sense that it does not move those involved toward the achievement of previously established objectives. Nonetheless, it sometimes preserves social relationships, minimizes conflict, and enhances personal integrity. It is a pervasive form of social action; one cannot remain a viable human being without making oneself accountable to others. The fact that human beings can never anticipate one anothers' actions with complete accuracy and sometimes fail to act as they intend assures that infringements, disruptions, and disturbances will remain an integral part of human life. Consequently, interpersonal accountability is and will remain a pervasive dimension of social life.

Chapter 7 Bargaining

Bargaining is such a common form of social activity that the exchange theorists posit bargaining as the basic form of social action. The exchange theorists claim that all other forms of social action and relationships flow from mercenary considerations (Homans 1972). It is true that calculations of cost and benefit infuse many social encounters. When we shop for items at a store or haggle with a salesman over the price of a used car, we make assessments of the benefits to be derived. Nonetheless, there is far more to social life than mercenary interests. Most exchange theorists fail to recognize the complex social foundations upon which bargaining rests.

Bargaining is restricted to human beings. As Adam Smith noted over two hundred years ago, "Two greyhounds, in running down the same hare, have sometimes the appearance of acting in some sort of concert" (Smith 1937, 13). He went on to note that "Nobody ever saw a dog make a fair and deliberate exchange of one bone for another with another dog. Nobody ever saw one animal by its gestures and natural cries signify to another, this is mine, that yours; I am willing to give this for that" (Smith 1937, 13).

The observations of Smith are as valid today as when he made them. Bargaining is distinctly a human endeavor. No other animals are capable of bargaining. Nor can young children bargain with one another. It is not until after young children have mastered symbols and developed consciousness of *mine* and *yours* that they are capable of bargaining. Bargaining is a rather complex form of social action that rests on a foundation of other social abilities. Contrary to the assumptions of exchange theorists, bargaining is not the foundation of human life. Nonetheless, bargaining is a common form of social action that can be observed in at least a limited form in all known human societies.

Social Foundations of Bargaining

Before human beings become capable of bargaining, they must first acquire the ability to coordinate their acts with others to achieve social objectives, have command of significant symbols, establish mutually recognized interdependence, respect the integrity of others, recognize another's interest in a service or good controlled by self, project a future of

84

offering a service or good willfully in exchange for another service or good, and anticipate benefits from rendering a service or transferring control of a good to another person. Young children are incapable of all these acts.

Children recognize their dependence on their parents before they recognize that others are sometimes dependent on them. After children have the ability to cooperate and use significant symbols, they can recognize mutual interdependence of self and others. When that foundation is established, the additional conditions of (1) mutual acceptance of the integrity of others, including the rights of ownership; (2) bilateral interest in a service or good controlled by another; (3) projection of a future of effecting an exchange; and (4) anticipating benefit from the exchange can be established.

When all these conditions are established, then, and only then, people can bargain. Each condition is always somewhat problematic. The thief does not accept the integrity of the other. If one person has no interest in a good controlled by another, no bargaining will occur. Reciprocally, each person must presume the other has an interest in a service or good she controls. Then both parties must project a future of rendering a service or transferring control of a good to the other. Bilateral anticipations of personal benefit structure bargaining.

Control of Services and Goods

Either the attitude that those with the might have the right to take or that all are obliged to share destroys the possibility of bargaining. Raiders, looters, and tribute takers extract; they do not acknowledge the right of possession. Sharing is all-encompassing in some primitive groups. In some nomadic hunting and gathering societies, whenever one person is successful in the quest for food, she is expected to share the fruits of the hunt with all others. In these groups, when one does not share with others, the others neither beg from her nor bargain with her. Instead they sanction her. They treat her as if she had committed a sin. It is impossible for bargaining to emerge as a distinctive form of social action when everything is shared by all.

Bargainers accept the prerogative of others to provide or withhold a service and to retain or relinquish control of their possessions. They accept ownership. Bargainers recognize and accept the distinction between yours and mine. If the relation between human beings and objects that constitute ownership are not acknowledged bargaining cannot occur.

Ownership is a categorical identity; it specifies that there is an enduring relationship between a person and an object. For example, the bicycle is mine. The connection between me and the bicycle endures until I act to change the relationship. To bargain for goods is to bargain for categorical identities. Before trading my car for a boat, I was a car owner; as a consequence of trading my car for a boat, I am no longer a car owner. But I have now become a boat owner.

Interest in Each Other's Possessions

An interest in another's service or goods is a necessary prerequisite for bargaining but, it does not assure that bargaining will occur. The interest in the services and goods of another must be constrained by the acceptance of the other's right to retain control of her possessions. If the interest is not constrained, then one person might attempt to extract the other's goods. The interest in the goods of another must be bilateral; each must be interested in something controlled by the other. If the interest is only unilateral, one of the conditions necessary for bargaining is not established.

Bargaining presumes differential control of services or goods; when all possess the same items, there is no reason to bargain. Bargaining is relatively uncommon within homogeneous groups. The greater the variation of the kinds of services and goods controlled, the more likely people are to bargain. Bargainers have differentiated interests that are compatible. The person who wishes to trade cotton for wheat must not only find someone with wheat but someone with wheat who is also interested in cotton. Only then is the condition of bilateral and compatible interests established.

Willful Transfer

The mutual belief that a transfer of services or goods can be accomplished by each willfully providing a service or relinquishing control of a good is also necessary before bargaining can occur. Those familiar with the intricacies of bargaining take this dimension of bargaining for granted. Nonetheless, the willful reciprocal transfer of services and goods is a very complex social act. It requires comprehension of ownership and considerable sophistication in aligning actions. Some appreciation of the complexity of willful transfer can be acquired by attempting to bargain with a two- or three-year-old child. Young children frequently attempt to take control of another's possession without offering anything in return. Other times, they will relinquish control of a good before the other has indicated a willingness to reciprocate in kind.

Children are instructed into the intricacies of willful reciprocal relinquishment of control in numerous ways. Sometimes it occurs when a child grabs a sibling's toy and a parent then intervenes. The parent may tell the child who took the toy that she cannot just take; that she must give something in return and that she must acquire the consent of the other before taking possession. The parent may then entice the child to offer one of her toys in return for the toy she wants. When children are first enticed to give while taking, they have no comprehension that the acquisition of control of a good is contingent on the surrender of a good to another. It is by performing these sequences several times and noting the outcomes that children become capable of giving while taking. The acts of giving and taking must be combined into a reciprocating social act before children acquire the sophistication necessary to initiate bargaining.

In order to bargain it is necessary that bargainers attend, at the minimum, to two shared foci. A attends to both the item she is offering and the item B is offering. Reciprocally, B attends to both the item offered by A and the item she is offering to A. Both bargainers must also link both of the shared foci to the social objective of exchanging control over them.

Bilateral Benefit

The anticipation of bilateral personal benefit structures bargaining. Not all bargains are beneficial for both parties. In some instances, neither party derives benefit from the exchange; other times, only one party derives benefit from an exchange. But often the welfare of both parties is enhanced. Both bargainers usually anticipate benefit when they begin bargaining.

Usually, bargaining is framed by the anticipation of mutual benefit. Each party to the transaction presumes the welfare of both will be served if an exchange is effected. Nonetheless, the anticipation of mutual benefit is not a necessary condition for the completion of an exchange. Each may be solely concerned with her own welfare and unconcerned with the welfare of the other.

Summary

Bargaining is a fragile form of cooperative behavior that can be produced only by individuals who have (1) learned and accepted the idea of ownership; (2) established compatible but different interests; (3) mastered the intricacies of willful transfer; and (4) come to expect benefit from effecting an exchange. An intense interest in a service or good of another person frequently entices people to violate the rights of owners. When that occurs, one of the structural dimensions necessary for bargaining is destroyed. Bargainers generally attempt to acquire the maximum benefit for the least cost. When both parties are concerned with minimizing their cost and maximizing their benefit the bargaining process often generates elements of hostility. The hostility in turn can lead one or both parties to abort the process.

The Act of Bargaining

As people acquire experience in bargaining and recognize benefits derived from the activity, the necessary foundation for them to initiate bargaining is established. Bargaining is initiated when two people mutually indicate to each other that they are interested in a service or good controlled by the other. When two persons mutually establish the fact that each is interested in a good controlled by the other and each indicates an interest in acquiring control of the service or good by relinguishing control of another service or good, the functional identities of bargainers are established. When the functional identities of bargainers are activated, each indicates that she is willing for the moment to consider the offer of the other. They are then socially situated as bargainers.

Offers and Counteroffers

Once people have socially situated themselves as bargainers, they produce offers and counteroffers. Congruent functional identities as bargainers are often activated by one approaching another and inquiring about the price of an item. Then the functional identities of bargainers are established at the same time as the offer and counteroffer sequence.

The offer and counteroffer sequence is at the heart of the bargaining act. Both individuals actively relate to one another and to the items offered by the other. It is common for both parties to make offers and respond to each other's offer — although in some instances only one party specifies the price with the other responding to the offer.

A person who inquires about a price or makes an offer indicates that she will give consideration to the other party's offer, but does not make a commitment to complete a bargain — only to attend to the other. It is mutually understood that either can withdraw at any time. Bargaining encounters are often aborted in the offer and counteroffer sequence. One party may decide that the offer of the other is unreasonable and leave.

The offer and counteroffer sequence sometimes consists of nothing more than an inquiry, a specification of the price by the other, with the inquirer abruptly indicating that she is no longer interested. In other encounters the offer and counteroffer sequence includes a series of offers and counters. Haggling is almost an inherent feature of the offer and counter-offer sequence.

Many other forms of activity are often produced during the offer and counteroffer sequence. It is common for one or both to attempt to persuade the other that what is being offered is of exceptional quality. It is also common for bargainers to claim they are honest and concerned about the welfare of the other. These insertions attempt to create a particular definition of the objects under consideration, of the bargainers, and of the benefits to be derived from completing a bargain. Statements about the qualities of items under consideration frequently dominate this segment of bargaining. But these insertions are not essential features of bargaining; they need not be produced. They are little more than window dressing.

Assessment of Value

Bargaining is a mixed-motive encounter. Each bargainer is dependent on the other, but at the same time each is primarily concerned with her personal welfare. Cooperation is necessary to complete a bargain; yet at the same time each is implicitly in competition with the other as each attempts to achieve the greatest benefit at the least sacrifice.

During the offer and counteroffer sequence, bargainers assess the worth of the services or goods under consideration. The assessment of each is made on the basis of anticipated satisfaction. The proximal shared future of completing a bargain structures the interaction of the bargainers, but the distal personal future of each bargainer structures the assessments made. If both make the assessment that their satisfaction will be greater if an exchange is completed than if one is not, then a necessary condition for the completion of a bargain is established.

Each bargainer knows that the other is bargaining for personal benefit, not for shared benefit. Personal futures, not social futures, dominate bargaining. Each recognizes the other is primarily interested in acquiring the greatest benefit possible for the least cost. It is that feature of bargaining that makes it such a volatile activity. The selfish concerns constrained by the necessity of acting with the other to achieve personal objectives frequently generate hostility and, on occasion, conflict.

Experienced bargainers assess the worth of objects on the basis of their personal distal future. They ask themselves: Will the consummation of an exchange provide greater personal satisfaction than the failure to complete an exchange? Not all bargainers assess the worth of objects on the basis of a distal personal future. Sometimes bargainers are impulsive; they assess the worth of an object on the basis of immediate gratification. Experienced bargainers often take advantage of impulsive bargainers.

Bargainers entice others to interact with them; they do not coerce. Each has the freedom to accept or reject offers and the opportunity to make offers. That, in conjunction with their interest in acquiring the greatest benefit at the least cost, entices most bargainers to be very attentive to the assessments of others. Each respects the autonomy of the other, but at the same time attempts to take advantage of the interests and needs of the other.

Agreements

When the functional identities of bargainers are activated they are linked to a specific set of shared foci, and to the social objective of completing a bargain. But before a bargain will be effected, an agreement must be reached. When the shared foci are goods and the bargaining is in the form of bartering, the agreement and the exchange of goods are often collapsed into a single set of reciprocating acts. For example, when a young boy offers a candy bar to another boy in exchange for his slingshot, if the candy bar offered is deemed sufficient by the owner of the slingshot, he may simply pick up the candy bar and turn over his slingshot. In such instances, the agreement and the exchange are completed with two reciprocating acts. In some instances, bargains are struck without any discussion.

In many other instances, however, the agreement and the exchange are constructed as separate social acts. First, the agreement is constructed and then the exchange of goods or services is effected. When one or both of the items under consideration are a service, then an agreement is reached and the services are rendered. The services may be rendered almost immediately or there may be a delay between the agreement and the delivery of services. In a similar manner, there may be a delay between reaching an agreement and the surrendering of control of goods.

When an agreement is reached, both are committed to complete an exchange of goods or services. To abort the process after an agreement has been reached will, at the minimum, generate a little ill feeling. A bargainer who attempts to back out on an agreement is likely to be called into account. Nonetheless, bargainers are not accountable to each other until after they have agreed to effect an exchange. The process can be aborted at any time during the offer and counteroffer sequence without either becoming accountable to the other.

The degree of accountability in bargaining is minimal. There is almost no accountability during the early stages. In addition, there is little accountability after a deal has been completed. If one later makes the assessment that she got the short end of the deal, that is her responsibility, not the responsibility of the seller. The only time accountability is a viable part of the bargaining process is between the time an agreement is struck and the delivery of service or transfer of goods.

The Exchange

The effecting of an exchange may be nothing more than each party surrendering control of her goods and assuming control of the goods offered by the other. When the exchange is limited to taking control of the other's goods, then that terminates the encounter. Bargainers may in fact continue to relate to each other after effecting an exchange, but if they do, it will be by producing some other form of social action. Or, in some instances, they may attempt to initiate another bargaining session centered on other goods.

When the focus of concern is service, then on the completion of an agreement the bargainers will continue to relate until the service is rendered. But the nature of their relatedness is transformed. They no longer relate as bargainers, but as giver and receiver of service. Whereas bargaining is a symmetrical form of social action, the giving and receiving of a service is an asymmetrical form of social action. The one who has sold a service is at the beck and call of the buyer until the service has been delivered. That is the case whether the service is sexual favors, labor, or medical treatment.

The consummation of bargains is usually a productive enterprise. When each party has greater satisfaction as the consequence of a bargain than would have been achieved if no bargain had been completed, then there is greater wealth than before. In that sense, bargaining is as productive as activities that transform raw materials into consumable goods. The acquisition of services and goods through trade renders all less self-sufficient and more dependent on others; yet at the same time, when mutual benefits are derived, the wealth of all is enhanced.

Illustration

In urban centers many services and goods are still distributed by bargaining. The street vendors of Hong Kong bargain, as do the denizens of markets in Latin America. Haggling over the price of a service occurs with some frequency in the United States. Real estate agents and car salesmen regularly bargain with customers; junkyard managers often bargain with clients. The following encounters between a manager of an auto salvage yard and customers are offered to illustrate bargaining.

The first encounter is with a customer who is a stranger (Allee 1982).

Customer: (Enters and establishes eye contact with dealer behind the counter.) Hello.
Dealer: Hello, what can I do for you?
Customer: What would you take for that '75 Camaro with front end damage?
Dealer: $1,500.
Customer: Little high, isn't it?
Dealer: You know what they're worth, everybody wants a Camaro.
Customer: Yeah, I know, but I priced a complete front end for $500, then you gotta add labor and paint.
Dealer: Well, I can't do better than that; I'll sell you a front end for $250. It needs some minor work.
Customer: Such as?
Dealer: Just a few nicks here and there. Chrome's good though.
Customer: Think there's any frame damage?
Dealer: Don't think so. (Pause) Tell you what. I'll guarantee the frame if you want the front end, too.
Customer: Would you take $1,650, for both?
Dealer: No, $1,700 would be as low as I could go.
Customer: Well, I gotta go look at some others. I'll check back.
Dealer: Ok.
Customer: Thanks.
Dealer: Uh huh.

The second encounter at the same junk yard is with a customer who is a friend of the owner (Allee 1982).

Customer: (Enters, makes eye contact with dealer and nods toward him with a smile on his face.)
Dealer: Hi, T---. What can I do you out of?
Customer: Got a left fender for a '79 Riviera?
Dealer: (Pauses a moment with reflective demeanor) No, but S---'s might have. (Walks over to citizen's band radio unit. Makes contact and converses with someone via radio for a minute. Turns back to customer.) They've got one for $150.
Customer: Jesus Christ D---. Now I know why you guys all drive Cadillacs. (Looks at observer and winks at him and grins.)
Dealer: (Grins.) You'd drive one too, if you were as smart as we are. (Laughs) Why don't you start selling parts instead of working on cars?
Customer: Naw, I'm not that crooked!

Dealer: Shit!
Customer: Are they firm on that price?
Dealer: Well, I might be able to get it for $125 'cause they owe me
              a favor or two. But if I do, I'm drinking whiskey next time
              you see me uptown.
Customer: Ok, you got me, but I don't know if I'm getting off any
              cheaper. I don't know anybody who can put firewater
              away the way you can. (Laughs)
Dealer: (Grins) Get outta here.
Customer: Call me when it comes in. (Turns to leave.)
Dealer: Ok, see ya later, T---.
Customer: Bye. (Walks out.)

Both encounters are contextualized social acts. Both the potential
buyer and the seller accept the integrity of each other; they mutually indicate an
interest in a good controlled by the other, project a future of effecting an exchange, and each anticipates benefit if an exchange is consummated. They
establish the functional identities of bargainers, produce offers and counteroffers, and make assessments of the worth of the items under consideration.

In the first encounter, the potential buyer and seller interact strictly as
bargainers. They do not reach an agreement. A bargain is not completed.

In the second encounter, the customer and manager also interact as
bargainers. They produce all the elements of sociation that constitute the
bargaining act except effecting the exchange; they reach an agreement but
do not consummate the act. They also produce several elements of sociation
that are not necessarily a part of bargaining. They affirm their friendship and a
distal shared future. These elements of sociation give the second encounter
a different tenor than the first encounter.

The encounter between the customer who a stranger also included an
element of sociation that is not essential to the bargaining act but is often
present. Namely, they characterized the items under consideration; they offered their respective definitions of reality. When the customer said, "Little
high, isn't it?" he offered his definition of the worth of the item. The dealer
countered with, "You know what they're worth, everybody wants a Camaro."
Each of them also make statements that attempt to establish a specific
definition of reality. For example, the dealer says, "It needs some minor
work," the customer inquires with, "Such as?" and the dealer offers the
specifics of "Just a few nicks here and there. Chrome's good, though."
These transactions that focus on the nature of the items under consideration are not essential features of bargaining encounters, but are often a part
of bargaining encounters.

The first encounter is, in comparison to the second encounter, a
relatively impoverished encounter. While the interaction in the first en-

counter is amicable, it does not contain the mutuality interlaced with the bargaining in the second encounter. Furthermore, the first encounter has no temporal depth. The bargainers have just met, and it is doubtful that either of them anticipate ever meeting again. The first encounter is typical of bargaining between strangers.

The customer and the dealer in the second encounter not only characterize the objects under consideration but also characterize each other. The customer implies that the dealer takes advantage of his customers when he states, "Now I know why you guys all drive Cadillacs." The dealer retorts by implying that the customer is not as sharp as he might be with, "You'd drive one too, if you were as smart as we are." These transactions are offered in a tone of voice that seats them as jokes. But most jokes offered within these situations have a grain of truth, or at least are regarded by those who offer them as having some basis in reality.

The interlacing of elements of mutuality with bargaining in the second encounter lessens the likelihood of anger, yet allows both to drive a hard bargain. Had these statements characterizing each other been offered in a deadly serious tone of voice and framed by an angry demeanor, conflict might have ensued. This encounter demonstrates that persons with a shared past can produce two distinctive forms of social action within a single encounter.

Summary

Bargaining is a form of social action that human beings have devised to distribute services and goods. It is always contextualized by the taken for granted structural dimensions of ownership, differentiated but compatible interests, and the anticipation of bilateral benefits. It is a composite form of social action. The typical bargaining encounter contains elements of competition subordinated to elements of cooperation. If the competitive features of bargaining are not subordinated to the cooperative features, hostility and perhaps conflict may come to the fore. The mixed-motive nature of the act makes it a fairly explosive kind of social action.

Self-interest, not collective interest, prevails in bargaining. The phrase "What is in it for me?" captures the basic orientation of bargainers. To bargain requires at the minimum a dyad, yet it is only minimally a collective endeavor. Shared interests are only minimally, if at all, present. When bilateral benefits flow from the act, the welfare of both is enhanced, but a concern with collective welfare is often absent. The primary orientation of bargainers is personal benefit, not collective concerns.

Bargaining is often complexly interlaced with other forms of social action. It can be interlaced with mutuality, solidarity, accountability, negotiation, and sociability. When persons relate to each other solely as bargainers, they treat each other as instruments with a will and respect each other's integrity and autonomy, but there is no emotional or temporal depth in the encounters. Bargaining often enhances the wealth of all, but it is not the foundation stone of social life. It has neither the temporal nor the emotional depth necessary to sustain human life.

Chapter 8   Interpersonal Negotiating

The terms *bargaining* and *negotiating* have been used interchangeably by some social scientists. For example, Rubin and Brown (1975, 2) state, "We propose to treat the terms bargaining and negotiating as synonymous throughout the book." Others have offered distinctions. Morely and Stephenson (1977), for example, note that bargaining usually refers to haggling over the worth of items, whereas negotiating usually refers to the process of securing agreements on a matter of common concern.

The two forms of social action have similarities. In addition, bargaining and negotiating are often intertwined within a given encounter. Nonetheless, bargaining and negotiating are two fundamentally different forms of social action. When persons confront each other solely as bargainers, each person is but a means for the acquisition of services or goods to the other. In contrast, negotiators are concerned with the welfare of the other, with their future relatedness as well as with their own personal welfare. Strangers frequently relate only as bargainers; friends and family members negotiate — although when friends and family members negotiate they may also bargain.

Generally speaking negotiating is more richly contextualized than bargaining. Some negotiations are produced in a relatively improvised context, but negotiations are usually contextualized by a robust shared past and a distal shared future. Although it is rare, on occasion people who have just met negotiate. But even then they have a shared future. Agreements hammered out by negotiators have shared ramifications; agreements by bargainers do not. The outcome of a bargain has consequences for each of the bargainers, but the consequences are not shared, they are personal.

More often than not, negotiators are well acquainted with each other and anticipate sharing a future of some significance. Negotiators focus on the nature of their future relatedness, whereas bargainers focus on the worth of services or goods. Negotiators establish their future relatedness as their shared focus and the resolution of their differences as their social objective. They then attempt to structure their future.

Negotiating, like bargaining, is a mixed-motive activity. In both, each participant has interests that are at variance with the interests of the other; and, in both, each participant recognizes the successful completion of the process requires cooperative action. Whereas personal concerns dominate

96

bargaining, collective concerns dominate negotiating. All negotiations contain an element of conflict. At the minimum there are disagreements as to how they are to relate in the future. The conflict may be mild or intense. Sometimes, people who have intense conflicts attempt to end them by negotiating. On other occasions, people attempt to resolve mild conflicts by negotiating only to have the negotiation session transform into intense conflict. On more than one occasion, negotiation sessions have ended in fist fights.

The Context of Negotiations

All negotiations are contextualized by (1) the projection of a shared distal future; (2) mutually recognized differences; and (3) the acceptance of the other as more or less an equal. In addition, most negotiations are contextualized by a robust shared past. Strangers rarely negotiate, and when they do, their negotiations usually focus on relatively insignificant issues — although on occasion strangers convene to negotiate significant issues.

A Shared Distal Future

Most negotiators simply presume a shared distal future. This is the case when marital couples resolve minor differences by negotiating. Both presume they will maintain their marriage. On occasions when the differences are profound, marital couples may explicitly discuss whether or not they are going to continue their marriage. If the dissatisfaction is intense and chronic, one partner might ask, "Do you wish to hold our marriage together?" More often than not, however, negotiators presume that they have a shared future and that presumption frames their negotiating.

A Shared Past

In sharp contrast to bargaining, negotiating usually has considerable temporal depth. Negotiators usually have an extended shared past and usually their relationship is significant for both of them. Bargainers often know very little about each other and do not care to become acquainted. Sometimes they know nothing of each other except that one is interested in selling and the other in buying. In contrast, negotiations are usually infused by elements of affection and dislike derived from their shared past and mutual concern with each other's welfare. Family and friendship relationships frequently provide the overarching context of negotiations.

The more extensive and intensive the shared past of negotiators the more robust the context that frames their negotiations. The negotiation sessions of people with a robust shared past are framed by many taken-for-granted factors. The robust shared pasts of marital partners allow them to resolve many of their differences by implicit negotiating.

Mutually Recognized Differences

Many people have mutually recognized differences but do not negotiate. Before people will negotiate, it is necessary for both to have an interest in removing their differences and subordinate their differences to their commitment to a shared distal future. It is the interplay between mutually recognized differences and a distal shared future that creates tensions in negotiations. The mutually recognized differences may be mild or severe. Roommates often have minor differences of opinion on how neat and tidy they are to keep their room. Occasionally, a married couple discover that each has betrayed the other, yet attempt to preserve their marriage by negotiating.

Whether the intensity of the differences is mild or intense, a "my side" and "your side" is established when the negotiators give their attention to their differences. The establishment of a "my side" and "your side" need not lead to the resolution of differences through negotiating. Both may recognize that the intensity of the differences is so great that negotiations are impossible. Then they may actively ignore their differences, disaffiliate, or fight over their differences.

Mutually recognized differences result in negotiating only when both parties acknowledge that they should attend to the differences and both parties indicate acceptance of the idea that they have a shared distal future. Negotiating does not automatically flow from disagreements. In many situations, mutually recognized differences lead to disaffiliation or conflict. Some people with a sustained relationship manage their differences by ignoring them. Close friends who differ vehemently on political issues may simply avoid discussing politics. Some differences can be managed by each accommodating to the other's opinion.

An Egalitarian Relationship

Masters and slaves rarely negotiate, at least not explicitly. The same is true of infants and parents. To negotiate with another implicitly establishes a symmetrical relationship, at least for the duration of the negotiation session. When one spouse is completely dominated by the other, they do not negotiate; one imposes his wishes on the other.

When people negotiate, not only is the integrity of the other accepted, but in addition each presumes the other capable of contributing to the solution of their disagreements. Negotiators resolve their differences by allowing each other to contribute to the solution; one does not impose a resolution on the other. Often, when people with an asymmetrical relationship attempt to negotiate, the negotiations break down and the more powerful party imposes his will on the weaker party. Young children and parents frequently open negotiations only for the parent to become frustrated and bring the session to a conclusion by dictating a resolution.

Elements of Negotiations

The completion of a negotiation session requires the production of (1) the functional identities of negotiators; (2) making proposals and counterproposals; (3) finding areas of agreements; (4) forging commitments that structure their future; and (5) closing negotiations. In addition, in all negotiations there is either a consensual taken- for-granted reality or the construction of a consensual definition of reality. A concern with reality often dominates negotiating sessions. Negotiators frequently have strong disagreements about their reality. These disagreements must be resolved if the session is to be brought to a successful completion.

Functional Identities as Negotiators

People establish functional identities as negotiators by making their future relatedness their shared focus, establishing the resolution of their differences as their social objective and mutually indicating a willingness to resolve their differences. Negotiators also indicate that they will take each other's standpoint seriously, assume some responsibility for structuring their future, and allow each other to propose solutions.

The shared focus of negotiators can be almost anything. One roommate may complain to the other about the fact that he is always using the telephone; or one spouse may complain to the other about his dereliction of responsibility. The complaint itself does not establish the issue as a shared focus. The other must indicate the complaint has some legitimacy and attend to the issue. Of course, sometimes the complaint is answered with a countercomplaint, and several facets of their relationship become their shared foci. If one responds that nothing can be done, then functional identities as negotiators are not established. Before an issue can become the topic of negotiation, both must acknowledge that it is possible to modify their relationship, that viable alternatives exist.

The overarching social objective is the resolution of disagreements and achieving consensus on their future relatedness. Negotiators manage both proximal and distal social objectives. The proximal objective is reaching an agreement; the distal objective is structuring their future relatedness. The distal social objective may be as all-encompassing as the total rearrangement of a relationship or as limited as two children negotiating which of them is going to ask their father if they can go to the playground.

When both parties indicate a willingness to take the standpoint of the other seriously, they thereby express respect for the other's standpoint and indicate the other is competent to offer solutions. Each indicates that he accepts the other as more or less an equal. The other's position is acknowledged as legitimate. Of course, during a session one may indicate that the other's stand on a specific issue is not legitimate. Then that issue may be dropped, or they may become embroiled in an argument over the legitimacy of the issue. Then the one offering that standpoint must either modify his position or convince the other of the legitimacy of the issue in question. Persuasion is often a major subprocess of negotiations.

Negotiators often call each other into account for their respective standpoints. For example, one spouse may state, "Why do you bring that up now? It isn't at issue here." Whenever accountability is introjected into a negotiating session, it stops movement toward the resolution of differences. Accountability is a past-oriented form of social action; negotiating is a future-oriented form of action. Many negotiating sessions transform into intense accountability sessions. When that occurs, the participants must reintroduce their shared future as the social objective if they are to resolve their differences. On some occasions, when negotiators call each other into account, the ill will between them becomes even greater.

Negotiators accept responsibility for structuring the future; they presume they have some control over their own lives. Each assumes some responsibility for future developments and allows the other to assume some responsibility. In short, they share responsibility for structuring their future.

On occasion, individuals refuse to enter into negotiations to avoid responsibility. For example, a father and his ten-year-old son were conversing about a minor ruckus created by the son. The father offered, "Let's talk it over and work it out." The son declined. The father attempted two or three more times to entice the son to discuss the situation. He even used the phrase, "Let's negotiate." The son finally retorted, "Naw, just tell me what to do and I'll do it." By refusing to negotiate and stating that he would do whatever his father instructed him to do, the son freed himself from responsibility — providing, of course, that he did as his father instructed. If any untoward developments followed, responsibility could be shifted to his father. Each negotiator implicitly, if not explicitly, presents himself as a responsible person; as a person who can and will exercise some control over his future behavior. Occasionally, as in the above example, individuals refuse to activate the functional identities as negotiators to avoid responsibility.

More often than not, it is the superordinate member of a relationship who refuses to allow the subordinate to negotiate. Students frequently attempt to negotiate with instructors. Sometimes instructors indicate a willingness to negotiate. But many issues are nonnegotiable. When students attempt to negotiate how they will do their term papers, instructors sometimes respond with, "In my class you do assignments as I want them done." In such encounters the superordinate presumes responsibility for structuring the future and refuses the subordinate the opportunity to contribute to programming the future.

When functional identities as negotiators are established, each has the prerogative as well as the obligation to contribute to the solution. Within a given session most of the solutions may be proposed by one party, but both have the opportunity to contribute proposals.

Proposals and Assessments

The proposal and assessment phase of negotiations is similar to the offer and counteroffer phase of bargaining. It differs in that in negotiations the content consists of statements about how the future might be structured, whereas in bargaining the content consists of what will be offered in exchange for what.

During the proposal and assessment phase negotiators search for a viable alternative to their current relatedness. Each proposal is evaluated. Sometimes the evaluation is explicit. One person might make a suggestion only to have it rejected by the other. In many transactions, however, one person offers a proposal followed by the other offering a counterproposal. When the second person offers a counterproposal, he implicitly informs the first person that the proposal offered by the first person is not acceptable.

The proposal and assessment phase of negotiations may be deadly serious or may be interlaced with elements of play. Negotiators frequently joke with and tease each other as they offer alternatives. This playful activity sometimes lessens the tension that is an inherent part of negotiating. Simultaneous laughter while disagreeing serves to inform both that they are in this together despite their differences.

Nonresponsiveness is a powerful activity once negotiators have begun making proposals. When a proposal elicits neither agreement nor disagreement, but only nonresponsiveness, the tension between negotiators increases. Moments of sticky silence often emerge when one person makes proposals and the other reacts like a fencepost. The expression of disagreement is often less stressful than is nonresponsiveness.

Consensual Reality

When people negotiate, there is either the presumption of a shared definition of reality or the negotiators construct a consensual definition of reality. When negotiators have a robust shared past and the issues negotiated are of minor significance, they seldom attend to questions of reality. They presume that they have the same conception of reality. But when negotiators do not have a robust shared past or when they have strong differences, then issues of reality often come to the fore.

Explicit attention to reality frequently emerges when one makes an assertion specifying the facts of the case with the other taking exception to the characterization offered. For example, one spouse may assert, "Well, that would work if you weren't so bullheaded." Assertions of that sort usually result in debates about the facts of the case. When the facts of the case become the shared focus, the negotiation process is held in abeyance until a consensual definition is established or until the topic is defined as irrelevant to the resolution of their differences.

Frequently, each negotiator attempts to impose his definition of the situation as the consensual reality. What are reasonable alternatives depends in part on the consensual reality agreed to. Consequently, negotiators often dispute the definition of the situation.

Issues of reality may focus on either the past, present or future. They often focus on the past. In many negotiation sessions the negotiation process is put on hold as the negotiators accuse each other of past crimes. Many spouses have attempted to resolve their differences and then transformed the negotiation session into a shouting match as each claims the other is responsible for their current difficulties.

These debates are highly evaluative. Often, each attempts to stigmatize the other; and the other reciprocates in kind. Sometimes these debates evolve into character contests (Luckenbill 1980), with each negotiator attempting to prove he can be nastier than the other. When that transformation occurs, it is likely that the negotiation session will transform into conflict.

The interjection of disputes about reality, especially those that focus on the nature of the past, impedes movement toward the construction of agreements and commitments. Rhetorical devices typically come to the fore as each attempts, usually without success, to entice the other to adopt his definition of the situation.

On occasion, when attention is focused on the past, it facilitates the successful completion of negotiations. Sometimes the parties acquire a greater understanding of the other's position and features of their relationship as the negotiation session unfolds. And sometimes negotiators become aware of dimensions of themselves they had not previously recognized. If that occurs, it can lead to a modification of assessments of the other's proposals.

When issues of reality focus on current or anticipated conditions, discussions of reality provide a foundation for firm solutions. For example, one negotiator may make a proposal with the other noting that because of certain external conditions, the proposal is not feasible. They may then formulate an alternative that takes into account the contingency noted. When that happens, movement toward an agreement is momentarily disrupted. But the disruptions are usually less severe and are less likely to degenerate into character contests when current and future contingencies are the focus of attention than when past events are made the shared focus.

Bargainers also frequently become involved in discussions of consensual reality. Sellers often assign great value to the item they are offering, and buyers often belittle what the seller has to offer. When that occurs in bargaining, it also disrupts the bargaining process. There is a fundamental difference, however. Bargainers may complete a bargain despite having basic disagreements on the facts of the case. In contrast, it is almost impossible for negotiators to bring their sessions to a successful conclusion unless they agree on the relevant facts.

Negotiators may direct their attention to the reality that encases their negotiations at any time. In the earliest stages, negotiators may address the issue of whether or not they have a shared distal future. In other instances, a concern with reality may not come to the fore until negotiators begin forging commitments. Then one may ask if a given commitment is realistic given prevailing conditions. In general, however, the establishment of a consensual definition of reality becomes predominate most often during the proposal and assessment stage of negotiations.

Agreements

Two quite different kinds of agreements are constructed in negotiations. One is agreements on their reality; the other is agreements on the viability of a proposal. Agreements on reality, of course, do not resolve differences; although they may provide a foundation for the construction of agreements. Usually negotiators are very sensitive to the difference between the two kinds of agreements — although on occasion negotiators indicate an agreement to a statement they thought was a characterization of reality only to learn the other interpreted it as an agreement to a proposal. If that is detected, the negotiators may construct a mininegotiation session within a negotiation as they work out their differences in interpretation.

For example, two women were negotiating which of them was going to speak to a university dean; neither wanted to do it. One said, "Well, you've talked with him before. It's best someone he knows approaches him." The other responded with a nod and "Uh huh." The first quickly stated, "OK, so you agree to go." The second responded, "No, no! I agreed I had done it before, not that I'd do it again." The first person attempted to transform an agreement focused on their reality into an agreement on a plan of action. The second person refused to allow the transformation. In this case, they continued to negotiate which of them was to speak to the authority. In some cases, however, persons who think they have expressed an agreement with a definition of the situation find themselves trapped into agreeing with a proposal.

Within a given negotiation, only a single agreement may be achieved; other times, complex series of agreements are made. When an agreement is reached, it does not necessarily specify the structure of the future. Often it only indicates that one facet of their differences has been resolved or that one part of a solution has been found. When multiple agreements are made, after the last one has been completed they may note that they have resolved their differences. They agree that they agree.

Forging Social Commitments

After agreeing on a solution to their mutually recognized differences, persons oblige themselves to act in the manner that has been jointly prescribed; they commit themselves to specific lines of action. Social commitments are a special form of agreement. When a social commitment is forged, one or both parties becomes obliged to carry out the program of action that has been constructed.

When constructing commitments, persons attend to the agreements they have constructed in the immediate past and link the immediate past to a distal future. The distal future projected may be almost immediate. For example, when two children negotiate a plan to "surprise" their mother, the commitment may be put into action almost immediately. Or the commitment forged may bind the two together for the rest of their natural lives. Marriage vows, for example, are social commitments that oblige both parties to each other and their community. Negotiators pledge their honor when they forge a commitment. If negotiators violate commitments, they acquire a reputation as dishonorable persons. When the plan of action at issue is a relatively insignificant point, the forging of a commitment may consist of nothing more than reciprocating OKs. For instance, two friends may resolve their differences over how they are going to spend a night on the town by agreeing to go to a bar. At the conclusion of the negotiation one may state, "Ok, we'll meet at Joe's at eight?" followed by, "Right, see you there." Or a married couple, after lengthy negotiating sessions, may review the set of agreements they have reached and with great emotion promise to abide by their agreements.

The construction of commitments is a serious activity. It is not completed in a playful context. During the earlier phases of a negotiation, playful activity may reduce tensions and reaffirm the solidarity of the group. But the settlement of their differences and the programming of their future cannot be consummated in a playful manner. When it comes time to forge commitments, negotiators take on a serious demeanor. Negotiators implicitly, if not explicitly, agree that the structuring of their future is important enough to require serious and thoughtful consideration (Sink and Couch 1986).

If playfulness is produced during the later stages of negotiation, when negotiators are forging commitments, the lack of seriousness will usually become their shared focus. One of the negotiators is likely to call the other into account with, "Let's get serious about this," or, "Are you going to be serious or not?"

When negotiations focus on relatively insignificant matters and are produced by persons with an extensive shared past, agreements and commitments may be produced simultaneously. There often is not a distinct set of reciprocating acts wherein each indicates he is honor bound to act as they have agreed. In these contexts, the negotiators have sufficient interpersonal trust to allow them to recognize that when an agreement has been constructed, each is simultaneously committed to the agreement.

When the commitment is divergent from the personal preference of one or both of the negotiators, the incongruity will typically be given explicit attention. One may say to the other, "I know that it is not your first choice, but can you live with it?" Usually, interpersonal negotiators avoid the construction of commitments that strongly conflict with personal preferences.

When a social commitment is made, the distal future has been at least temporarily structured by and for the negotiators. Subsequent developments may result in the reopening of negotiations, and not all negotiators are honorable. For the moment, however, a micro social structure has been constructed that orders their future.

Closing Negotiations

Once the commitment is made, the negotiators discontinue concerning themselves about what is to be done. They may directly implement the resolution or may attend to other concerns. If they bring their time together to an end, they will construct a closing (Leichty 1986). They will not simply turn their backs on each other and go their separate ways. Instead, they will mutually indicate to each other that while they are terminating their time together, they recognize that they have a shared future.

If the issue at hand is relatively unimportant, both negotiators may recognize that as soon as the commitment is made, they are finished and simply turn their attention elsewhere. If the negotiators have attended to important differences, and they have successfully resolved them, they will make statements such as, "Well, I guess that does it, right?" If the query is agreed to, both recognize that their negotiations are at an end.

Not all negotiations are successful. Many negotiators terminate their sessions without forging commitments. Then they may turn their attention to the specification of the time and place of the next negotiating session. If they have disagreements centering on the time and place of the next session, they may negotiate when and where they will meet. When a negotiating session is unsuccessful, and they cannot agree on when to reopen negotiations, the encounter may be brought to a conclusion by one simply turning away and leaving.

If the negotiation session is successful, the negotiators usually celebrate their achievement before terminating their time together; the celebration may be nothing more than mutual smiles. They thereby inform each other of their shared satisfaction with the outcome. When they jointly celebrate their achievement, they assure one another that they have a solid commitment to a shared future. For the moment, differences have been pushed into the background, and similarities have emerged in the foreground. When negotiations end without a celebration, the security of the commitment is questionable.

Summary

Like bargaining, negotiating is a mixed-motive form of social action. It contains elements of both conflict and cooperation. In contrast to bargaining, one objective of negotiating is to remove the conflictual elements. Successful negotiations remove some of the uncertainty and chaos of life. Negotiating is one procedure for rendering the ever problematic world somewhat less unstable. It is not the only way that human life acquires structure. But it is one of the more important ways of creating micro social structures. Even within the most rigid authoritarian structures, there is usually some room for negotiating and renegotiating social arrangements.

Not all coordinated activity flows from negotiations. Much of the time human beings simply coordinate their activity with each other on the basis of taken-for-granted structures. When college students attend the first class meeting of a course, for example, they seldom negotiate with the professor the content of the course or how they are to behave toward each other. Procedures are offered by the professor and accepted by the students. Students and professors do negotiate some minor features of their relatedness.

Negotiations are "time out" activities. Negotiators discontinue their established routines and turn their attention to working out their relatedness. If each and every social act was preceded by negotiating how the activity was to be performed, nothing much would ever be accomplished. Nonetheless, negotiating provides procedures for human beings jointly to structure their future whenever it has been rendered problematic. It is an alternative to the asymmetrical imposition of social order.

Negotiators respect each other. Both regard the other as competent to contribute to the structuring of the future and as honorable. Negotiating is an alternative to coercion and asymmetrical control. It is a form of social action that human beings have developed and use to create social orders without one party imposing his will on the other.

Chapter 9   The Structure of Action and Relationships

Social life is both processual and structured. Some social scientists focus primarily on the processual dimensions of social life; others focus primarily on the structural dimensions of social life. The two emphases are not inherently incompatible. In fact, a comprehensive account of social life requires the analysis of social processes, the elements of sociation produced in social encounters, the social relationships that human beings use to contextualize social encounters, and the elements of sociation that compose social relationships. The preceding chapters focused on social processes and the elements of sociation that compose various forms of social action. The chapters following this one describe and analyze social relationships. Both the preceding chapters and the following ones adopt a third-party and analytical standpoint and focus attention on dyadic transactions, how two people fit together their actions to produce social events and objects.

George Herbert Mead (1934, 1938) was the first student of social life to call for the analysis of social processes. He emphasized the social, sequential, and temporal nature of human conduct. He noted that each of us acquired our minds and identities by participating in social activities. He also noted that human conduct not only occurs across time but in addition that human action is informed by past experience and structured by projected futures. Mead also recognized that human beings first become competent in the production of units of social action and later acquire the competencies to construct and use social relationships.

Mead did not develop a set of concepts that specified the elements and structure of social action. That was achieved by research that focused on how individuals moved from a state of acting independently to acting interdependently (Miller, Hintz, and Couch 1975). That research identified the six elements of sociation—copresence, reciprocal attentiveness, social responsiveness, functional identities, shared focus, and social objective— that must be produced for members of a dyad to cooperate. Simpler forms of social action—the chase, conflict, accommodation, etc.—are composed of particular combinations of some of these six basic elements of sociation. Complex forms of social action—interpersonal accountability, bargaining, and interpersonal negotiating—are composed of these six basic elements plus additional ones.

108

The specification of these elements and how they are linked to each other provide a general conceptual framework for the analysis of social action, but they are not adequate for the analysis of social relationships. Many social scientists have focused on social relationships. Few have given much attention to the specification of the elements of sociation that constitute social relationships. Instead they have concentrated on the consequences that flow from specific relationships. For example, Marx advanced the thesis that ownership—the control of the means of production—was an asymmetrical social relationship that resulted in owners exploiting nonowners.

Many social scientists who focus on social relationships adopt a point in time, as opposed to an across-time standpoint, when they analyze social relationships. They presume that social relationships are constant. They fail to recognize that social relationships, like all human creations, exist only in human action. Nonetheless, they have a point. Social relationships, in contrast to units of social action, are enduring. Today's father—son relationship, which is a subform of the parental relationship, is much the same as it was several decades ago. In general, it is social relationships that provide constancy; they give stability to human conduct. Nonetheless, they, like social encounters, are human creations. One of the fundamental differences between social encounters and social relationships is that social encounters are ephemeral, whereas social relationships are, relatively speaking, enduring.

Some social scientists who focus on social relationships, especially the structuralists (Althusser and Balibar 1970), advance the thesis that social relationships cause social action. These social scientists assign little significance to the analysis of social action. They claim that social action merely flows from social structure or that social encounters are mere reflections of social relationships. The more reasonable position is that the actions produced in social encounters both reflect and have an impact on social relationships; social relationships are learned and produced in social encounters and in turn contextualize social encounters. Nearly all social encounters are contextualized by one or more social relationships that people activate when they establish social contact.

Social Action

The structure of social action almost constantly changes as human beings establish, maintain, modify, and break contact with one another. Social activities are not chaotic; they, as well as social relationships, have structure. Nonetheless, the structure is a dynamic one that is constantly evolving and devolving; it has little constancy. But there is a sequential order in the production of the elements of sociation in all social encounters. For example, people cannot establish a social objective until after they have established a shared focus. When we can specify the necessary order for the production of the elements of sociation that constitute the various forms of social action, we increase our understanding of social conduct.

Each form of social action, including social panic, is composed of distinctive elements of sociation. The structure of each social encounter, ranging from a simple chase to a complex interpersonal negotiating session, is a combination of (1) the elements of sociation established; (2) the sequential order in which the elements are produced; and (3) the dimensions of temporality employed as people take each other into account and align their individual lines of action with each other to produce a course of social action.

Each element of sociation may be established and maintained symmetrically or asymmetrically. The elements of sociation established by young children and adults are usually asymmetrical. A primitive social encounter is created when an infant produces an act that is noted and responded to by an adult. A somewhat more complex social encounter is created when an adult initiates action toward an infant and the infant attempts to align her action with that of the adult. The behavior of infants and young children is often erratic, however. One moment a child may call for attention, only to let her attention drift before the adult acts toward or with respect to the child. On other occasions, one moment the child is very responsive; the next moment the child may be indifferent to the actions of the adult. The production of coordinated action by a young child and an adult usually requires that the parent be very attentive and responsive to the child's action. Whether the young child or the adult initiates contact, the adult usually provides more of the content than the child when adults and children coordinate their actions.

As children acquire command of their movements and the ability to anticipate, they can respond in a more consistent manner to the actions of adults; their behavior becomes less erratic. In the process, children become more capable of producing their "half" of an element of sociation. As children acquire the ability to respond to the initiations of adults and the ability to be attentive and responsive to others, the social encounters produced by children and adults move toward symmetry. The movement toward symmetry is a long drawn-out process.

Even after children have acquired the ability to specify social objectives, the interaction between children and adults usually remains asymmetrical. For example, when the small boy calls for his mother to zip up his coat, it is the mother who provides the bulk of the action. The child cooperates by adopting a passive stance, while the mother zips up his coat. In these and many other transactions between children and adults, the child does not contribute half of the content; the action is asymmetrical. Yet the action is reciprocally aligned. Both child and parent attend and are responsive to each other, and both contribute to the achievement of social objectives.

When adults carry on conversations, the listener usually produces listener's responses. Most adult listeners nod, smile, and say, "Uh huh" as speakers provide content. When the speaker discontinues, the listener takes her turn (Dittman 1972). Conversations between adults are often symmetrical; each person more or less equally contributes content. When an adult attempts to carry on a conversation with a young child, however, the interaction usually is asymmetrical. The child often not only fails to contribute half the content but sometimes fails to respond at all to the content provided by the adult. When that occurs, the adult often asks the child such questions as, "Did you hear me?" or "Do you understand?" to elicit responsiveness. Such questions are relatively rare when adults converse. Adults are, generally speaking, more responsive to the activities of others than are young children.

When children begin to interact with other children, they move from participating in asymmetrical interaction to participating in symmetrical interaction. Of course, when children first begin interacting with other children of the same age, their concerted action often dissolves when one or both of them fail to produce their half of an element of sociation necessary to maintain coordination. It is the limited ability of young children to sustain elements of sociation that makes the interaction between young children so erratic.

In general, as children socially mature, they move from the asymmetrical production of elements of sociation to the symmetrical production of elements of sociation. But units of social action produced by two adults may be very asymmetrical. If one person is more interested in the other person than the second person is in the first, their reciprocal attentiveness and social responsiveness may be very asymmetrical. In a similar manner, if one adult is more interested in achieving a social objective, say, resolving their mutually recognized differences than the other, their interaction also is likely to be asymmetrical.

Whether the interaction is symmetrical or asymmetrical, some of the elements of sociation are established in a definite sequence. The sequential order that holds for children acquiring mastery of elements of sociation tends to follow the same sequence as when two adults produce a unit of social action. Before children can produce congruent functional identities, they have to master social responsiveness; similarly, before two adults can establish congruent functional identities, they must become socially responsive. That order cannot be reversed.

The establishment of an element of sociation that is a prerequisite for another element of sociation does not assure that the other element of sociation will be established. The establishment of mutually recognized differences and the projection of a shared distal future, for example, does not assure that a proposal-response sequence will follow. The establishment of mutually recognized differences and the projection of a shared distal future are prerequisites for the production of proposal-response sequences, but they do not cause proposal-response sequences.

Social action not only occurs across time; human beings use their personal, common, and shared pasts to project personal, contingent, and shared futures. The pasts used by human beings inform their action, and the projected futures guide the action produced in the immediate situation. Human beings constantly use their pasts to project futures that structure their actions in the immediate situation.

Both shared pasts and common pasts give structure to social action. For example, the boy who has repeatedly "played catch" with his father by rolling a ball back and forth can quickly and smoothly produce that unit of social action with his father. If the youngster attempts to "play catch" with another boy, who does not have that past, it is unlikely that they will be able to coordinate their actions. At least they will not be able to produce that unit of social action quickly and smoothly. But if the other boy has played catch in that manner with his parent, then the two of them have common pasts. That will allow for easier coordination of action than if they do not have common pasts.

As the pasts of children become elaborated and as they refine their abilities to project futures, it become easier for them to construct complex units of social action. Their behavior acquires more structure and becomes less erratic.

When children acquire command of distal futures, the complexity of the units of social behavior that they can construct undergoes a qualitative transformation. For example, when children first master the ability to bargain, they often bargain implusively. They organize their actions to achieve immediate gratification. They do not organize their behavior in the immediate situation on the basis of long-range implications of an exchange; instead they organize their behavior on the basis of a proximal future. After children acquire the ability to project distal futures, they can assess the implication of an exchange on the basis of anticipated long-range consequences. Their bargaining transforms from impulsive bargaining to rational bargaining.

As children acquire the ability to produce symmetrical elements of sociation and to subordinate their actions in the present to distal futures, they also learn to categorize others and themselves. As they acquire consciousness of how categorical identities are linked, they become aware of social relationships. When children acquire mastery of linkages between categorical identities, they enter the world of social structure.

Social Relationships

Consciousness of categorical identities provides the foundation for the entry of children into the world of social structure. Children become capable of contextualizing their activities within social relationships as they become aware of the commonalities in the linkages between categorical identities across situations. The two sets of categorical identities that most children master early in life are those that link them to their parents and those that connect them with their playmates. When a young boy recognizes that the patterns of activity that he and his parents produce are similar to the patterns of behavior other children and their parents produce and that these patterns of behavior are linked to the categorical identities of child, mother, and father, he becomes conscious of the social relationships that constitute a nuclear family. Similarly, when a young girl acquires command of the categorical identity friend and recognizes that the activities she and her playmates produce are similar to those of other children who play together she acquires consciousness of the structure of friendship.

Children establish patterns of action with their parents and their friends before they acquire consciousness of the relationships. The acquisition of consciousness of relationships requires the adoption of a third-party point of view toward sets of categorical identities. Just as the emergence of consciousness of self requires the adoption of the standpoint of another toward self, consciousness of relationships requires the adoption of a third-party point of view toward the connections between at least two categorical identities. For example, when a father tells his son that he should share with his friend, the parent attempts to entice the child to adopt a third-party point of view toward the connections between the child and his playmate. These instructions specify that one of the dimensions of friendship is sharing.

All social action contextualized by social relationships is based on two parties consensually assigning themselves and each other categorical identities and agreeing on how the two categorical identities are linked to each other. The degree of agreement on how the categorical identities are linked is not always complete. It ranges from encounters where there is almost total agreement on how the two categorical identities fit together to encounters where people violently disagree on what are the proper linkages between categorical identities. Even the closest friends occasionally have disagreements on how friends should act toward each other.

One of the distinctive features of social relationships is the anticipation of constancy. The parental relationship begins to emerge when both parent and child begin to anticipate that their relationship will endure. Of course, in most instances that anticipation informs the actions of the parent long before it informs the actions of the child. The mutual recognition that their association extends into the distal past and mutual anticipation that it will endure into the distal future are two basic elements of all parental relationships.

After people have become conscious of a social relationship, they can activate it whenever they establish social contact and mutually recognize each other's categorical identities. The activation of social relationships is not automatic. Sometimes people disagree on whether or not a given relationship is relevant to the immediate situation. For example, two friends at the same auction might find themselves bidding on the same piece of furniture. One of them might regard the competitive bidding as acceptable, whereas the other might regard it as a violation of the friendship and discontinue bidding.

The action taken toward children and the actions of children are structured by social relationships before they become conscious of relationships. Parents use their conception of the parental relationship to organize their actions toward children long before children become aware of social relationships. The actions of the parent have an impact on the child. The behavior of the child will reflect the actions of the parents toward her. The parents' conception of the parental relationship thereby structures both the actions of the parent and the actions of the child. But the activity of the child in the early years is not structured by the child's conception of the parental relationship.

Most parents assume that they have certain prerogatives and responsibilities toward their children. They simultaneously assume the child has prerogatives—the right to be cared for, fed, and protected. Then, as the child matures, she is assigned responsibilities. When the child acquires command of the categorical identities of parent and child and their linkage, she becomes a full- fledged participant in the maintenance of the parental relationship. When a mother retorts to her child's request with the question, "Why should I?" and gets the response, "Because you are my mother" the child has at least partial command of the parental relationship.

Most children first acquire command of the categorical identities and linkages that compose family relationships. They often use their conceptions of family relationships to organize their play. They pretend to be fathers, mothers, babies, etc. How children organize their actions within these pretend relationships reflects their understanding of them. Three young children, about four years old, two girls and one boy, were playing house in the backyard. They pretended that a large packing crate was a house. One of the girls took on the identity of mother, the other of baby, and the boy that of father. They pretended it was time for the father to go to work. The boy kissed the girl playing mother good-bye, mounted his tricycle, and rode around the corner of the house. He stopped, dismounted, and sat down on the lawn for a few minutes. Then he got up and wandered into the garage and looked around. His actions seemed undirected, as if he did not know what to do. He returned to his tricycle, fiddled with it a while, and sat down again for a few minutes. Then he mounted his tricycle and returned to the packing crate.

In the meantime, the mother had swept out the packing crate and put the baby to bed in a corner of the crate. When the boy returned, he was met with, "What are you doing here?" He shrugged in response to the query. The pretend family structure collapsed when the boy suggested they go play in the nearby swings. After a moment's hesitation, first the girl playing mother, then the one playing baby, followed his lead.

The girl playing mother had a conception of the activity that was linked to the categorical identity of mother. The boy had only a vague conception, if any, of what activity was linked to the categorical identity of father when the father was not in the house. He knew fathers left home to go to work, or at least to go somewhere, but he seemed to have no idea of what fathers did when away from home.

When people activate social relationships, whether in the real world or the pretend world, they mutually establish congruent categorical identities and attempt to perform the functional identities implied by the categorical identities. Often the functional identities flow smoothly and easily from the categorical identities. But on other occasions people are unsure of the actions called for by a categorical identity. Other times, they are incompetent; they cannot effectively produce the functional identity called for by the categorical identity. Not all professors are competent; neither are all students.

Most of the time, the social action contextualized by social relationships is so routine that little conscious attention is given to it. Each person acts as anticipated, and no thought is given to either the categorical identities, the fit between them, or the fact that the behavior is structured by a mutually activated social relationship.

The importance of a social relationship often is not recognized unless the relationship is rendered problematic. For example, it is when a romantic relationship is in the process of disintegrating that people usually become most aware of its significance; when a parent dies, we become very conscious of the parental relationship. On a more mundane level, we routinely activate exchange relationships with salesclerks. It is only when we misidentify another customer as a salesclerk that we become conscious of the necessity of activating an exchange relationship to complete simple economic transactions.

Usually on the basis of either shared pasts or categorical identities displayed in appearance, we are able to activate the appropriate relationship, complete our transactions with others, and go on our way. These highly routine encounters are possible only because we and others have acquired command of complex sets of relationships that we use to structure our social activities. Routinized activity, especially with strangers, is highly dependent on establishing consensual categorical identities and agreeing with each other on how these categorical identities are linked to each other.

Consider the following situation: A policeman is standing at an intersection and preventing drivers from turning down one of the streets. When a driver approaches, she and the policeman make visual contact, immediately establish consensual categorical identities and the driver acts as instructed by the policeman. All the policeman has to do is make a gesture that the driver should proceed on the other street, and the driver complies. Suppose, however, that a driver approaches and attempts to go down the street blocked by the policeman. The policeman steps in front of the car and the driver stops. The policeman asserts, "No one is allowed down this street." Further, suppose the driver states, "But I'm Bill Jones, a detective." The policeman might or might not allow the driver to proceed. He might insist that the driver offer evidence of his categorical identity.

Then suppose the driver is not capable of offering any evidence that he is a detective. Any number of different scenarios might unfold. The two of them might get into an argument, the driver might finally abide by the directives of the policeman, the policeman might back down, or a third party might be called upon to intervene.

Even if the driver produces some identification, the policeman might not allow him to proceed down the street. The policeman might take it upon himself to keep all, including detectives, from the scene. Then the two of them are likely to get into a hassle over who has what prerogatives and responsibilities in the situation. The lack of order that flows from such encounters is the consequence of those involved not being able to activate a consensually accepted social relationship.

Often there are disagreements or uncertainties on either the categorical identities to be activated in a situation or how the categorical identities are linked to each other. When that is the case, if people are to contextualize their interaction within a social relationship, they have to turn their attention to establishing a consensual definition of what categorical identities are relevant and how the categorical identities are linked to each other. Sometimes consensus is achieved by one persuading the other on what identities and linkages are relevant; at other times, they negotiate an acceptable solution.

In general, we regard social relationships as facets of our environment that have an existence above and beyond the immediate social encounter. We tend to forget that they are human constructs. But social relationships, like units of social action, are social productions. They are more complex than units of social action, and they are more enduring. Each social encounter endures only for the length of time it takes to produce it. In contrast, social relationships endure across situations. A father and a son retain their parental relationship from one social encounter to the next.

Of course, like all human constructs, social relationships change. Some change very slowly over long periods of time, but on occasion some relationships are changed cataclysmically. The father—son relationship that prevails in the United States is much the same as the father—son relationship that prevailed two hundred years ago. Of course, it has changed some. The king—subject relationship that prevailed in 1770 between the king of England and the residents of the American colonies was eradicated by the American Revolution.

Nonetheless, social relationships in general give constancy to human action. They provide us with ways to effectively accomplish many objectives. Conversely, they also constrain us. If the current social relationships were not replaced with others, however, the complex social world we are all a part of would not be possible.

Nearly always, when a set of social relationships are under attack or fading from the scene, some take the position that the social order is crumbling. And, in a sense, that is correct. A social order is crumbling. Sometimes the preexisting social order is being replaced by an alternative social order. Sometimes the emerging set of social relationships provides human beings with greater opportunities; other times, only greater constraints. Usually, whenever social relationships are transformed, both new opportunities and new constraints are established.

For example, the abolition of the social relationships that constituted slavery was regarded by some, especially slaveowners, as a serious threat to social order. The assessment of that transformation by others, especially the ex-slaves, was somewhat different.

Some regard social relationships as chiseled in stone; others regard them as the bane of human existence. Some in the latter group would abolish all social relationships. The more reasonable position is to recognize that they are human constructs and to analyze them; then, on the basis of the analysis, assess them; then, perhaps modify, transform, eradicate them, or create new ones.

One of the primary tasks of social scientists is to offer an analysis of social relationships. The knowledge generated by social scientists can then be used to modify and eradicate social relationships and perhaps to develop new relationships that provide human beings with new opportunities and fewer constraints.

Summary

Both units of social action and social relationships have structure. The structure of social action is composed of the elements of sociation people establish, the order of their establishment, the pasts that inform the coordinated activity, and the futures projected. The structure of social relationships consists of the categorical identities people activate when they make contact with each other, the linkages they make between the categorical identities activated, their common or shared distal pasts that inform their ongoing activity, and the distal futures projected.

When people acquire command of social relationships, their interaction is structured on two levels—on one level, by the dynamic elements of social action that are constantly evolving and transforming as human beings join together their individual lines of action to construct a course of social action, and on another level, by the relatively constant structural elements of sociation that compose social relationships that endure across social encounters.

Each new member of a society enters a preexisting social structure. For the first few years of life, she is unconscious of that structure. Each child first acquires the ability to join her actions with others to produce simple units of social action; then the ability to produce more complex units of social action; then acquires command of social relationships. Children cannot acquire consciousness of social relationships until after they have acquired command of categorical identities.

After children have acquired command of social relationships units of social action continue to be structured by the elements of sociation produced in the immediate situation. In addition, their action is structured by the relationship they activate when they align their actions with the actions of others. The acquisition of these abilities proceeds from the simplest to the more complex. After command of social relationships is achieved, then the more complex, the social relationships, are usually activated as soon as people make social contact. The social relationships activated on contact then contextualize the units of social action produced.

To state the process somewhat differently, individuals first acquire command of the ability to produce units of social action, then they acquire command of social structures. The social relationships that compose the social structure then structure social encounters. Neither units of social action nor forms of social relationships have an existence other than that of human beings willfully taking each other into account and organizing their actions in concert. Yet the structuralists, those who conceptualize social action as flowing from the structure, do have a point. Most of the social relationships that we use to structure our social conduct existed in much the same form as they currently do before any of us were born. In a sense, we are all products of the social relationships that preceded us and will endure beyond our lifetimes.

Chapter 10 Parental Relationships

Each of us was the focal point of complexly patterned activities structured to protect, care for, and instruct us for the first several years of our
lives. When we entered the world, each of us was encased by at least one
parental relationship; most of us have been a part of a series of parental
relationships. We did not actively contribute to these relationships for the
first several months of our lives. We were merely objects of concern; some
of us were treated as precious objects, others were not so fortunate. But all
of us received the care necessary for our survival.

The parental relationship is universal; it is a necessary part of the social
structure of all societies. At least some of the newly born must be encased
by a parental relationship if a society is to survive. The assignment of the
primary responsibilities of caring for and instructing infants and children
varies greatly from society to society (Murdock 1949). But in all societies a
set of persons are designated the caregivers of each infant. In most, but certainly not all societies, the biological parents have primary responsibility
for protecting, caring for, and instructing their children for at least the first
few years.

There is also great variation across and within societies in the content
of parental relationships. In some societies, infants are constantly hovered
over; in others, they are treated indifferently. But in all cases, if the infant is
to survive, some person or set of persons must provide the material
necessities to sustain life; they must also provide the instruction necessary to
transform human organisms into human beings.

The earliest parental activity is primarily structured by the objective of
assuring the infant's biological survival. In the process of receiving the care
necessary for survival each infant is also exposed to repetitive sequences of
behavior that allow her to formulate anticipations, acquire significant
gestures and symbols. Until infants acquire some control over their actions
they are only objects encased in a relationship. They do not contribute to
the relationship. In the early months infants' caregivers routinely act
toward them for their benefit, but infants do not act toward their caregivers; there is no coordination of activity. The amount and nature of the
contact between the infant and others is completely dependent on others. If
the caregiver refuses to attend to the infant, there is little the infant can do.

In the typical parental relationship, adults are fairly attentive and responsive to the infant. That allows the child to acquire command of significant gestures. The infant who has mastered significant gestures then becomes an active part of the relationship. The infant can then call for others to attend to her. Some parents come running; others take their time; and some ignore most of the gestures of the infant. If the caregivers are exceedingly attentive and responsive, the infant may become a little tyrant, demanding and receiving attention. The infant's power, of course, is contingent on the caregivers' willingness to subordinate themselves to the child. If the caregivers refuse to attend and respond to the infant, she will not mature into a competent social being.

The parental relationship is asymmetrical, but it is not an authority relationship. Adults have far greater abilities and resources than infants. In one sense, that places parents in a superior position. Nonetheless, young infants cannot comply with the demands of adults. If infant and adult are to coordinate their actions, the adult must subordinate herself to the initiations of the infant. Only after the infant acquires control of her body and command of significant symbols can the infant comply with directives issued by caregivers. Prior to that the child cannot be part of an authority relationship.

Both biological maturation and participation in repetitive sequences of reciprocating acts contribute to the infant's becoming incorporated into parental relationships. When the infant acquires significant gestures the relationship is no longer merely a function of the activities of adults toward the infant, but slowly is transformed into a mutually constructed relationship. Both infant and caregivers contribute to their relationship.

A mature parental relationship is present when two people (1) mutually acknowledge a differentiated shared past; (2) mutually acknowledge that one has greater resources and/or abilities than the other; (3) categorically differentiate themselves and link themselves to each other; (4) mutually accept asymmetrical responsibilities; and (5) project a distal future of lessening their differences. Some parental relationships endure for only a short time; others endure for decades. A short-lived and relatively insignificant parental relationship can be established by one person noting that another is having difficulty in completing an act, the first person offering to help the other, the second person accepting the help offered, and the termination of their relationship on the successful completion of the act. The parental relationship may endure only for a few moments. At the other extreme, the relationship that exists between a father and daughter often endures for decades, contains a shared past extending over many years, is encased by an indefinite shared distal future and infused with mutual affection. Whatever the intensity and duration of parental relationships, all are structured in part by the projection of a distal future of the subordinate (child) acquiring greater ability to perform activities and greater autonomy. It is the projection of a future of the subordinate acquiring mastery of activities and greater autonomy that most clearly distinguishes the parental relationship from other asymmetrical relationships.

There are great differences in the quality of parental relationships. Some of them are the source of pleasure for both parties; others are stressful to both parties. Some parents and children are attracted to each other; others are relatively indifferent to each other. Whatever the qualitative dimensions of the relationship it exists only when there is mutual recognition of their shared past and the projection of a shared future of continuing affiliation with each other. Deserted children, for the moment, are not part of a parental relationship. If they are rescued by someone and the rescuer adopts the child and projects a future of caring for the rescued child, then an association is initiated that might mature into a robust parental relationship.

In a robust parental relationship the parent and the child become part of each other's taken-for-granted world. The parent presumes she will continue caring for the child, recognizes the child's dependency on her and organizes action toward the child to promote the child's security and autonomy. Reciprocally, the child presumes that her parents will continue to care for her, recognizes her dependency on the parents, at least from time to time relies upon the protection and care offered, and acquires skills that provide greater autonomy.

Most parents and other caregivers, but certainly not all, derive satisfaction from their parental relationships. Reciprocally, most children, but again certainly not all, derive security and pleasure from the relationship. But these qualities are not necessarily a part of parental relationships.

Differentiated Shared Past

As parents provide the necessities of life and nurture the child, parents and child construct a differentiated shared past. Each transaction between a parent and an infant adds to their shared past. For the first months of life, the parent contributes most of the content to their shared past. As the child acquires command of significant symbols she begins to contribute content to their shared past. Each parental relationship has a shared past that contains unique elements. Yet the shared pasts of all parental relationships are differentiated. The superordinate (parent) provides protection, care, and instruction; the subordinate (child) receives protection, care, and instruction.

As the parties of each parental relationship elaborate their differentiated shared pasts, each subsequent encounter between them becomes more richly contextualized. Their ability to anticipate each other's intentions increases. They thereby become capable of fitting together their actions to produce complex units of coordinated action smoothly. Each unit of coordinated action produced by the members of a parental relationship is structured by an objective, and each unit of social action is informed by the shared past of the relationship.

The shared past of some parental relationships are infused with mutual attraction; others contain elements of fear by the child toward the parent and resentment of the parent toward the child. The ideal parental relationship supposedly is one of mutual affection and trust. But many parental relationships have a shared past that is highly ambivalent. Some children both love and hate their fathers; some parents both worship their children and regard them as burdens.

All parental relationships continually change. Some parental relationships remain relatively constant for long periods of time, but all transform. Some transformations are incremental; other transformations are cataclysmic. Most toddlers acquire greater mastery of significant symbols each day. The acquisition of that ability slowly transforms the relationship young children have with their parents. In contrast, if the parents of a teenager suddenly discover that their child is a drug addict, the relationships between parents and teenager may be cataclysmically transformed.

The shared past of the parental relationship is originally one of great differentiation. As the relationship continues and the child matures, both biologically and socially, the degree of the differentiation lessens. In general, parental relationships move from asymmetry toward symmetry.

When mutually satisfying experiences are extended, the parties to a relationship become attached to each other and dependent on each other. Mutually satisfying parental relationships provide security for the subordinate and a purpose for being to the superordinate. Members of highly satisfactory parental relationships are sometimes reluctant to allow their relationship to mature; they sometimes attempt to resist the changes that are an inherent part of the relationship.

Conversely, when the relationship contains antagonistic elements, one or both parties may avidly anticipate terminating or transforming the relationship. Members of stressful parental relationships usually wish to minimize the differentiation on which the relationship is based. One of the paradoxes of parental relationships is that when both members derive pleasure and security from their parental relationship movement towards symmetry is often inhibited; whereas if neither derives pleasure or security from their relationship, movement towards symmetry is often hastened. Many parental relationships are infused with ambivalence.

Acknowledged Differentiation

A differentiated shared past and mutually recognized differences in competencies evolve simultaneously as the infant enters the parental relationship. At first the infant has no awareness that others have the ability to do things that she cannot do. The typical infant probably has command of a fairly complex set of significant symbols before it dawns on her that her caregivers can accomplish many things that she cannot. As the child acquires command of significant symbols, she becomes aware of her dependency on others. As the child acquires consciousness of her dependency, the relationship acquires the added dimension of mutually recognized asymmetrical dependency. The parent, of course, takes this dimension of the relationship for granted from the beginning.

Infants have little choice but to acknowledge that others have abilities they do not have and to relate to others on the basis of that difference. But children classified as severely autistic fail to acknowledge these differences. Autistic children are indifferent to the efforts of others to do things for them (Schreibman and Koegel 1975). They, in effect, deny that their welfare depends on others. Of course, if they are to survive others must protect and care for them. In cases of extreme autism, however, the child does not become part of a parental relationship. These children refuse to relate to others on the basis of their dependency on others. Such children may remain objects of concern, but if they do not willfully make themselves available to others to receive protection, care, and instruction; they do not become part of a parental relationship.

Nearly all children, from time to time, refuse to acknowledge their dependency on their parents and thereby prevent, for the moment, the activation of the parental relationship. That is often frustrating to the parents. Parents frequently note the efforts of their children and offer help only to have the offer rejected. For example, a father noted his daughter having difficulty putting on her coat; he offered help, only to have the offer rejected. The father then manhandled the child, putting her coat on her and buttoning it up. The child went limp and did not respond to the actions of the parent. The parental relationship was for the moment denied. Instead, a momentary tyrannical relationship was established.

In another instance, a father noted his child having difficulty with a jigsaw puzzle and "helped" the child by putting a piece in place. The child responded with, "Don't! Let me do it. I know how." The parent attempted to activate the parental relationship, only to have his bid rejected.

Reciprocally, parents must also acknowledge their differences and relate to the child in part on that basis. When a child asks a parent for aid or instruction, and the parent refuses to acknowledge the request, the relationship is, for the moment at least, held in abeyance. And, of course, the extreme form of rejection of the parental relationship by the superordinate is when the parent deserts the child. The parental relationship, like all relationships, is only activated when two or more willfully relate to each other in a congruent manner. Parental relationships do not automatically endure. Each party must willfully relate to the other to maintain a parental relationship. In general, however, as a shared differentiated past becomes elaborated and both parties repeatedly acknowledge their asymmetrical dependence, the relationship becomes taken for granted by both parties.

In the typical parental relationship a multitude of interactional sequences are encased by the mutual recognition of differentiated competencies. For example, each time a daughter approaches her mother and asks, "Show me how" and the mother acknowledges the request, the parental relationship is reaffirmed. Reciprocally, the relationship is often reaffirmed by the caregiver approaching the child and offering help. Again, of course, the child must accept the bid before the relationship is reaffirmed.

The parental relationship of a parent and young child is highly asymmetrical. In that sense, the relationship is similar to tyrannical relationships. And, of course, parents sometimes institute a tyrannical relation between themselves and their children. But in the early years it is impossible to institute a tyrannical relationship. The infant is incapable of complying with the demands of the parent, despite threats. One of the fundamental differences between parental and tyrannical relationships is that either the superordinate or the subordinate can initiate social objectives within the parental relationship. The parent can offer to help or instruct the child or the child can call for help or instruction from the parent. Only the superordinate in the tyrannical relationship programs the future. Masters tell slaves what to do, and slaves comply; slaves do not program the future for either their masters or themselves.

Yet when a transaction is completed within a parental relationship, both subordinate and superordinate acknowledge their differentiation. The early child—adult transactions within a parental relationship are based on functional differentiation. Both recognize that only one of them is capable of performing certain acts. As the shared past of functional differentiation becomes more elaborate and the child acquires command of symbols, categorical differentiation emerges.

Categorical Differentiation

Each child, as she becomes incorporated into the parental relationship, learns to classify herself as a child (baby) and one or more others as caregivers (mother and father). Firm sets of reciprocal expectations become attached to the categorical identities. The pattern of relatedness that parent and child establish is linked to the mutually recognized categorical identities. Each regards both other and self as objects, as well as subjects. The child and parent, then, do not merely relate to each other in a differentiated and patterned manner, instead they take each other into account as distinctive entities. Most children and their caregivers attach consensual expectations to their categorical identities. The consensuality is always a manner of degree. In some relationships, consensuality of expectations approached totality; they almost completely agree on how they are to relate to each other. In other parental relationships, only minimal consensuality is established.

When the parties to the relationship have consensus on the nature of their relatedness, each of their transactions is framed by the categorical relationship. Their relationship becomes objectified. The superordinate and subordinate categorize their relatedness. Fathers refer to their child as "my child"; and daughters refer to their fathers as "my father". Both usually conceptualize their relatedness as having a continual existence independent of their actions. Each regards their relatedness as constant, as something that will endure.

Of course, as the relationship matures, their conceptions of it will be modified. For example, when a mother states to her daughter, "You are a big girl now, you can buckle your own shoes" she is indicating that their relationship should change. Nonetheless, the overarching relationship of mother—daughter continues to endure. The categorical relationship continues on unless one explicitly rejects it, or unless they mutually terminate it.

Another level of complexity is added when the daughter recognizes that other children have a relationship with their parents similar to the one she has with her own parents. When children acquire consciousness of the relationships between other children and parents that are similar to their own relationship with their parents, they acquire a universal categorical relationship. They then use that universal relationship to assess their own relationships. That level of sophistication is achieved, for example, when a child informs her father, "But Betty's daddy plays basketball with her."

The acquisition of a universal categorical relationship provides a foundation for the negotiation of the relationship. Prior to this, the relatedness between parent and child is taken for granted. It may be accepted or rejected, but not negotiated. Children who become aware that their parental relationships have some things in common with those of other children, but also some distinctive features, may attempt to negotiate the relationship they will have with their parents. If parents are willing, they can make their relationship their shared focus, and negotiate their relationship. The relationship then is not something that is simply taken for granted but something that can be modified.

Of course, parents with their greater resources, can reject the offer to negotiate and insist the child accept the relationship as offered. Then the subordinate has the option of withdrawing from the relationship. That option is not a viable one for young children; it becomes more viable as the child moves toward social maturity. Even then, however, given the cost of modern education and an interest in completing college, many young adults remain in a subordinate position far longer than they deem appropriate.

Some parental relationships are established without a shared past. For example, the young man who enters into an apprenticeship with a master craftsman thereby activates a parental relationship that does not rest on a shared past. Of course, as the apprenticeship unfolds, he and the master construct a shared past that becomes a part of their relationship. In the typical parent—child relationship, a shared past precedes the emergence of awareness of categorical differentiation. But even that relationship can be initiated by first establishing a categorical relationship. The parental relationship is sometimes established in this manner when older children are adopted.

Asymmetric Responsibilities

The burden of responsibility between infants and parents is solely on the parents. The parents, of course, are not accountable to the child, nor is the child accountable to the parents. The assurance that the parents fulfill their responsibilities depends on a combination of (1) the parents adopting a communal standpoint toward themselves and their child and holding themselves accountable for acting as responsible parents; and (2) other members of the community monitoring and holding the parents accountable for their responsibilities. In the early years of life, the child is not accountable. As the child acquires abilities and sophistication, the original asymmetrical responsibilities of parental relationships slowly transform. Responsibilities become more symmetrical.

In general, as long as the parental relationship endures, it is the superordinate who is primarily accountable, at least from the point of view of the larger community. Children are sometimes relieved of responsibility by other members of the community with phrases like, 'What could you expect of the child, given his parents?'

One of the major internal transformations of the parental relationship is the assumption of responsibility by the subordinate. In the early stages the superordinate presumes responsible for her behavior, the behavior of the child, and the outcome of their transactions. As the child acquires control of herself and awareness of the consequences of her actions for others, she becomes more responsible for her actions. Often there are disagreements between superordinates and subordinates on who is responsible for what. Sometimes the subordinate wishes to assume more responsibility than the superordinate will allow; on other occasions, the subordinates are reluctant to assume responsibility.

In the following transaction, the child assigns the mother greater responsibility than she is willing to assume. The child is a seven-year-old boy.

The boy had just awakened and had come into the kitchen where his mother was conversing the another adult. The three exchanged greetings and then the mother placed a container of milk, a bowl, three boxes of cereals, and utensils on the table. The son sat at the table and surveyed the items on the table.

Son:	I want Raisin Bran.
Mother:	There isn't any.
S:	I want some, I want Raisin Bran.
M:	I told you. There isn't any.
S:	Why didn't you get some at the store? (Somewhat indignant.)
M:	No one told me they wanted any. (Offered indifferently.)
S:	You're spoze to get it. I want Raisin Bran! (Delivered as a mild shout.)
M:	(Turns and stares at her son.) Aren't you the one that eats it?
S:	(Stares back at his mother. Makes no other response.)
M:	You're the one that eats it. Right?!
S:	Uh, huh. (Lowers eyes.)
M:	Did you tell me we were out?
S:	Uh, uh.
M:	Well, don't dump on me. If you want Raisin Bran for breakfast, you'll have to tell me when we're out. It's your own fault you don't have Raisin Bran. (Turns away and resumes conversation with other adult.)
S:	(Stares at his mother in bewilderment. Starts to say something. Stops and reaches for a box of breakfast cereal.)

The child attempted to place responsibility on his mother for the absence of Raisin Bran. From his standpoint, the absence of the desired cereal was his mother's fault. His mother refused to accept the responsibility. She informed her son that it was his responsibility to tell her when all of the cereal had been consumed. The son did not explicitly accept the responsibility, but it seems likely he was made aware that his mother would not assume the responsibility. The implication was that the son must accept some responsibility for dealing with the external world.

In general, as parental relationships mature and move toward their termination, the subordinate assumes greater responsibility for his own welfare and the superordinate is relieved of some of the responsibility. The movement toward the symmetrical allocation of responsibility is often the center of disagreements and conflict, and sometimes results in the abrupt termination of parental relationships.

The acquisition of responsibility by the subordinate takes many different twists and turns. Superordinates sometimes lay a heavy trip of responsibility on the subordinate. More than one parent has accused a child of being responsible for the parent's mental breakdown. Sometimes children accept the responsibility assigned them, sometimes they reject it, and sometimes they are confused.

Distal Futures

Two very different distal futures structure parental relationships. On the one hand, members of a parental relationship project a future of maintaining their current mode of relatedness for some time; on the other hand, the future of terminating the relationship is also projected. In the early stages, the future of continuing the relationship predominates; as social maturity is approached, the future of terminating the relationship comes to the fore. One of the distinctive features of the parental relationship is that a distal future of bringing the current form of relatedness to an end is a viable dimension of the relationship. When the child becomes as competent as the parent or the student as competent as the teacher, the reason for the relationship has disappeared. That, of course, does not automatically terminate the parental relationship. One or both parties to the relationship must take action that brings the relationship to an end.

The subordinates of parental relationships often find the relationships confining and eagerly look forward to termination. Others are reluctant to leave behind the security of the parental relationship. Reciprocally, some superordinates of the relationship look forward to the termination of the relationship; others resist the termination of the relationship. Satisfactory parental relationships usually become infused with ambivalence as the relationship approaches termination.

Terminating the Relationship

Some societies have initiation ceremonies that mark the end of parental relationships. There are no ceremonies explicitly designed for that purpose in modern societies, although graduation exercises and birthdays partially fulfill that function. In some instances, the parental relationships between parent and child is at least radically transformed, if not brought to an end, by the child's moving out of the house. In other cases, it slowly fades away.

One paradoxical feature of parental relationships is that those that are the most satisfying usually create the most stress when the relationship approaches termination. If the parties to the relationship have become alienated from each other, then they usually are pleased to bring the relationship to an end. But if both have found the relationship a source of satisfaction, the termination of the relationship is often a time of both sadness and joy. Many parents are both saddened and delighted when their children strike out on their own.

Sometimes a parental relationship transforms into a paternal relationship, or at least becomes infused with elements of paternalism. A parental relationship predominates when the transactions within the relationship are directed toward increasing the autonomy of the subordinate. But when the superordinate acts to preserve the asymmetrical relationship by aiding the subordinate when the subordinate does not wish to to helped or when the subordinate calls for aid or instruction when it is no longer necessary, the relationship moves toward paternalism. On occasion, both parties find the asymmetrical features of the parental relationship satisfying and continue to contextualize their transactions by activating the parental relationship despite the fact that their original differences in competencies have been eradicated. Many mothers wait on their children long after the children are capable of waiting on themselves and many children call for their parents' protection and aid when it is no longer necessary.

The gratitude many subordinates feel toward superordinates often makes them reluctant to terminate the relationship. Grateful children often continue the relationship because of their fear of hurting the feelings of their parents. If gratitude by the subordinate is coupled with the superordinate's enjoyment of the relationship, they may continue to contextualize their encounters by activating the parental relationship.

The termination of a parental relationship is sometimes inhibited by the mutuality that infuses many parental relationships. In some instances, parent—child mutuality begins with teasing, matures through play and games, and culminates with each enjoying the company of the other. Some fear that the termination of the parental relationship will bring to an end, or at least lessen, their mutuality.

But perhaps the feature that most often makes it difficult to terminate parental relationships is the solidary embeddedness that often is a vibrant part of a satisfactory parental relationship. When the subordinate and superordinate coordinate their actions to make the subordinate more competent, they often produce elements of solidarity. The two thereby become merged. The elements of solidarity elicited in most parental transactions are minimal, but the accumulative impact is for the subordinate and super-ordinate to merge into a single unit.

Consider the following example: The mother is instructing her four-year-old daughter on how to complete a task. The daughter is attentive and responsive as the mother verbally instructs her and demonstrates how to accomplish the task. Then the mother sits back and says, 'Now you try it.' The daughter attacks the task, while the mother carefully watches. The daughter accomplishes the task, and a smile comes over her face. Simultaneously, the mother also smiles, lightly claps her hands, and asserts, 'You did it!' The daughter then claps her hands as her smile turns into a wide grin. The daughter snuggles up against her mother, who welcomes her with open arms. The daughter then asserts, 'We did it. Didn't we, Mommy?' The mother responds, 'We sure did,' as they snuggle against each other.

As transactions of this sort are multiplied many times over between parent and child, their parental relationship becomes interlaced with solidarity. The interlacing of a parental relationships with elements of solidarity provides a foundation for transforming the parental relationship into a solidary one. Nonetheless, some parents and children are fearful of transforming their parental relationship into a solidary one; they suspect it might lessen their affiliation with each other.

In many instances, the original parental relationship between parent and child is transformed into a solidary relationship. But when that occurs, traces of the parental relationship typically remain. The following transaction is between an eighty-year-old father and his fifty-five-year-old son as the son prepares to leave after a visit:

Father:	What route are you taking?
Son:	I thought I'd take 212.
F:	In weather like this, be careful. Maybe you ought to stay on the freeway?
S:	I suppose you're right, the freeway would probably be safer.
F:	Yeah, especially if it keeps on raining.
S:	Yeah, I guess I'll take the freeway.
F:	Be careful.
S:	I will.

The father expresses concern for the welfare of the son and offers a suggestion that the son accepts; they jointly activate elements of paren-talism. When two people have had an asymmetrical relationship of several years duration that has been mutually satisfactory it is difficult to transform the relationship into a symmetrical one.

Summary

In all parental relationships the overarching objective is to lessen the dependency of the subordinate by making her more competent and ultimately to terminate, or at least transform, the nature of the relationship. The parental relationship is a necessary social form if the human species is to endure. It provides the structure necessary for transforming helpless infants into competent adults. There is variation across societies as to who is responsible for nuturing and instructing the young. But in all societies specific adults are designated as those responsible for caring for specific children. Unless human infants are encased by preexisting parental relationships they are very unlikely to survive, and if they did survive, they would be very unlikely to become competent members of society.

There is tremendous variation in the duration, intensity, and breadth of parental relationships. Some, such as that between a student and instructor in a college class, endure but a semester and have little intensity; others, such as those between parents and their children, often endure for decades, generate and sustain intense emotions, and contextualize a wide range of activities.

The more intense and enduring parental relationships are usually interlaced with ambivalence. Not all parent—child relationships are interlaced with ambivalence, but many of them are. The ambivalence stems from the nature of the relationship. To consummate the relationship successfully the subordinate must repeatedly subordinate herself to the superordinate to acquire skills that will provide greater autonomy. That is often both simultaneously irritating and satisfying to the subordinate. Reciprocally, the obligations of attending to, caring for, and instructing the subordinate often are both joyful and burdensome for the superordinate. If the transactions contextualized by a parental relationship are successfully completed, and if the long-range objective of achieving symmetry is achieved, the relationship can be the source of much satisfaction for both parties.

The asymmetrical nature of the relationship, its intensity, and the solidarity and mutuality that infuse many parental relationships almost assures that enduring parental relationships will be interlaced with both resentment and gratitude. It is not surprising that both subordinates and superordinates of parental relationships often are both sad and glad when the relationship is terminated or transformed. All social relationships contain paradoxical elements, but the parental relationship is more paradoxical than most.

Chapter 11 Solidary Relationships

Solidary relationships are universal; they are found in all human societies. Solidary relationships are the foundation for our humaneness. Parental relationships are, in one sense, more basic than solidary relationships. Parental relationships are necessary for the survival of infants. But solidary relationships are necessary to transform human organisms into human beings. Human organisms that never become involved in solidary relationships do not become human beings. It is through the production of elements of solidarity that human beings become merged *with* each other.

Elements of solidarity infuse our lives. Nearly all human collectivities contain elements of solidarity. Even groups and organizations that are in the process of disintegrating contain elements of solidarity. Elements of solidarity are commonly intertwined with other relationships. Solidary relationships provide the foundation on which accountable and authority relationships rest. On occasion, people relate almost entirely on the basis of their solidary relationship. For example, in August 1945, when Japan's surrender was announced, the solidary relationship among the citizens of the United States came to the fore. Multifaceted and complex layers of solidarity were produced as the nation celebrated its victory. For a short time all, other relationships were pushed to be background as Americans framed their interaction with each other by activating a nationwide solidary relationship.

Whenever two persons jointly respond in a similar way to some event, an element of solidarity has been produced (Sehested 1975). When two young women who are strangers note a handsome young man striding by, smile in appreciation, and note each other's smiles, they produce an element of solidarity. The two women may never see each other, but for a moment they responded in unison. They indicated to each other that they had the same reaction to a shared focus. For a moment, they were unified ("solid") in their standpoint toward the young man.

Momentary shared responses do not establish a solidary relationship. In such encounters people merely establish a momentary solidary responsiveness. Each is aware that both responded to something in a unified manner, but they have no shared past and no shared future, nor do they think of themselves as constituting a social entity.

A robust solidary relationship is present when two or more people (1) have a mutually recognized shared past of responding in unison; (2) project a shared future of acting in unison beyond the immediate future—a distal shared future is projected; (3) categorically characterize themselves as having a collective identity that distinguishes them from others; and (4) have established an egalitarian mode of relating among themselves. Each of these dimensions can vary in both intensity and extensiveness. And, of course, one, two, or three of these dimensions may be absent. But people with a robust solidary relationship have an extended shared past with emotional depth, project a shared future of "forever," regard themselves as sharing a collective identity, and treat each other as equals.

A solidary relationship may be as transitory as that which prevails when two people find themselves in the same circumstance, project a future of acting in concert to change their circumstances, locate themselves as having a shared problem to resolve, and relate as equals as they resolve their difficulties. For example, two strangers who find themselves trapped together in an elevator are likely to establish a temporary solidary relationship as they attempt to free themselves from their predicament.

Other solidary relationships endure for a lifetime. The prototype of an enduring and robust solidary relationship is that of lifelong friends. In some families the primary relationship is solidary; other families have only minimal elements of solidarity.

Many enduring associations rest on a foundation of solidarity; others contain only minimal elements of solidarity. Healthy friendships rest on solidarity. Other associations endure that contain almost no solidarity. For example, two local businessmen may repetitively deal with each other despite the fact they hate each other's guts. If each is the only source of a needed resource for the other, however, they may continue to associate on the basis of their compatible mercenary interests.

Some individuals live a life almost devoid of solidary relationships. The social isolate who avoids contact with others or has been rejected by all others may not be part of any solidary relationships. Nonetheless, in order for that person to have the skills necessary to live a solitary life, he had to have previously participated in some solidary activities. Command of significant symbols is acquired by acting solidarily with others.

Most of us are part of a series of solidary relationships of varying degrees of intensity with our siblings. Most of us are also part of a solidary relationship that includes all other citizens of our native countries. Some solidary relationships are of minimal robustness and limited to two people; others encompass thousands, are robust, and multitiered. When two devout Catholics who are lifelong friends attend a religious celebration at the Vatican, they activate an intense solidary relationship that on some dimensions is shared by only the two of them. As they participate in the celebration, however, they are also participating in a solidary relationship that encompasses millions of others. Two non-Catholic friends who attend the celebration out of curiosity also activate a solidary relationship, but one of far less intensity and expansiveness than that of the two devout Catholics.

Shared Solidary Pasts

When two people note that each of them has responded in a similar manner to some event, an element of solidarity is created. Their solidary response may provide the foundation for a solidary relationship. Of course, in the vast majority of cases, a solidary relationship does not emerge from the solidary responses produced in fleeting encounters. To return to our example of the two young women smiling in unison, it is conceivable that they might strike up a conversation. If they did strike up a conversation, it then becomes possible, but not probable, for them to develop a solidary relationship. It is certainly more likely that they would establish a solidary relationship if they responded solidarily to the young man than if they had not. If one of them smiled while the other frowned in disgust at the handsome young man it is very unlikely that their responses would serve as the initial step toward the forming of a solidary relationship.

Solidary responsiveness is often a vibrant part of transactions framed by parental relationships. An element of solidarity is sometimes produced by a parent and child when the parent notes the response of the child to some event and then responds in a similar manner. If the child notes that the response of the parent is similar to his own, an element of solidarity has been generated. Parents and children frequently establish elements of solidarity by babbling and cooing in unison. Of course, not all parental relationships are infused with solidarity. Some are infused with anxiety, disgust, and even fear.

When parents and children repetitively respond in unison, they become merged with each other; they become embedded with one another. The interjection of solidarity into the parental relationship modifies the relationship between parent and child. Parental relationships are asymmetrical; solidary relationships are symmetrical. As the relationship between parent and child becomes infused with solidarity, they relate both asymmetrically and symmetrically. Most parent–child relationships become more symmetrical as parents and children construct a solidary past. If a solidary past is not established, then there is no foundation for the transformation of their association from a parental one into a solidary one.

Solidary pasts are multitiered. They have three distinct levels. First, each element of solidary responsiveness is originally past oriented. The unified responses are linked to events that have occurred. Second, each instance of solidary responsiveness enriches and extends the shared past of those who are solidarily responsive. Third, after an extended solidary past has been constructed, it encases each subsequent solidary response.

For example, two strangers seated next to each other at a basketball game responded in unison with loud cheers when the home team scored a basket to take the lead early in the game. Their first unified cheer was not contextualized by a solidary past. But they continued to applaud the efforts of their team and occasionally responded in unison. As they did so, they extended their solidary past. That solidary past contextualized their cheering during the latter part of the game. By the second half, they were making comments to each other as well as cheering the exploits of their team.

Dramatic instances of solidary responsiveness are frequently elicited in problematic undertakings. The audience cheers the successes of the home team and suffers agony when it is defeated. In a similar manner, hunters, whether modern pheasant hunters or primitive nomadic hunters, are solidarily responsive to their successes and failures.

Groups, organizations, and nations schedule programs for the explicit purpose of reaffirming their solidarity. The communal firework displays associated with the Fourth of July in the United States elicits oohs and aahs from the gathered multitude. These events, if successfully completed, reaffirm the unity of the collectivity and sometimes expand the solidary relationship to incorporate more people.

Intense solidary responsiveness is most commonly produced by people who have a robust solidary past. On occasions, however, intense solidary responsiveness is produced by strangers. Two strangers traveling together, may uncover the fact that both are ardent trout fishermen and that they have fished some of the same waters. They are likely to produce many instances of solidary responsiveness as they swap tales of their fishing exploits. In a similar manner, strangers who are fans of a rock band produce intense units of solidary responsiveness when they attend a concert.

Many instances of solidary responsiveness are to events that are external to those who respond in unison. But human beings also construct solidary pasts by responding in unison to their own actions. For example, two young men turned over their snowmobile and buried it in a snowbank. After an extended struggle, they extracted it from the snow. When they finally freed it and placed it upright, they cheered in unison. They were solidarily responsive to their accomplishment. When people respond in unison, they display their unity and become merged with each other. The merger is often very transitory, but for the moment they demonstrate their solidarity with each other.

Most instances of solidary responsiveness are enjoyable, but do not have profound significance. But solidary responsiveness is accumulative. If those who are solidarily responsive continue their association and continue to be solidarily responsive, they may become so unified that they think of themselves as a unit. The mutual embeddedness that results from an elaborate solidary past can be so great that neither wants to be separated from the other.

The more robust the shared solidary past, the greater the security of the members. People with a robust solidary past trust each other; each knows how the other has responded to a variety of happenings and is quite certain how he will respond to future developments.

The development of a solidary past is essentially a universe of touch phenomenon. Common standpoints are often indicated by appearance or stated in discourse. For example, when two strangers make contact and each notes the other is wearing a lapel pin indicating membership in the American Legion, they are likely to presume they hold many sentiments in common. At the moment of contact, however, they do not have a solidary past. It is very likely that if they strike up a conversation and discuss the American Legion, they will be solidarily responsive. They thereby begin to construct a solidary past that could mature into a solidary relationship. When people construct a solidary past, they display shared feelings toward shared foci. People can inform each other in discourse and appearance that they have shared sentiments, but these transactions do not provide the depth and authenticity that the simultaneous expression of strong emotions provide.

Some standpoints are so intense and universally shared within a society that it is difficult to imagine anyone taking any other standpoint. The idea of cooking and eating human flesh is so universally responded to negatively in Western societies that most of us cannot imagine ourselves eating human flesh. Yet the members of some societies have consumed human flesh. The intense repulsion most have to eating human flesh reflects the almost universal solidary standpoint that prevails in modern societies.

When a standpoint is universally shared and routinely reaffirmed by solidary responsiveness, that standpoint is almost automatically elicited whenever certain events are observed. For example, a concern with the welfare of little children is almost universal. Whenever we see a child suffering, most of us "instinctively" empathize with the child. These so-called instinctive responses have a social, not biological, foundation.

It is shared and common solidary pasts that are the foundation of social morality. Our sense of right and wrong stems from our solidary pasts. Those who have been incorporated into social units that preach and practice kindness toward all human beings have a different morality from those who have been incorporated into social units that regard outsiders as less than human. But in both instances what is regarded as moral and immoral has a social foundation.

Distal Futures

Many solidary relationships emerge without the members of the relationships explicitly projecting a shared distal future. Friendships often mature from becoming acquainted through hanging around together to a robust solidary relationship. Often those who establish a solidary relationship never discuss their distal future. Their shared past becomes extended, and they just take it for granted that they will continue to associate with each other.

On occasion, a solidary relationship is initiated by people convening on the basis of a common interest to undertake unified action. For example, someone might post a notice for all interested in forming a rugby team to meet in Room 108 at 7:00 P.M. If a number of persons appear and a rugby team is formed, it is very likely a solidary relationship will emerge. In that case, the first step toward the construction of a solidary relationship was taken by the projection of a distal future, not by the construction of a solidary past. Of course, as the rugby team practices and plays other teams, the members will produce a solidary past. If they do not produce a solidary past, the team will disintegrate.

Many partisan groups are formed by someone projecting a distal future of modifying some governmental policy and calling for others to join in the effort. Those who originally convene do not have a solidary past, but many have pasts that contain common experiences. Of course, as they convene and plan for their future endeavors, they will construct a solidary past. If they do not construct a solidary past of some robustness, the undertaking will not be successful.

The future is routinely discussed in all solidary relationships. Friends discuss what they are going to do tomorrow or the next weekend or how they are going to spend their vacations. Members of partisan groups regularly plan their tactics and strategies. When people have a robust solidary relationship, however, a shared distal future of some sort is simply presumed. The members of the relationship take it for granted that they have a shared distal future and that they will act in unison to achieve it. The content of their shared future is often discussed, but not its presence or absence. Members of robust solidary relationships seldom explicitly discuss the future of their relationship. They presume that their relationship will endure. In fact, when the relationship itself becomes a topic of discussion, it is likely that the solidary relationship is in jeopardy. When one member of a solidary relationship asks another, "Are you with me or not?" the relationship has become somewhat problematic.

Solidary relationships, like all relationships, change. Some intensify, others disintegrate, and some continue on much as they have for indefinite periods. A solidary relationship may become problematic as the result of internal or external developments. On occasion internal developments make solidary relationship problematic. One member of the relationship may become disenchanted with the other and seek out alternatives.

On other occasions, solidary relationships are rendered problematic by external developments. For example, a member of a group of young unmarried male friends might inform his friends that he is going to marry. This makes his position within the friendship group problematic; it may even make the solidary relationships between other members of the group problematic.

Robust solidary relationships have temporal depth that extends into both a distal past and a distal future. The more extended the solidary past and future, the firmer the relationship. Both a shared past and a shared future are essential dimensions of robust solidary relationships.

Collective Identities

Members of solidary relationships conceive of themselves as an entity. Their relationship is objectified; they locate themselves as a unit. They are members of the Couch clan, liberated men, citizens concerned with the environment, or The Gang. The boundaries separating them from others may be precisely and firmly drawn or may be loose and easily penetrated. But at the minimum, members have some consciousness of existing through time as a distinct social unit.

Members of an emerging solidary relationship sometimes accumulate an extended shared past of responding and acting solidarily before they objectify themselves. Children act solidarily with their parents and siblings for some time before they begin thinking of themselves as part of a particular family. In a similar manner, two high school girls may hang out together for some time before they become conscious of themselves as a distinctive pair. Often members of a newly forming solidary relationship construct a shared solidary past of considerable depth before they categorically differentiate themselves from others.

People who have common categorical identities do not automatically have a solidary relationship. Neither the physically handicapped, blacks, nor blue-eyed residents of a community have a solidary relationship by the mere fact of having a common categorical identity. Categorical identities held in common sometimes provide the initial foundation for the construction of solidary relationships, but common categorical identities do not by themselves establish a solidary relationship. If individuals with a common categorical identity construct a solidary past and project a shared distal future and begin to think of themselves as a distinct social entity, then they establish a solidary relationship.

When a number of individuals label themselves and are designated by others with a label, they become an objective unit — an entity that is separated in some way from others. When a plurality of people have established themselves as a distinctive social unit, each of them can then subsequently present themselves to outsiders as acting in behalf of a collective interest. Reciprocally, they are acted toward by others as members of a viable collectivity.

The categorical collective identity of most solidary relationships arises as a consequence of both internal and external action. Sometimes the collective identity is largely a consequence of internal actions. That is often the case for newly forming partisan groups. Those who organize themselves to advance the cause of a political candidate usually first convene and act in unison independent of any action taken toward them. At their meetings, as they plan their future, it is likely that the issue of what are they to call themselves will emerge. Then they are likely to select a label for themselves. In such cases, the collective identity is the consequence of internal actions. If they then confront the external world and others refer to them by the label they have chosen for themselves, the collective identity is validated. Reciprocally, a number of individuals may convene without any consciousness of constituting a distinctive collectivity. But if others began referring to them as "the young turks," they may then refer to themselves as the young turks. When they do that, they have validated their collective identity.

Once a collective identity is established, the members often use plural pronouns when discussing their activities. Members of solidary relationships use the pronouns we, us, and our in referring to their activities and interests. Their use of collective pronouns further validates their collective identity.

The categorical collective identity of solidary relationships has both a subjective (or acting) dimension and an objective (or passive) dimension. The subjective dimension, the "we" of solidary relationships, emerges as the consequence of the members of the relationship initiating collective action. For example, when a collectivity boycotts a local chain store, it provides a foundation for the emergence of the "we" dimension of the solidary relationship. Subsequent to the action, the members of the relationship will speak of the event as something "we did."

The "we" dimension of solidary relationships is founded on and validated by the members of the relationship exercising their collective will. The projection of a shared future, the structuring of the action to bring to fruition their social objectives, and the accomplishment of shared objectives all contribute to the validation of the "we" dimension of solidary relationships.

The objective or passive dimension of the collective identity emerges as the consequence of actions taken by others toward the collectivity. The "us" of solidary relationship is the consequence of shared experiences of the relationships that results from actions taken by others. As one high school student put it, "We didn't think of ourselves as anything distinctive until the teachers began referring to us as the 'frivolous five.'" The "us" dimension of solidary relationships objectifies a shared past that has been constructed in transactions between the members of the solidary relationship and outsiders.

A solidary relationship cannot be established solely by external objectification. For example, outsiders may classify two people as sharing some characteristic. The targets of the classification are thereby collectively categorized by others. But unless they acknowledge the classification, construct a solidary past, and project a solidary future, they do not have a solidary relationship. Collective classifications by others may stimulate the development of a solidary relationship, but external collective classifications do not create solidary relationships. The construction of solidary relationships requires that those who constitute the relationship willingly relate to one another and act as a collectivity.

Egalitarianism

Solidary relationships are essentially symmetrical. All members of the relationship acknowledge a shared past of some significance that was jointly constructed; project a shared future in which they will experience similar, if not identical, consequences; and at the minimum recognize that on at least one issue they take the same standpoint. They recognize that they have shared sentiments and interests and will act in unison to achieve their shared interests.

Members of a robust solidary relationship are like "peas in a pod." For example, members of a vibrant women's movement are likely to display the same standpoint when discussing women's issues. Outsiders are likely to comment, "Talking to any one of them is like talking to any other; they all take the same position."

Of course, solidary relationships are composed of diverse people. But diversity and ranking are minimized. Members of robust solidary relationships make a special effort to deny their diversity. Members of some solidary relationships wear the same clothing; they attempt to appear identical to the external world and to deny differences.

Their unified standpoint toward issues frames their interaction with each other. They acknowledge and accept the prerogative of all to participate in structuring their future. Members of a solidary relationship do not impose their wills on each other. If one member of a robust solidary relationship deviates from the collective interests, it is the collectivity that acts toward the deviant, not individuals.

Members of solidary relationships, especially partisan groups, often differentiate themselves to achieve their collective objectives more effectively. For example, members of a group devoted to the election of a political candidate nearly always construct a division of labor. Some devote their time to registering voters, others to seeking out campaign funds, and still others to promoting the cause of their candidate in the mass media. Their differentiated actions are framed by their collective interests. The action of each member is given meaning on the basis of what they, the plurality who compose the relationship, are attempting to accomplish.

One of the paradoxes of the solidary relationship is that when the members of a solidary collectivity differentiate themselves and undertake special responsibilities, it generates experiences that are unique to each specialty. That often erodes the solidary relationship. Those who seek additional funds have different experiences than those who register voters. One consequence is that the division of labor often becomes the source of differences. It may result in the fragmentation of the collectivity. Mothers and fathers usually have a solidary relationship that focuses on the welfare of their children. In many families, however, there is a division of labor. One enters the labor market and provides the income for the family, while the other assumes primary responsibility for domestic tasks. A common consequence is for the division of labor to undermine their solidary relationship.

The undermining of the solidary relationship that often flows from a division of labor can be counteracted by scheduling events that emphasize their solidary relationship. Partisan groups schedule picnics, parties, and celebrations to reaffirm their solidary relationship. During these affairs, the members of the relationship are solidarily responsive to a variety of events; they revalidate their collective distal future and their collective identity.

The division of labor that is usually present within solidary collectivities often leads to the emergence of subsections of solidary relationships within the larger collectivity. For example, the members of a football team usually have a solidary relationship that encompasses all members of the team. But the solidarity among the starters is usually more robust than the solidarity among the substitutes. In a similar manner, the linemen often have a more robust solidary relationship than they do with members of the backfield.

Altruism

One of the more redeeming qualities of human beings is that sometimes they will sacrifice their own personal well-being to further the well-being of others. Of course, at other times they commit the most vile acts toward their fellow human beings. For example, in World War II, some Germans who manned concentration camps and sent millions to their death also made great sacrifices to further the well-being of their families, friends, and neighbors. And, of course, many Germans made the ultimate sacrifice by giving their lives in defense of the Third Reich. The continuation of human societies depends on people assuming some responsibility for the welfare of others out of compassion. If every individual always acted solely for personal benefit, human life could not endure.

Several explanations have been offered for altruism. They range from those of sociobiologists (Wilson 1975, 1978) to those of exchange theorists (Piliavin, Piliavin, and Rodin 1969, 1975). The sociobiologists claim that altruism has a genetic base, that the same factors that explain the altruism of insects also account for human altruism.

The honeybee stings intruders. The bee loses its stinger and soon dies, but the survival of the swarm is made more likely. In a similar, manner when a soldier throws himself on a grenade, he sacrifices his life, but other members of his troop are more likely to survive. There are similarities. In both instances one organism loses its life and makes the continuation of the collectivity more likely. Nonetheless, the two "altruistic acts" have an entirely different foundation. The action of honeybee does not deserve the designation *altruism*. There is no evidence that honeybees intentionally sacrifice their lives for the well-being of the collectivity.

The behavior of bees is genetically structured and is not intentional. The act of the soldier rests on a foundation of solidarity and is an intentional act structured by a concern for others. The altruism of human beings is not structured by genetic factors.

Others have attempted to explain altruism on the basis of exchange theory. Explanations of altruism based on an exchange calculus simply do not fit the facts. Human beings rather frequently assume responsibility for the welfare of others at some cost to themselves. Of course, people also do things for others with the intention of acquiring benefit.

Many actions that benefit others are the consequence of a variety of factors, including anticipated personal benefit. But the altruistic act is based on compassion and structured by the objective of benefitting another. Many other factors besides compassion influence whether or not one person will aid another. One is the severity of the sacrifice. It is more likely that a person will aid another when the sacrifice is minimal than when there is high risk of great sacrifice.

Altruism stems from solidary relationships. People who have a robust solidary relationship are more likely to aid one another than those without a solidary relationship. Altruistic acts range in significance from one person's sharing a tasty morsel with a friend to individuals sacrificing their life for others.

The significance of solidary relationships for assuming responsibility for the welfare of others is illustrated by the following two events.

Kitty Genovese was murdered in the Bronx in New York City, and the killing was witnessed by thirty-eight people. One of the distinctive features of the murder was that none of those who witnessed it intervened. One of the thirty-eight called the police. That person called the police after he had called a friend for advice. He then went to the apartment of another resident and asked her to make the call.

As the affair has been reconstructed by the police and newspaper reporters (Rosenthal 1964), Kitty Genovese returned to the apartment complex where she lived about 3:30 A.M. She was attacked in the parking lot. When she was stabbed, she screamed, "Oh, my God, he stabbed me! Please help me!" Some lights in apartments went on. One man shouted, "Let the girl alone!" The assailant left. The lights went out. The assailant returned and found Kitty Genovese attempting to get to her apartment. He stabbed her again. She cried, "I'm dying! I'm dying!" Lights went on again; some residents opened their windows and looked out. The assailant got into his car and drove away. But he returned again and found her slumped at the foot of the stairs. He stabbed her a third time. The police were called about twenty minutes after the beginning of the attack. They arrived on the scene two minutes after receiving the call. Kitty Genovese was dead.

These events occurred in one of the better neighborhoods of New York City, an area with few reports of crimes. Several of the people who witnessed the attack were interviewed afterward; some refused to be interviewed. One woman said she and her husband did not do anything because "I didn't want my husband to get involved." Another person when asked why she hadn't called the police, shrugged and said, "I was tired, I went back to bed." None of those interviewed displayed much, if any, compassion for their neighbor.

Compare that affair with the following one: Several years ago, I was pheasant hunting in a rural area of Iowa. I and a companion were driving on a blacktop road in my brother-in-law's pickup truck. Two shotguns were in plain sight. A car passed us and turned around about a quarter of a mile up the road. The driver approached us with his left arm extended, indicating he wanted us to stop. I stopped. He drove up next to me and asked, "Isn't that Earl Hesse's truck?" I said, "Yes, he is my brother-in-law." The driver nodded acceptance and drove on.

I recounted the incident to my brother-in-law and described the driver and the car. My brother-in-law was not certain who had stopped me. A few days later, he asked an acquaintance if he had stopped someone driving his truck. His acquaintance said, "Yeah, I didn't think it was stolen, but I thought it might have been. When the guy said he was your brother-in-law, I figured it was OK."

Many factors contributed to the difference in responses in these two situation. But it seems likely that one of the major differences was the pervasiveness of solidary relationship in the two communities. The residents of the apartment complex in the Bronx were almost entirely unknown to one another; they were essentially strangers. The person who stopped me was a lifelong resident of the community, as was my brother-in-law.

The difference in behavior cannot be accounted for by the risk involved. The residents of the apartment complex would have risked little by calling the police. The person who stopped me probably saw the two shotguns in the pickup.

It is doubtful that the man who stopped me did it to acquire benefit. He had told no one about it until quizzed about it by my brother-in-law. The most reasonable explanation is that he assumed some responsibility of his neighbor's welfare. He and my brother-in-law did not live close to one another, but each thought of the other as a member of the same community.

In contrast, only one of Kitty Genovese's neighbors (they were only geographic neighbors, not social neighbors) assumed any responsibility for her welfare. Those who turned on their lights and the two or three who shouted at the killer expressed a little concern, but little compassion.

The difference in the pervasiveness of solidary relationships in the two communities seems to be at least a partial explanation for the differences in response.

Altruism is almost routine in collectivities that have a robust solidary relationship. Members of primitive hunting and gathering groups take it for granted that when food is available, all will eat. The members of some families routinely act for each other's benefit; they suffer agony when other members of the family fail and rejoice when they are successful. These responses stem from their solidary relationship. To be compassionate requires that we merge ourselves with others. If we cannot feel with others, we are unlikely to assume responsibility for their welfare. Compassion is one of the basic social emotions. It rests on a foundation of solidarity. When there is no solidarity, there is no compassion. When there is no compassion, there is no altruism.

Summary

Human beings construct many different relationships. Each person is a part of a series of parental relationships before she becomes part of solidary relationships. Parental relationships are necessary to assure the survival of each child; but solidary relationships transform human organisms into human beings. Social solidarity is the bedrock on which the social structures of all human societies rest.

In small, primitive groups of hunters and gatherers, the only two sets of social relationships that are fully developed are parental and solidary relationships. Primitive bands of food gatherers do not have complex accountable, authority, exchange, or tyrannical relationships. Their lives are structured largely by parental and solidary relationships. As primitive nomadic food gathering groups seek out the necessities of life, they construct a vibrant solidary past. When they migrate from place to place, they travel together and respond and act in unison. Even when one person, say, an adult male, stalks a game animal, all members of the band relate to the action in a solidary fashion. The success of the hunter is important to all. If the hunter is successful, they all respond in unison; they reaffirm their solidarity.

The intense solidarity that pervades many primitive groups is sometimes referred to as tribalism. In these groups, as long as they are successful in extracting the necessities of life, an intense tribal solidarity frames nearly everything they do. Intensive and extensive solidarity also pervades collectivities of modern societies. Generally speaking, however, citizens of modern societies do not experience the intense solidarity that prevails in many primitive bands.

As the size of a social unit increases it becomes more difficult to maintain an intense solidary relationship. The collectivity then either fragments or a division of labor based on other social relationships emerges. If the collectivity fragments, of course, there are two social units instead of one. If a division of labor emerges, the collectivity may continue as a distinctive entity, but solidarity ebbs.

Nationalism and religious groups are modern social groupings that contain large numbers of individuals primarily on the basis of a solidary relationship. These particular forms of solidary have been and continue to be a source of much human joy. But they also have been the source of much human suffering. A monolithic solidarity that encompasses all and frames all action is stifling. Monolithic solidarity has also provided the foundation for members of some groups to take the most vile actions imaginable toward outsiders and any insiders who deviate from the morality of the collectivity. Nazism was a vibrant form of national solidarity; the ancient Aztecs justified their capture and killing of surrounding groups by appealing to the collective welfare of the Aztec state. Currently, Americans and Soviets seem willing to eradicate each other in order foist their respective views of morality on the rest of the world.

Chapter 12 Accountable Relationships

Whenever people establish copresence, they become interpersonally accountable. Each is obliged to be aware of the consequences of his actions for the experiences of others. Sensitive people note the consequences of their actions for others and offer an account to others whenever their actions disturb another person. Those who are insensitive to the consequences of their actions for others do not offer an account, but are likely to be called into account by those they disturb. Interpersonal accountability is encased within immediate encounters; interpersonal accountability does not extend across encounters.

In contrast, when people have an accountable relationship, their accountability extends beyond the immediate encounter. Those with an accountable relationship are not merely accountable to each other for the action they take within the immediate encounter, but also accountable for actions they take when separated from each other. Solidary relationships provide a foundation for the construction of accountable relationships. Accountable relationships emerge when two or more people with a solidary relationship construct a division of labor and a social commitment (Strauss 1985, Weiland 1975). Some accountable relationships are of short duration and are based on a minimal division of labor; others endure indefinitely and are based on a complex division of labor.

Accountable relationships are a part of the structure of such diverse social units as families, basketball teams, work groups, and legislative bodies. When people have an association that endures across encounters, they usually are accountable to each other in two different but intertwined ways. First, each person is expected to exercise his initiative to facilitate the achievement of the social objectives of the collectivity. Second, each person is assigned specific responsibilities. For example, the members of a high school basketball team are accountable to one another on two levels. First, each member is obliged to perform as well as he can to assure victory. If one player fails to pass the ball to a teammate who has an open shot, he becomes accountable. Second, each member of the team has the categorical identity of guard, forward, or center. Each of these positions has attached to it distinctive responsibilities. The guards are primarily responsible for bringing the ball up the court. If one of the guards fails to perform his duties, he is

146

likely to be informed that if he continues to fail to perform the duties linked to the categorical identity of guard, he will be replaced by someone else.

Members of accountable relationships are categorically differentiated and assigned obligations linked to their categorical identities. The file clerk in an office has different duties from the receptionist. Each set of obligations is linked to both a categorical identity and the objectives of the collectivity. File clerks, receptionists, and others are obliged to perform their duties to assure that the office will achieve its collective objectives.

When people are part of an accountable relationship, they are both embedded with and obliged to one another. They have both a collective identity based on their solidary relationship and special identities that allocate each of them specific responsibilities and prerogatives. For example, the members of Martin High School basketball team have a collective identity, and each player has a special identity of guard, center, or forward.

An accountable relationship is established when persons with some degree of solidarity (1) categorically differentiate themselves; (2) agree that each is responsible for specific activities; (3) are knowledgeable about each other's actions; and (4) adopt a consensual standpoint when assessing their own and each other's actions.

Accountable relationships are committed relationships (Weiland 1975). In order for people to construct commitments they must have either a foundation of embeddedness or mutually agree that a third party will judge the actions of each. Friends construct accountable relationships on the basis of their embeddedness; strangers construct accountable relationships by mutually agreeing to the terms of a contract with the understanding that a third party will interpret and enforce the terms of the contract if any dispute arises.

Each member of an accountable relationship is an object to himself as well as to others. All members of an accountable relationship can make each other's and his own actions their shared focus. They consensually acknowledge that each has distinctive responsibilities and the adequacy of each member's performance will be evaluated from a shared standpoint. When the guard on a basketball team makes either an outstanding pass or throws the ball out of bounds, all, including the guard who committed the act, judge the action from much the same standpoint. When the responsibilities linked to a categorical identity are performed in a routine manner, then usually no one makes an explicit evaluation of the action.

An element of trust, based on solidarity, is present in most accountable relationships. The members of these accountable relationships promise to the other member(s) of the collectivity that they will take on certain responsibilities. The commitments are mutually agreed to by those who compose the relationship. Accountable relationships that include a third party need not involve any trust, only agreement on who is to serve as the third party.

Some accountable relationships rest largely on a solidary relationship; others, largely on faith in the third party. Friendship is usually primarily a solidary relationship intermixed with elements of accountability; the associations between members of a bureaucracy are usually largely accountable relationships linked to a third party. In some cases, the only element of solidary present within bureaucratic associations is the mutual recognition that all are employed by the same bureau. Sometimes the members of accountable relationships do not have either a solidary past or a shared distal future. In some instances the mutual recognition that both are employed by a larger collectivity is the only element of solidarity that frames their accountable relationship.

Many accountable relationships emerge without conscious intent. Many times, people become acquainted and then become friends. In the process they construct both a solidary relationship and a diffuse accountable relationship. In contrast, other accountable relationships are explicitly negotiated. The negotiations may be as incidental as those constructed when two men plan a fishing trip. The two friends might agree that one of them will furnish the boat and the other will buy the beer and bait. Then, when they reconvene the next day, each is accountable for the performance of responsibilities. If the one who agreed to buy the beer and bait fails to do so, his performance will be judged by both the other person and himself from much the same standpoint.

Of course, when one member of an accountable relationship fails to live up to his responsibilities, quite often he takes a somewhat different standpoint toward his failure than other members of the relationship. But unless there is at least some agreement on what constitutes an adequate performance of responsibilities, an accountable relationship cannot be constructed.

Some accountable relationships endure for only a short period; others endure indefinitely. A group of hunters might agree that they are more likely to be successful if half the group walks around a herd of deer and spooks them toward the others, while the second half lie in wait. Each segment is responsible for fulfilling its obligations. If those who had the responsibility of spooking the deer toward the others fail to give the deer a wide enough berth and frighten the deer away, they will be blamed for the group's failure.

When marriage vows are exchanged, the bride and groom promise to "love, cherish, and honor" each other indefinitely. They become accountable to each other, and the two of them become accountable to the larger community, for an indefinite period.

Accountable relationships have three distinct temporal periods. At time 1, members of the relationship differentiate themselves, define or negotiate their respective responsibilities, and each makes a commitment to act in a specific way at time 2. At time 2, each person performs or attempts to carry out his responsibilities. Then at time 3, an assessment is made of the adequacy of each performance. In many accountable relationships, the responsibilities of each person are only specified in general terms; in others, they are specified in detail.

Internal Differentiation

The internal differentiation of accountable relationships may be implicit or explicit; and it may be personal or formal. Generally speaking, when people have a robust solidary relationship, the internal differentiation of accountable relationships is implicit and personal; whereas within account-able relationships encased by only categorical solidarity, the differentiation usually is explicit. Close friends with a robust solidarity simply assume each will be a responsible person. When that implicit assumption is violated, then the accountable dimensions of friendships usually are made explicit or the friendship disintegrates.

For example, each friend usually assumes that the other one will not spread vicious gossip about the other. If one friend hears the other has been spreading gossip, the one who has been the victim is likely to ask first if it is true—call for a report from the other—and then call the other into account if it is true. When that occurs, their accountable relationship is made per-sonal and explicit. In contrast, the internal differentiation of bureaucracies is usually explicit and formal. Each new employee of a bureaucracy is given a distinctive categorical identity. His categorical identity may separate him from all other employees or may be an identity he shares with some other employees. In either event, each employee is explicitly and formally dif-ferentiated from some other members of the collectivity and assigned specific responsibilities and prerogatives.

The collective identity predominates in solidary relationships, in ac-countable relationships, differentiated identities come to the fore. The col-lective identities of solidary relationships and the differentiated identities of accountable relationships are not mutually exclusive. Whether the solidary or accountable dimensions predominates often depends on the context. In many arguments between married couples, the accountable dimensions of their relationship are made very manifest. But if a third party intervenes, the solidary dimensions of their relationship are likely to come to the fore as both of them turn on the third party and inform him that their problems are none of his business. When members of a group attend and act toward out-siders the solidary dimensions of their relationship usually comes to the forefront; but when they attend to internal affairs the accountable dimen-sions usually premominate.

Assignment of Responsibilities

Within purely solidary relationships, individuals are not assigned responsibilities. When social objectives are sought, all act in unison. But many social objectives can be more effectively achieved if some perform one set of tasks while others perform other tasks. A division of labor is an inherent part of accountable relationships (Strauss 1985, Weiland 1975).

Members of accountable relationships mutually recognize that the actions of each has consequences for others. When the accountable relationship is encased by a robust solidary relationship, the responsibilities of each person are usually taken for granted; they often are not explicitly constructed. When an accountable relationship is constructed by people who do *not* have a robust solidary relationship, then usually the creation of an accountable relationship is marked by a set of reciprocating acts wherein each explicitly promises to perform specific tasks sometime in the future.

Members of accountable relationships are burdened with tasks. The burdens are not necessarily unpleasant. Parents are obliged to care for their children; some parents find caring for their children a delight, although most, from time to time, find the task burdensome. Teachers may enjoy teaching, but sometimes find their obligations burdensome.

Members of accountable relationships are objectified when they are assigned categorical identities that differentiate them from one another. In addition, when an accountable relationship is explicitly constructed, the actions to be taken by each party are also objectified. The behavior linked to each categorical identity is given unity. For example, the young lad who has agreed to serve as a batboy for a baseball team has specific tasks that he is to perform. Unless the tasks linked to each categorical identity are explicitly specified, it is difficult to make judgments as to the adequacy of the performance.

The burden of responsibility linked to categorical differentiation is recognized by all who have been part of accountable relationships. The realization that the special responsibilities are linked to distinctive identities sometimes makes identities unattractive. People may delay or avoid marriage because they do not wish to assume the responsibilities of husband and wife. Others may decline assuming positions of responsibility to avoid becoming the focal point of evaluation.

Individuals may act for the welfare of others on the basis of either a solidary or an accountable relationship. When the action is based on compassion, it rests on a foundation of solidarity; when the action fulfills an obligation, it rests on an accountable relationship. When a citizen goes to the aid of another in need, his actions stem from communal solidarity; when a policeman gives aid to a citizen in need, his actions also stem from a base of communal solidarity, but, in addition, he has been obliged to give aid to citizens.

The mutual differentiation of self from others, the linking of responsibilities to categorical identities, and the monitoring of self by others and self create a distinctive relationship between self and other. Within accountable relationships, each member is an object as well as an actor. Many of our categorical identities are based on accountable relationships. "Thus, it is in accountable relationships that the object (me) part of the self is constructed" (Weiland 1975, 91).

Not only are the parties to accountable relationships made objects, but as they act to fulfill the responsibilities linked to each identity, they and others evaluate their performance. When the performance is judged to be outstanding, it is a source of credit and pride; when the performance is judged as less than adequate, it is a source of blame and guilt. The reputation accumulated within accountable relationships is a personal one. If the reputation is positive, it is the source of satisfaction; if negative, it is a source of dissatisfaction. Repetitive good performances within accountable relationships provide persons with secure and satisfying self-conceptions.

Monitoring

It is necessary for people to monitor one another's performance or acquire information about the performance to maintain an accountable relationship. In some accountable relationships the actions of all are readily apparent. In many accountable relationships, however, at time 1 a commitment is made, then at time 2 the parties to the relationship are separated from each other and reconvene at time 3. In those instances, members of the relationship cannot monitor each other's behavior. Then at time 3 they must make assessments of the adequacy of each other's performance on the basis of the outcome or on what the other reports having done.

When accountable relationships rest on a robust solidary relationship, members of the relationship may not make any great effort to monitor each other's action when they are separated at time 2. They trust each other. When an accountable relationship does not rest on a firm solidary base, then monitoring of the other person's performance during time 2 often is an important facet of the relationship.

Members of accountable relationships constantly monitor themselves and constantly assess their own performances. People who are firmly embedded in a robust solidary relationship usually are severe evaluators of their own actions; they are conscientious. When members of a robust solidary relationship construct a division of labor, each party usually does his utmost to fulfill obligations.

Sometimes members of accountable relationships are under high surveillance; in other relationships only a low level of surveillance prevails. And the level of surveillance varies from occasion to occasion within a given accountable relationship. For example, the defense attorney is under high surveillance by both clients and other interested parties when he performs in the courtroom. But when he acts in behalf of a client behind closed doors to plea-bargain the case, he is under low surveillance. When surveillance is low, people have the opportunity to be irresponsible. Some take advantage of the situation.

A group of close friends may undertake a small business venture and designate one person to be in charge of the group's finances. It is likely that they will only incidentally monitor the person who manages their funds. In contrast, a number of crooks who form a gang to commit a robbery might allow one person to keep the loot to be dispersed at some later time. All are likely to be concerned about the actions of the one who has the loot in his possession.

If other parties to an accountable relationship that rests on a foundation of minimal solidarity do not know what one party is doing, it is impossible to maintain a viable accountable relationship. Those who are the focus of intense accountability based on a low level of solidarity frequently hide from other members of the relationship. If it is impossible to acquire information about the actions of those persons it is impossible effectively to call them into account. Members of bureaucracies frequently attempt to shroud their activities in mysticism to lessen their accountability to both fellow workers and clients. The uninformed cannot effectively call others into account. Ignorant clients are a blessing.

Standpoints and Objectives

When people construct accountable relationships, they implicitly presume or explicitly agree that they have a consensual standpoint and a shared objective. When members of a partisan group assume and assign differential responsibilities, they presume all share the same standpoint toward the issue at hand and all are interested in achieving the same objectives. In a similar manner, when a person is employed for a special task, it is implicitly presumed, if not explicitly negotiated, that he will assume the same standpoint as the employer and act to achieve the employer's objective. For example, when one goes to a physician for medical treatment, it is presumed that the physician regards illness as undesirable and will attempt to cure the malady.

When accountable relationships are constructed on a foundation of robust solidarity, often there is almost complete consensus of standpoints and objectives. When the relationship is constructed on less than robust solidarity, for example, when an accountable relationship is constructed by strangers, there is often little consensus of standpoints and objectives. When that condition prevails, not all will adopt the same standpoint when they assess their and others' performance. Lawyers, for example, often employ different standards in assessing the adequacy of their performance than do their clients.

Members of an accountable relationship often assess the adequacy of their own performance differently from the assessment by others. Individuals are often more lenient in assessing their performance than others are. Students frequently conclude that their performance on an essay examination is more adequate than does the instructor. The opposite also occurs. On occasion, a person is more stringent in assessing his own performance than others are in assessing the performance. Stringent self-assessments of performance are usually associated with accountable relationships that rest on a robust solidary relationship.

Formalized Accountability

The absence of complete consensus on standpoints and objectives usually means that there is less than complete consensus on the criteria to be employed in the assessment of performances. A common consequence is that when important accountable relationships are established that do not have a foundation of a robust solidary relationship, the criteria for the assessment of performance becomes formalized. Lawyers, physicians, and other professionals generate official codes of conduct. In a similar manner, bureaucracies usually have formal criteria that are used to assess performances.

When the responsibilities of an accountable position and the criteria to be used in assessing performances are formally specified, people often become more concerned with conforming to the formal criteria than with social objectives. Some bureaucrats become so concerned with the formal criteria that they no longer judge their performance on the basis of movement toward objectives. Instead they adhere to the regulations and ignore objectives.

Consider the following example: A student was informed by an assistant dean that he would not receive his degree because he had not completed the required eight hours in social science. The regulations listed several freshmen- and sophomore-level courses that fulfilled the requirement. The student had taken two of these courses, one a three hour course and the other a four hour course. In addition, he had taken two advanced courses in sociology. He was informed by the dean that the advanced courses did not fulfill the requirement. The student contacted the instructor of one of the courses. The instructor was of the opinion that the advanced courses should count toward the fulfillment of the requirement. The instructor called the assistant dean. The conversation included the following exchanges.

Instructor: How come you are withholding approval of graduation for Don Jones?

Dean: As I told him, he has completed only seven of the required eight hours.

Instructor: But he has taken six additional hours in sociology. Don't they count?

Dean: No, they are not listed as courses that fulfill the requirement.

Instructor: What difference does that make? He has taken more than the required hours in social science.

Dean: That may be, but unless he has taken the designated courses he can't graduate.

Instructor: Why was that requirement established in the first place?

Dean: I don't know. I don't make the rules.

Instructor: Wasn't the rule made to assure that all with a liberal arts degree be exposed to a wide range of subjects?

Dean: That may be, I don't know. Like I said, I don't make the rules.

Instructor: This is absurd. The guy has more than fulfilled the spirit of the requirements and you are keeping him from graduating by enforcing the letter of the law.

Dean: (angrily) Look! I said I don't make the rules! If he hasn't fulfilled the requirements, he can't graduate. And that is that!

Instructor: We'll see about that!

The instructor assessed the situation from what he presumed was the objective of those who had instituted the requirements. The dean assessed the performance of the student on the basis of the formal criteria.

When accountable relationships are formalized, it lessens ambiguity. Responsibilities are more clearly delineated, as are the criteria for assessing performances. Paradoxically, the formalization of the responsibilities and criteria often entices people to become less concerned with objectives and more concerned with adhering to the regulations. The two concerns are not necessarily in conflict, but often they are.

Bureaucratic organizations epitomize accountable relationships. In the extreme case, the only dimension of solidarity present is mutual recognition that all are employed at the same agency; there is little in the way of a solidary past or a shared future. Bureaucratic systems consist of titles (categorical identities) linked together on the basis of compatible obligations. Individuals are recruited for previously defined positions and to fulfill specific obligations. Maintenance of a position requires the fulfillment of objectified pattern of behavior. The file clerk is responsible for filing; the typist, for typing. There is an implicit assumption that each specialist contributes to the social objectives of the organization. Yet each is often more concerned with performing his obligations than with the overarching objective of the organization.

Bureaucrats live a solitary life. The file clerk goes about the job of filing quite independent of the actions of the typists and both act independently of maintenance personnel. While all are part of a larger system, they fulfill their functions primarily by acting as individuals, not as a collectivity. They often act in one another's presence, but seldom with one another. Cooperation is achieved on the basis of a formal allocation of responsibilities, not on the basis of reciprocal attentiveness and social responsiveness. Bureaucrats are responsible people, not responsive people.

Once a social system is in place that is composed almost entirely of accountable relationships, often there is little or no solidarity within the organization. The typical file clerk is hired and assigned tasks. He may work in the presence of others, but seldom works with them. Shared experiences are few. Each file clerk does have experiences that are common to those of other file clerks, but more often than not, they work in other rooms.

If perchance two file clerks make contact with each other, their common pasts provide a foundation for them to construct a solidary relationship. But the solidarity generated in this manner is a reaction to their accountable position within the system; it is not based on mutually coordinated action within the system. On occasion, persons who have extensive common experiences on the basis of their accountable relationships within an organization form new organizations. The new organization, such as a labor union, often is a response to the larger system; and the action structured by the new organization is usually against the organization, not action to promote the original objectives of the organization.

Symmetry

Whereas solidary relationships implicitly, if not explicitly, deny differentiation, accountable relationships rest on a foundation of explicit differentiation. One person, *A,* is one type of object while another person, *B,* is another type of object. One is the father and the other, the mother; and they have different responsibilities. Accountable relationships are based on differentiation, however, they may be symmetrical. An accountable relationship is symmetrical when the burdens and rewards linked to each position are equal.

Differentiation does not automatically create asymmetry, but it establishes a condition that often leads to asymmetry. Whenever there is differentiation, the burdens of one are likely to be greater than the burdens of another; and the prestige acquired by one is likely to be greater than the prestige acquired by the other. For example, the pitcher on a Little League baseball team is saddled with greater responsibility than the left fielder; and he also has more opportunities to acquire prestige than the left fielder.

One consequence is that the establishment of an enduring accountable relationship, even when it rests on a foundation of robust solidarity, creates conditions that often lead to disagreements, conflicts, and alienation. One member of the relationship is likely to conclude that his burdens are greater than the burdens of the other, or that he acquires fewer rewards than he deserves. That may lead to the renegotiation of the division of labor, or it may result in eroding the solidary base and ultimately fragmentation of the group. The continuation of a symmetrical accountable relationship wherein there is a sustained and significant division of labor is difficult.

To maintain an accountable relationship that entails sustained and significant division of labor without external constraints requires the reaffirmation of the solidary relationship from time to time. Members of partisan groups, religious groups, and other groups that depend on voluntary membership routinely convene to reaffirm their solidary relationship. They hold ceremonies, rituals, and parties during which they deny their differences, reactivate their collective identity, are solidarily responsive, and reassert their collective objectives. If they do not so, it is very likely that many of the members will become alienated from the group.

Summary

Accountable relationships appear to be pan human; they can be found in all human societies — although apparently in some primitive groups accountable relationships are of minor significance (W. Miller 1955, Spindler and Spindler 1971). Within some societies, the only accountable relationships of any significance are those attached to the kinship structure. The social structure of some primitive societies is largely limited to parental and solidary relationships.

In many societies, the members act to promote the welfare of others on the basis of compassion, not on the basis of obligations. And if people do not act out of compassion to protect or help others, they are only minimally held accountable. In such societies, those who are not compasssionate may be avoided or shunned, but they are not called into account.

In Western societies, accountability is part of the relationship between parents and children. Children are accountable to their parents; they are expected to live by the dictates of their parents. That is such a taken-for-granted part of the parent—child relationship in Western societies that some have difficulty imagining it as not part of all parent—child relationships. Nonetheless, in some societies children are only minimally accountable to their parents. In some societies, if a little girl becomes dissatisfied with her parents, she is likely to leave her parents to attach herself to other adults. She does not thereby become accountable to her new "parents." Nor are parents necessarily accountable to their children or to the larger community for caring for their children. In all societies, the parents or some other adult kin generally are expected to care for children. If they failed to do so, they may not be called into account by other adults. Parents who do not give adequate care to their children are likely to be the topic of gossip in such societies, but they are not called into account.

If American parents do not give proper care to their children the neighbors, welfare agencies, police, and court are likely to step in and relieve the parents of the children. The accountability of children to their parents and that of parents to the larger society for the welfare of their children is presumed to be part of the parent—child relationship in America. But accountability is not part of parent—child relationships in all societies.

Any division of labor results in different experiences. In the traditional family where the mother was responsible for caring for the home and children and the father for earning the necessary income, the mother and father had different experiences as each fulfilled her or his obligations. Those differences very often led to an erosion of solidarity. As long as each member of an accountable relationship regards the allocation of responsibilities as more or less equal and the rewards associated with each set of responsibilities as equal, however, the division of labor need not lessen the solidarity.

When there are differences of opinion on what constitutes an adequate performance of the obligations, and if these differences are expressed, accountable relationships usually undermine solidary relationships. The husband and wife who regard each other's performance as inadequate and make their assessment known to each other run the risk of undermining their solidarity.

When members of an accountable relationship explicitly evaluate each other's past behavior, it is usually alienating. Those who focus on each other's obligations soon find themselves disenchanted with one another. Unless there are external constraints that hold the relationship together, the relationship is likely to disintegrate when the adequacy of performance comes to the fore.

The construction of an accountable relationship is not divisive. When people negotiate responsibilities, there is a degree of flexibility. Each voluntarily commits himself to perform certain obligations. But when commitments have been forged and each monitors the actions of the other, a different state of affairs prevails. The past is commonly regarded as something that has a fixed existence. Most do not regard the past as something that can be negotiated. Either something occurred or did not occur; either one is at fault or the other is.

Consequently, when the assessment stage of accountable relationships is reached, and one regards the performance of the other as inadequate the person who is being assessed usually must choose one of four options. He can attempt to demonstrate that he did perform adequately. If he successfully demonstrates his performance was adequate, he then places the person who made the negative assessment on the defensive. Transactions of that sort are likely to erode solidarity. A second option is to agree that he did not fulfill his obligations. He thereby stigmatizes himself and places himself in a one-down position. A third option is to lie, to claim that he did fulfill his obligations, even though he did not. That option sometimes gives temporary relief. But in the long run it is likely to erode the relationship. Furthermore, presenting a false front erodes the self of the liar. The fourth option is simply to deny that an accountable relationship exists between himself and whoever is calling for an account.

These consequences stand in sharp contrast to those that flow from assessments made within a solidary relationship. When assessments of the past performances are made from the platform provided by a solidary relationship, the collective identity of those composing the relations is reaffirmed. The issues are discussed in terms of what *we* did or might have done or in terms of what happened to *us*. Assessments made from that position are likely to elicit solidary responsiveness and strengthen the relationship, not weaken it.

The construction of all cooperative action requires the surrender of some autonomy. Persons must attend to others and to some extent subordinate their acts to the actions of the other if they are to coordinate their actions. The construction of an accountable relationship is a cooperative act. Both parties take part, but one of the distinctive features of accountable relationships is that not only is autonomy surrendered in the ongoing present but a commitment is made to abide by the dictates of the group in the future. Both a degree of present and future autonomy is surrendered whenever an accountable relationship is constructed. That feature of accountable relationships is why accountable relationships are actively avoided by some people. Some avoid marriage because, as they phrase it, they want to keep their freedom.

The division of labor inherent in accountable relationships may promote solidarity. For example, when a number of persons divide up responsibilities, they may be more successful than they would have been without a division of labor. If the division of labor is recognized as contributing to their effectiveness, their internal differentiation can enhance their solidary relationship.

Individuals who are both embedded with and accountable to each other are obliged to each other. They adopt the standpoint of the other when assessing their own actions. But accountable relationships that rest on only categorical solidarity, for example, employees of bureaucracies, generate a self-interest morality. The typical response of one bureaucrat to another is, "That is your problem, not mine." That it could be "our" problem seldom occurs to those embued with a bureaucratic mentality.

Chapter 13 Authority

Authority relationships rest on a foundation of solidarity and accountability. When people establish an authority relationship, they categorically differentiate themselves, assume distinctive responsibilities and prerogatives, and agree to relate in an asymmetrical fashion. One person is designated the focal point of the relationship. That person has the responsibility and prerogative of coordinating and supervising the actions of others. For example, foremen have the prerogative to, and are obliged to, direct the actions of the work crew.

In many social encounters the first question asked, at least implicitly, is, Who is in charge? When workers come to their place of employment, all know who is in charge, who is to direct and supervise their activity. When we appear in court to plead a traffic citation, we recognize that the traffic judge is in charge. On occasion, there is uncertainty about who is in charge. When a group of tourists congregate at the entrance of the White House for a tour, they mill about until the tour guide appears. When the guide appears and announces herself as a guide, nearly all validate her identity by focusing their attention on her and abiding by her directives. As the tour unfolds, she directs and monitors their actions.

Whether the authority relationship takes the form of the judge and defendant in a courtroom, a boss and workers, or a tour guide and tourists, one person is the focal point of the encounters. All other members of the encounter are accountable to the focal person and the person occupying the focal position is accountable to others. Some authority relationships are extremely asymmetrical; others only slightly asymmetrical. Some endure for years, if not decades; others endure for only brief encounters. Some authority relationships rest on a foundation of robust solidarity; others, on only categorical solidarity.

When several young people congregate on a playground to play a softball game, they often select two persons to choose sides. When that occurs, an authority relationship is established. The relationship between the two captains and the others is only slightly asymmetrical; the only prerogative and responsibility the captains have is to select sides. The authority relationship may not endure any longer than the time it takes for them to choose sides.

In contrast, when a newly hired man assumes his position within a bureaucracy, his relationship with both his supervisor and his subordinates is very asymmetrical; and that relationship may endure for years. When the newly hired first assumes his position in a bureaucracy, usually only categorical solidarity underlies the authority relationships. After the new man assumes his position, he and his subordinates and he and his superordinates may construct a shared past that may enrich their relationship with elements of functional solidarity. Or they may construct a shared past filled with antagonism and fear. If the latter happens, then their authority relationship continues to rest on only categorical solidarity.

In authority relationships, someone is authorized to direct a collective effort. The authorization can be accomplished in several ways. One is by members of a collectivity selecting one of themselves to serve as the focal point. For example, when the residents of a neighborhood congregate to take community action, they are likely to select someone to chair their deliberations. Managers of companies are selected by a board of directors and authorized to run the company. The managers in turn delegate some of their responsibilities to their assistants. Authority relationships are often multitiered.

Authorization is a collective accomplishment. Both the person assigned command and others agree to the selection. The authority-to-be may offer himself as a candidate for the position and thereby initiate the authorization process, but unless his offer is acknowledged and validated by others, he is not authorized to assume the position of command. Reciprocally, others may offer a person a position of command, but unless the recipient of the offer accepts it, no authority relationship is established.

Authority relationships are social products; they are not the consequence of unilateral action. A person may impose himself on others by coercion and threats, and others may accede to the threats. An asymmetrical relationship is created in such encounters, but it is not an authority relationship; it is a tyrannical relationship.

Authority relationships are established by a plurality of people (1) categorically differentiating themselves; (2) assigning the responsibilities and prerogatives of coordinating the effort of the collectivity to someone; (3) projecting a shared but differentiated future; and (4) mutually committing themselves to relate in an asymmetrical fashion.

Categorical Differentiation

The categorical differentiation of authority relationships implies categorical ranking as well as functional differentiation. At the minimum, one person is made the focal point for the group and is conferred an element of prestige. When two children of a grammar school class are selected to choose sides for a spelling bee, they are categorically differentiated; for a short time at least, they rank above other members of the class. Once the spelling bee is under way, they become just two more members of the teams.

In other authority relationships, the ranking endures and is extreme. Distinctive and enduring rankings prevail in military units. Officers are authorized to exercise many prerogatives denied enlisted personnel. The responsibilities and prerogatives of prisoners and prison guards are entirely different. But the relationship is authoritarian; it is not tyrannical. The guards are accountable; the prisoners have some prerogatives. In many instances, this particular relationship approaches tyranny. As long as the guards are accountable to someone for their behavior toward prisoners, however, an authority relationship is maintained.

Communication via appearance is nearly always a viable facet of enduring authority relationships. Military units invest each person with an insignia that clearly specifies a categorical identity. Each encounter between members of military units is contextualized by the insignia. Captains are to defer to colonels, and privates are to defer to captains. The responsibilities and prerogatives of each rank are communicated via appearance each time members of the military establish copresence. The display of categorical identities in appearance relieves people of the necessity of establishing their ranking in discourse.

In a similar manner, the relative ranking, the prerogatives of each rank of members of a bureaucracy, are usually communicated in appearance. When employees of a bureaucracy contact one another their interaction is contextualized by their rank in the bureaucracy. Usually both are aware of their respective ranking on the basis of their shared past or categorical identities displayed in appearance. On occasion, however, they do not know each other's title. Then they will usually establish their categorical identities in discourse.

The consensual categorical identities that frame encounters within highly asymmetrical authority relationships are usually unambiguously established the moment people make contact. When the colonel looks up from his work and establishes reciprocal attention with a private, he and the private are immediately aware of which of them will defer to the other. On occasion, subordinates in highly asymmetrical relationships fail to note the categorical identities of their superordinates. When that occurs, they are usually reminded rather forcefully to give rank its due respect. On some occasions, subordinates are insubordinate; they refuse to defer to their superordinates. Whenever that occurs, the relationship itself becomes the focus of attention. Then the relationship may be renegotiated, or it may disintegrate.

Responsibilities and Prerogatives

It is the authority's responsibility and prerogative to coordinate and supervise his own and his subordinates' actions to achieve the social objectives of the collectivity. For example, when two children are selected by their classmates to choose up sides, those selected are obliged to make selections, and they have the prerogative of making any choices they wish. If one fails to make selections or is slow to select, he is likely to be called into account by his classmates. Reciprocally, he has the prerogative of making the selections. Others may suggest who should be chosen next, but the captain has the final say. He also has the prerogative of issuing directives, and others are obliged to comply with the directives. Of course, subordinates sometimes question the prerogatives of authorities and on occasion attempt to usurp the prerogatives of their superordinates. A subordinate member of a work crew who issues an order, attempts to usurp the prerogatives of the foreman.

In authority relationships the superordinate has the responsibility for programming the future. The president of a corporation, for example, is responsible for developing plans to assure the success of the organization. The asymmetrical responsibilities and prerogatives of authority relationships usually saddle the authority with primary responsibility for the achievements of the group. One consequence is that within authority relationships the superordinate tends to receive most of the credit for successes and most of the blame for failures. Most authorities willingly accept credit for the successes of their organizations, but many are reluctant to accept blame for failures. Both responsibility for success and failure may be negotiated.

The relative ranking of members of authority relationships are often taken for granted, but the specific responsibilities and prerogatives attached to each categorical identity are frequently the source of disagreements, and on many occasions they are negotiated. Teachers frequently presume they have prerogatives that students do not wish to concede to them; reciprocally, students often presume they have prerogatives that teachers do not think they have. Prerogatives and responsibilities often are not clearly delineated. When that is the case they are likely to be the source of disagreements, ill feeling, and negotiation.

Even when there is consensus within an authority relationship on the relative ranking of the members, dissatisfaction is often experienced by both superordinates and subordinates. Superordinates frequently complain about the heavy burden of authority. They often feel they are not justly rewarded for responsibilities. Reciprocally, subordinates must comply with the directives of their superordinates. They frequently find that irritating in even the smoothest authority relationships.

Asymmetrical Accountability

All members of authority relationships are accountable but superordinates and subordinates are differentially accountable. For the most part, the accountability of subordinates is directly to their superordinate. Superordinates monitor the actions of their subordinates and assess their performances. Reciprocally, superordinates are partially accountable to their subordinates. In multitiered authority relationships, for example, the military, the authority is often only incidentally accountable to subordinates. He is primarily accountable to his superiors. Within multitiered authority relationships, superordinates are often more concerned about their accountability to their superiors than they are with their accountability to subordinates. When that condition is present, many superordinates are relatively indifferent to calls for accounts from their subordinates. Foremen, for example, often find themselves caught betwixt and between their supervisors and their crews. Still other authorities are almost entirely accountable to their subordinates.

Presidents of local groups serve at the pleasure of their members. The president of a local voluntary club is only accountable to other members. An authority who is accountable to subordinates usually exercises constraint when issuing directives.

In multitiered structures, those in middle positions often find themselves the targets of incongruent calls for accounts. Their superiors use one set of criteria in evaluating their performance; their subordinates use different criteria. As a consequence, occupants of middle positions frequently find themselves caught in a bind. Their superiors usually evaluate them primarily on the basis of the accomplishments of their unit. In contrast, their subordinates usually evaluate them primarily in terms of how the authority relates to them. These two different standpoints frequently result in quite different evaluations.

The effective coordination of the activity of subordinates in groups of any size requires the authority to monitor the activities of subordinates. An authority who cannot effectively monitor subordinates will not acquire the information necessary to coordinate their actions and call them into account. Generals, supervisors, and police chiefs must be able to monitor the actions of their subordinates. If they cannot monitor the actions of the subordinates the activity is likely to become disorganized. Subordinates must be available so that the authority can initiate encounters with them and issue directives and guidance, but it is not necessary for the subordinate to monitor the actions of the superordinate.

The differential monitoring and accountability of superordinates and subordinates was neatly demonstrated in a study of transactions between the supervisor and workers at a student cafeteria (Philby, 1983). The workers were students employed part-time; the supervisor was a full-time employee of the university. The supervisor had a small, glassed-in office at one end of the cafeteria line. From her office she could easily observe most of the activity on the serving line. When the supervisor was in her office, the workers could observe her only if they turned in that direction. Most of the time, their attention was focused on the people passing through the line and the food trays in front of them.

On occasion, the supervisor left her office; most of the transactions between the supervisor and workers were initiated by the supervisor. Usually the workers quickly complied with the instructions, requests, and directives of the supervisor. Occasionally a worker would attempt to ignore or deflect a directive, but nearly always these efforts were unsuccessful. In one instance, the supervisor approached a worker and stated, "Walt, we need you in the dishroom. We're one short." The worker replied, "But what about Jeff?" The worker made no other response, he did not turn to establish eye contact with the supervisor. The supervisor, in a firmer tone, replied, "We need him here. We need you in the dishroom and someone can watch this." At that point the supervisor briskly turned away. The worker slowly left his station to comply with the directive.

Many transactions between this supervisor and workers focused on assessing the current state of affairs. In one instance, the supervisor left her office just as customers began proceeding through the line. She queried one worker with, "John, how many pans are you ahead?" The worker replied, "Three." The supervisor moved on a few steps and asked another, "Is everything OK with desserts?" She received an affirmative reply. In neither case did the supervisor and worker make eye contact. In these and similar encounters, the supervisor reaffirmed her authority and acquired information.

Most of the encounters were routine. But on occasion things went amiss. Then the supervisor issued forceful directives. In one instance, the supervisor noticed a worker playing with empty ice cream cartons. She left her office, walked up next to the worker (who had not detected her) and asked, "Where do empty ice cream containers go? Do you know where they go?" The tone was bitter and mocking. A grin of embarrassment came across the worker's face. He replied, "Yeah. They go right over there," and he pointed to the garbage bin. The supervisor, with a stern face and her arms crossed, directed, "Then throw them away." She sharply turned away. The worker mumbled as he deposited the empty containers in the garbage bin.

Each authority has a personal style, but in all authority relationships it is necessary for the authority to monitor the activity of subordinates, note disruptions in the movement toward the collective objective, and from time to time issue directives.

Nearly all authorities acquire more information that is relevant to the group's activities than do subordinates. In general, authorities also acquire more information about the workers than the workers acquire about the authority. One consequence of those differences is that within enduring authority relationships, the authority tends to acquire more information than the subordinates. In some instances, authorities deliberately withhold information from their workers. When the authority has more information than the subordinates, that places the authority in an advantageous position whenever any subordinates attempt to negotiate their responsibilities and prerogatives.

Shared and Differentiated Futures

Members of authority relationships have both shared and differentiated futures. When the members anticipate that all will share equally in the benefits of their accomplishments, a shared future contextualized their action; when they anticipate that the rewards will be differentially allocated, actions within an authority relationship are contextualized by a differentiated future. In most authority relationships, the futures projected are both shared and differentiated. The assembly-line workers at General Motors and the top executives presume that the continued success of the organization will yield both of them benefits; however, the benefits reaped by the top executives are usually greater than those of the assembly-line workers.

When all are working for the same objectives, it provides a foundation for solidary responsiveness between superordinates and subordinates. Workers and their bosses frequently shout in celebration when a difficult task has been successfully completed. Both the foremen and workers of construction crews sometimes joyously celebrate their successes and agonize when they fail. In contrast, when the anticipated futures are highly differentiated, those anticipating little reward for success are often indifferent to their accomplishments. When an assembly line breaks down, the workers often cheer, and the supervisor is distraught.

Commitment

The authority relationship is a committed one. Both subordinates and superordinates willfully enter authority relationships; both adopt a similar standpoint that rests on a foundation of solidarity and commit themselves to relate in a prescribed manner. Commitments can be constructed only by people who can adopt a third-party standpoint toward their relatedness.

Those who construct an authority relationship may not be solidarily embedded with one another, but at the minimum they presume that both of them are embedded in the same general social framework. Authority relationships have a moral dimension. Consequently, all who subscribe to the same morality can make judgments on the propriety of the actions of both the authority and the subordinates. In contrast, tyrannical relationships are immoral; no boundaries of propriety encase them.

The commitments that frame authority relationships specify the directives the authority can issue. Most significant and enduring authority relationships are activated by the parties completing a ritual that defines the parameters of their relationship. Military recruits take an oath when they enter the military; the president of the United States takes the oath of office; and in traditional marriage ceremonies, the bride swore to "obey" her husband-to-be when she became his wife.

These rituals are "public" events. Either they are performed before an audience or a representative of the public administers them or both. Significant authority relationships are three-party affairs- --the two who constitute the relationship and the public (witnesses). Furthermore, there is the presumption that all three parties to the relationship are part of a larger, encompassing solidary relationship. The construction of the commitment, then, is encased by a presumed solidarity within which the members of the relationship bond themselves to each other in a specific manner.

Nazi Germany constructed a political structure that rested on an extreme form of authoritarianism interlaced with tyranny. The generals of the army were required to swear personal loyalty to Hitler. Hitler was obliged to work for the welfare of Germany, but there was no third party to enforce Hitler's obligations. Toward the end of the war, some of the generals concluded that Hitler had violated his oath of office. They organized an unsuccessful rebellion against him. The fact that parties to authority relationships make commitments does not assure that the commitments will be honored. Many superordinates and subordinates violate their commitments.

The social structure of Nazi Germany is instructive. It demonstrates some of the pathologies associated with extremely authoritarian relationships. Extremely authoritarian relationships relieve subordinates of responsibility for their actions. Immediately following Nazi Germany's defeat, many of those responsible for killing and torturing others pleaded that they were not responsible, that they were merely following orders. Some avoided being called into account; others were brought before a world court and made accountable for their actions.

Extremely asymmetrical authority relationships, such as those that prevail in the military, relieve subordinates of responsibility. In relationships of that sort the subordinates' only responsibilities are to be attentive to the superordinate and comply with the directives the superordinate issues.

Milgram's Studies

Stanley Milgram conducted a series of studies of obedience. He was appalled by the unquestioning obedience of many of the subordinates in Nazi Germany. He was especially intrigued by those who did violence to other human beings. His revolutionary experiments touched off an extended controversy about obedience, authority, and laboratory studies.

Milgram did not conceptualize his research as focused on authority relationships; instead he focused on the actions of subordinates within an authority relationship. He thereby made his unit of analysis the acts of individuals, not relationships and transactions between people. The following account of Milgram's studies is derived from Miller's (1986a) reanalysis of Milgram's research. Whereas Milgram focused on obedience, Miller attended to the relationship that contextualized the actions of Milgram's subjects.

As Milgram stated it, his prime concern was "How far the participant will comply with the experimenter's instructions before refusing to carry out the actions required of him" (Milgram 19744, 3). Milgram completed eighteen studies. Each study varied some dimension of the authority relationship. But in all the studies, individuals were recruited to take part in a study of "punishment and learning." When volunteers came to take part in the study, Milgram told them that he was studying punishment and learning. As each volunteer arrived a second person, who was waiting in the laboratory and looked like another volunteer, was presented to the naive volunteer as another volunteer. The second person was in fact a shill. After the study was outlined, the naive volunteer and the shill drew lots to determine who was to be the learner and who the teacher. The drawing was rigged so that the naive subject always became the teacher. The subject—teacher was then informed that the learner would be shocked each time he failed to give the proper response. The subject—teacher was placed in the shill— learner's "electric chair" and administered a shock of 45 volts. Most of the subject—teachers estimated that the shock they received was stronger than 45 volts.

Then the shill—learner was strapped into the "electric chair" and the subject—teacher was seated before a control panel that had thirty switches. The switches were labeled from 15 volts to 30 volts and on to 450 volts. Labels ranging from "slight shock" to "DANGER- SEVERE SHOCK" were attached to the control panel. The shill—learner was instructed, then the "test" was administered. Each time the shill—learner gave an incorrect response, the subject—teacher was directed to administer a shock to the shill—learner. The subject—teacher was also instructed to increase the voltage of the shock by 15 volts each time the learner gave an incorrect answer. This pattern continued until the subject refused to administer the shocks or until the 450-volt switch was reached.

In the first experiment, the shill—learner did not say anything. At certain points in the "tests," there was pounding and kicking on the wall that separated the shill—learner from the subject—teacher. At 315 volts the shill—learner discontinued making responses, and there was no more pounding or kicking on the wall. Twenty-six of forty subjects (65%) continued to comply with the instructions of the experimenter until the 450-volt switch was reached.

In another study, the same general situation was constructed, but the shill—learner and the subject—teacher were seated in the same room. They did not face each other, but if they turned their heads, they could establish eye contact. In that condition, sixteen of forty subjects (40%) obeyed the orders of the experimenter until the 450-volt switch was reached.

Milgram varied the feedback from the shill—learner to the subject—teacher, whether or not the experimenter was in the same room with the subject—teacher or gave orders through an intercom, the sex of the subject—teacher, the location of the study, the identity of the shill—learner, and the presence of a third party. Complete compliance of the subject—teachers to the experimenter's orders ranged from a high of 65 percent when there was no verbal feedback from the shill—learner to a low of 5 percent when a third participant, who was also a shill, refused to comply with the orders of the experimenter.

The fact that Milgram conducted the studies outraged many. They regarded the studies as unethical. The subjects were tricked into thinking that they had caused severe pain to another human being. (They were, of course, informed afterward that the shill—learner had not been shocked, had not suffered.)

Some people have attempted to minimize the significance of the findings. They have argued that the findings are suspect because the subjects "knew" they were not really causing another to suffer. A viewing of Milgram's (1965) film indicates that most, if not all, of the subjects thought they had caused severe pain. In any event, attempts to minimize the significance of Milgram's finding by arguing that it was only an experiment or that the subjects really knew they were not hurting another misses the point.

The fact that subordinates in an authority relationship will follow orders that cause others great suffering is not unknown in the everyday world. The guards at the concentration camps in Nazi Germany routinely followed orders to kill other human beings. When volunteers for a firing squad are called for, some people volunteer. And, of course, members of the military routinely follow orders that will have the consequence of killing other human beings. Yet, not very many people routinely torture and kill others.

At least a partial explanation of the actions of Milgram's subjects, and some of the actions of others who inflict suffering on their fellow human beings, can be offered by recognizing some of the features of authority relationships. That, of course, does not excuse those who follow the directives of authorities to inflict suffering on others.

First, not all of Milgram's subjects obeyed his orders. Some rebelled. In all situations, 35 percent or more of the subjects refused to comply with all of Milgram's directives. Conversely, in one study in which subjects were required to press the skill-- learners's hand on a shockplate to assure that the shock was received, 40 percent complied with Milgram's orders. Yet the fact that a significant percentage of the subjects refused to obey demonstrates that obedience is not an automatic response even in the most authoritarian relationships. On occasion, soldiers have refused to serve as members of a firing squad; and some citizens have refused to serve in the military.

The situation that Milgram constructed was not as authoritarian as the military, but it was nonetheless an extremely authoritarian relationship. Furthermore, probably unintentionally, Milgram constructed a situation wherein his subjects were placed in a bind where they had to violate a commitment to avoid inflicting pain. Some chose to abide by their commitment, whereas others were compassionate and rebelled.

The social science laboratory is an authoritarian situation (Sehested and Couch 1986). All who volunteer to take part in such studies are aware that they are expected to follow the directions of the experimenter. The laboratory as a physical entity, of course, does not establish an authority relationship. But it does provide a background that serves to give some legitimacy to the orders issued by an experimenter. Of far greater importance is the fact that the experimenter, or someone acting as his delegate, initiates an authority relationship when a call for volunteers is issued. Those who respond indicate that they are willing to enter into an authority relationship with the experimenter.

The experimenter — authority and subject — subordinate explicitly agree to a time and place for reconvening. At the minimum, they implicitly agree that when they convene at the laboratory, the experimenter will direct the actions of the subject, and the subject will comply with the directives of the experimenter. They may discuss and/or negotiate what action will be called for by the experimenter. It is usually presumed that the subject will not be asked to take any actions that are unethical or that will cause suffering.

In Milgram's studies, when the subjects appeared, the purpose of the study was explained to them and they were paid for appearing. Both the subject and the shill then proceeded to comply with the directives and instructions of the experimenter as they became situated within the experimental context. The directives were issued by the experimenter, the authority. All complied with the directives that situated them in the laboratory. That kind of compliance can be observed at any airport, dentist office, waiting room, or classroom. The directives are benign; no one suffers more than incidental inconvenience as they follow the orders issued by the public address announcer at an airport. In a similar manner, those who took part in Milgram's study were following routine directives as they became socially situated into the highly authoritarian context of the "official study."

The first orders issued by the experimenter as the study got under way were also relatively benign. As a consequence of the directives issued in the early stages of each experiment, each subject became firmly located as a subordinate in the authority relationship. Furthermore, subjects were informed that while the shocks were painful, they would not cause any lasting damage.

Then, as the situation unfolded, subjects became aware that they were causing extreme pain. Milgram violated the implicit parameters of the authority relationship; subjects were called on to act in a harmful and immoral manner. Most, if not all, of the subjects indicated that they did not wish to continue to comply with the experimenter's directives. Milgram did not report any subjects who readily complied with all directives.

At various points most, perhaps all, of the subjects attempted to renegotiate their commitment. Some at least attempted to return the fee they had received for taking part. Milgram refused to take back the payment the subjects had received. Consequently, the subjects were in a bind. Either they had to continue to act in a harmful way toward another human being or violate their commitment to the experimenter. Some chose to continue to cause pain to the shill—learner; others violated their commitment. Those who discontinued denied the legitimacy of directives issued by the authority.

The experimenter presented a nonnegotiable position. He stated that the subject had no choice but to continue to act as directed. Some subjects mustered up their courage and rebelled.

Other subjects continued on. Several of them, again perhaps most of them, then attempted to negotiate responsibility for the consequences of their actions. One of Milgram's subjects, for example, asked, "Who is going to be responsible if that guy in there gets hurt?" The experimenter stated that he (the experimenter) was responsible and then directed the subject to comply with the directive. When both experimenter and subject agree that the experimenter is totally responsible for the consequences, the subject becomes an irresponsible actor. Subordinates in extremely authoritarian relationships often are rendered irresponsible. For example, workers sometimes ask their boss if the boss is going to take responsibility for the consequences of a worker's action. If the boss and worker agree that responsibility for the outcome will be assumed by the boss, then the worker has become nothing more than an instrument of the boss. He becomes an irresponsible human being.

The social situation created in the typical social science laboratory study is not merely an authority relationship, it is in fact a highly authoritarian situation (Sehested and Couch 1986). Furthermore, Milgram constructed situations that extenuated the authoritarian dimensions of the laboratory situation. He created a situation where the subjects explicitly committed themselves to act as subordinates, masked his intentions, proceeded to entice subjects to proceed from compliance to benign directives to compliance with malevolent directives, refused to renegotiate the parameters of the relationship, and when called upon, attempted to relieve the subordinates of responsibility for their own actions.

Milgram's work is a powerful demonstration of how easy it is to elicit compliance to the directives from authority when the action is contextualized by a highly authoritarian relationship. It demonstrates that compliance to obligations will often override compassion; at least, compassion for strangers.

The significance of the authority relationship for explaining the behavior of Milgram's subjects is suggested by the following scenario: Suppose someone with the appearance and demeanor of an uneducated janitor had the same laboratory setup as Milgram. She has no categorical identity to offer other than "someone interested in punishment and learning." Then, somehow, she entices an untenured assistant professor and the dean of liberal arts into her laboratory to serve as subjects. They draw lots to see who will be the teacher and who will be the learner. The untenured professor is the teacher and the dean the learner. Then the experimenter begins to issue the same directives as the experimenter did in Milgram's studies. How many untenured professors would proceed through all thirty switches until they reached 450 volts?

Milgram stresses the fact that the subordinates in authority relationships view themselves as agents, as merely the extension of the will of the superordinate. There is some merit to that interpretation, but it is not adequate. To an extent, some of the subordinates did locate themselves as agents. But they were more than agents. Some, in postexperimental interviews, stated that they were not responsible, that they were merely following orders. But they also suffered. Some giggled and laughed hysterically. Some claimed they were not themselves. Most, if not all, displayed some compassion for their victims. They were more than merely an extension of the will of their authority; they still empathized with their victims.

Not all who cause suffering while acting as ordered empathize with their victims. Compassion is not an automatic response to the suffering of others. For instance, some Nazi functionaries seemed to enjoy their work; some took delight in torturing and killing others. But as Hannah Arnedt notes, most of the cruelties inflicted on victims were routine acts—evil was made banal. Those who gassed the inmates of the concentration camps were merely doing their job. They acted as directed. Perhaps an important part of that structure was the development of an ideology that defined the victims as something less than human. When the targets are defined as nonhuman, compassion is less likely to be elicited.

In Milgram's studies, those who failed to comply with the directives of the experimenter did not merely disobey, they also rationalized their disobedience. They provided an explanation for their failure to comply. In one case, the subject indicates that he is going to quit. The experimenter responds by assuring the subject that while the shocks are painful, they do not cause permanent damage. The subject—teacher retorts, "Well, that's your opinion. If he does not want to continue, I'm taking orders from him." The experimenter counters with, "You have no other choice, sir; you must go on." The subject asserts, "If this were Russia maybe, but not in America," and terminates the experiment.

Subjects who refused to comply with directives that called for them to administer electric shocks did *not* disavow the authority relationships between themselves and the experimenter. They only refused to comply with directives calling for them to administer shocks. They still remained situated within an authority relationship; they continued to locate themselves as subordinate to the experimenter. When the subjects refused to comply, the authority relationships were "reactivated" on another level. The experimenter then debriefed them by explaining the "true" purpose of the study. These transactions between the subjects and experimenter were still contextualized by the mutually recognized categorical identities of authority and subordinate.

To disavow the authority relationship completely, a subject would have had either to leave the situation—flee the scene—or locate himself as an equal with the experimenter. The adoption of the latter position would have required subjects at least to indicate they were willing to challenge the legitimacy of the experimenter's identity. On occasion, subordinates challenge the authority of the superordinate. To accomplish this, it is necessary for subordinates to indicate to superordinates that they are not legitimate occupants of a position; that their categorical identity will no longer be recognized. The explicit rejection of the authority of a superordinate in any authority relationship also implicitly denies that a solidary relationship exists between superordinate and subordinate.

Milgram's dramatic studies raised the consciousness of people about some facets of human life. Some have attempted to interpret them as uncovering dark and evil facets of human nature. Such an interpretation is at best misleading. It is possible to design situations that would elicit compassionate acts instead of compliant acts. If such studies were completed, some might conclude that human beings are blessed with a compassionate trait. That conclusion would also be misleading.

Milgram created an almost pure set of authority relationships. Authority was brought to the fore relatively uncluttered by other relationships. Like the chemist who isolates a pure chemical, Milgram distilled social relationships and isolated almost pure authoritarianism. He was not entirely successful. A significant percentage of his subjects failed to comply. Lack of complete compliance stemmed from the subjects' interjecting elements of other social relationships into Milgram's laboratory. When the subject stated, "If this were Russia maybe, but not in America," he located himself in a larger solidary relationship that justified his lack of compliance.

The elements of sociation that Milgram activated in his laboratories were similar to those constructed between drill sergeants and military recruits. Military recruits enter into an authoritarian social structure. They are then explicitly assigned the categorical identity of subordinate and instructed into the intricacies of compliance linked to that categorical identity. Some rebel, but most learn to comply. If their training is successful, they do not reason why, but do or die.

So long as military relationships are encompassed by a solidary relationship that legitimates the actions of the military, the death and destruction created by soldiers is regarded as moral. If the encompassing solidarity begins to disintegrate, as it did in the United States during the Viet Nam War, then some question the morality of those who issue and comply with directives to kill others.

Benign Authority

One popular justification for authority relationships is that they are necessary to create and maintain social order. In fact, some popular interpretations of social order equate authority relationships with social order. Such an equation ignores the fact that there is a social order in egalitarian solidary relationships. The order is different, but order is as much a part of the relationships that prevail among close friends as it is a part of the relationships that prevail between privates and captains in the military. The foundation of the order is different. In the solidary relationship, there is the presumption of equality; in the authority relationship, the members are categorically differentiated and hierarchically ranked.

Not all categorical and hierarchical differentiations are malevolent; many are benign. Members of parental relationships are categorically and hierarchically differentiated. It would be impossible for human societies to endure without parental relationships. In an extension of that frame of thought, some have argued that authority relationships are also necessary in order for societies to endure. Some must be allocated the authority to assume the responsibility of directing and coordinating the actions of others. Committee meetings, families, work groups, and a multitude of other convenings of human beings seem to require the establishment of at least a mild form of authority.

When we enter the dentist's office, we activate an authority relationship. We cede control of the situation to the dentist. We open our mouth for inspection at the dentist's command. Similarly, we board the airplane at the command of the public address announcer. We abide by the directives of the policeman when leaving the parking lot at the conclusion of the football game. In these and many other social encounters, some one or limited set of others issues directives that are for the most part complied with to facilitate the achievement of social objectives. Not all comply with the directives. Sometimes, when leaving the parking lot, another driver ignores the directives of the policeman and sneaks in ahead of us. That usually elicits resentment; he should obey like the rest of us.

Summary

The establishment of all authority relationships is based on two or more persons indicating they will assign significance to the actions of each other and will relate to each other in a reciprocal but asymmetrical manner over a period of time. One distinctive feature of authority relationships is the asymmetrical surrendering of self-control. One party is conferred the prerogative of directing the actions of another. The boss may issue directives to the worker, but the worker does not have the prerogative of directing the actions of the boss.

Both parties to authority relationships agree to an asymmetrical division of labor. Compliance is a burden placed on the subordinate; responsibility for programming and coordinating the action of the collectivity is the burden placed on the superordinate. The burdens may be equally constraining and demanding, but the content of the burdens is different. The superordinate assumes primary responsibility for the accomplishment of objectives; the subordinates are responsible for acting as directed.

Some refuse to assume the responsibilities linked to positions of authority. Others become disenchanted with the "burden of office" and resign. Still others are judged incompetent and have their prerogatives stripped from them. In general, however, positions of authority are sought after, and those who occupy them usually attempt to retain them.

Subordinates in enduring authority relationship often become alienated. They would prefer to disaffiliate themselves from their position. Some do. Others remain subordinates because of external concerns. Many workers are alienated from their jobs, but remain. Some dream of acquiring a position of authority within the organization. Some are successful. Some line workers become foremen; some office clerks become managers. Others retain a lowly position as a result of external factors, for example, they are obliged to provide an income for themselves and others. If they have no other occupational opportunities, workers often retain their positions despite their alienation from the relationship.

Enduring authority relationships inherently generate some conflict between superordinates and subordinates. Superordinates assess the well-being of the relationship primarily on the basis of the achievement of objectives. Many conclude that the achievement of objectives is facilitated by the quick and ready compliance of subordinates. Reciprocally, subordinates are more likely to evaluate the relationship on the basis of the degree of subordination required. If the subordination is extreme, if they are little more than an extension of the wills of their superordinate, they are apt to become alienated. They are then likely to be slow in complying with the directives of the authority. The failure of subordinates to respond quickly and readily to directives is often a source of irritation to superordinates.

Some authority relationships, of course, endure in much the same form indefinitely. None is completely static. Most enduring authority relationships, such as those between bosses and employees, coaches and team members, officers and enlisted personnel, and prison guards and prisoners, tend to evolve toward tyranny unless safety measures are built into the relationship. Authorities usually have command of more information and resources than do their subordinates. If control of information and resources by the authority is relatively complete, then an authoritarian relationship may become tyrannical. If the control of information and resources is less than complete, then subordinates in extremely authoritarian systems are likely to withdraw from the relationship—flee the scene—or challenge the authority.

The only proper response to authority is alienation; The only proper response to alienation is revolution; The only proper revolution is the abolition of authority.

Chapter 14 Romance

Romantic relationships receive far more attention in the mass media than any other relationship. Several magazines are devoted to romantic problems, nearly every daily newspaper has a column that offers advice to the lovelorn, many publishing companies do a brisk business in sex manuals, and books are regularly published that are entitled some variant of *"How to Meet the Right Guy (Gal)."* Despite all the attention romantic relationships receive, they are poorly understood. Perhaps by approaching romantic entanglements, not as unexplainable, but as a particular form of human relationship some light may be shed on romance.

One of the obvious qualities of romantic relationships is that they are both highly pleasurable and painful. Those in the throes of a robust, pleasant romantic relationship are ecstatic; they are on top of the world. Those in the midst of a breakup of a robust romantic relationship sink to the depths of depression. Some claim it is better to have loved and lost than not to have loved at all. But some who have loved and lost conclude it is best to avoid love.

Romantic relationships are inherently contradictory. On the one hand, romance is the source of variation, excitement, and adventure. On the other hand, relationships are constant. Constancy generates boredom. When all is certain, interest tends to fade. It is very difficult simultaneously to maintain variation and constancy. Romantic relationships attempt to give stability to exciting and ever changing experiences; that is almost an impossibility.

When two people find each other attractive and exciting, they sometimes establish a romantic relationship. They thereby attempt to give stability to their association with each other. They are enticed to form an enduring relationship to obtain and provide excitement and sensual satisfaction. But as a relationship is formed, the shared past they construct often removes some of the variation and uncertainty from encounters. A viable part of romantic relationships tends to fade away as the relationship matures.

Romantic relationships do not seem to be universal; at least, robust romantic relationships are not constructed in all societies. Degrees of sensual play, intimacy, sexual arousal, and sexual satiation are present in all societies, but in many societies the romantic relationship is poorly developed. And in societies where romantic relationships are common, not

177

all in the society experience them. Some are fearful of falling in love and avoid romantic entanglements; others never have the opportunity.

Sexual encounters are not equivalent to romantic relationships. Rape certainly is not romantic. Sexual encounters usually are a viable part of romantic relationships, but many romantic relationships endure without benefit of sexual intercourse; reciprocally, many routinely have sexual intercourse without benefit of romance.

Romantic relationships take many different forms; some are relatively mild, others are very intense. Robust romantic relationships are (1) based on sensual play; (2) establish emotional and physical intimacy; (3) include repetitive lovemaking encounters; (4) produce sensual satiation; and (5) project intimacy indefinitely into the future. Each of these qualities can vary independently of the others. Some people have a love relationship that contains relatively little intimacy, while the other qualities of the relationship are fully developed. In others, one or both of the partners fails to obtain sensual satiation.

Romantic relationships, like solidary relationships, are inherently egalitarian — although in many of them one party is dominant while the other is submissive. To construct a robust romantic relationship, however, both parties must willfully and regularly make themselves highly available to the other. If one party imposes herself on the other, or maintains the relationship for ulterior motives, it deadens the relationship.

Whereas other relationships often include large numbers, each romantic relationship tends to be exclusively dyadic. On occasion, triads and larger groups have established and maintained romantic relationships, but they are rare. The intense sensations and interpersonal dependency of robust romantic relationships make it difficult for a romantic relationship to contain more than two people.

In modern societies it is widely presumed that romantic relationships provide the foundation for marriage and extend into marriage. But romance is not inherently associated with marriage. In fact, some people regard romance and marriage as antithetical; and they may have a point. Marriage is an accountable relationship; it implies constancy, obligation, and seriousness. Romance is based on variety, attraction, and playfulness.

In a cliche, a romantic relationship is established when the right chemical reactions occur when two people encounter and stimulate each other. The chemical analogy is an appropriate one. Many chemical mixtures are explosive. Similarly, romantic relationships often are explosive.

Sensual Play

Sensual play is a particular kind of mutuality. It is produced when two people find each other sensually attractive, publicly indicate their mutual attraction, and stimulate each other. Sensual play occurs whenever two people are more attentive and responsive to each other than required by the situation and at least hint that they have a passing sensual interest in the other. Each suggests the possibility of intimate and perhaps sexual contact.

Sensual play can occur almost anywhere — on elevators, at church, at work, on the street, in taverns, at gatherings of extended families, and in the privacy of a bedroom. Sensual play permeates gatherings populated by unattached young people.

The production of sensual play requires two people to indicate that each finds the other at least passingly attractive. Sensual play blossoms when both hint they have an interest in becoming intimate with the other. Many instances of sensual play do not proceed beyond the mutual expression of sensual appreciation. That was the case in the following transaction: A basketball player scored a goal. As he turned to run down the court on defense, an attractive female fan caught his eye. She blew him a kiss. The player smiled and winked at her. He quickly assumed his position on defense. They probably had no subsequent contact with each other. Each momentarily expressed attraction to, and appreciation of, the other.

To construct more significant transactions of sensual play the parties must maintain copresence and intermittently attend and respond to each other. People put themselves on display for others of the opposite sex (or the same sex in the case of homosexual encounters) and note the attention and responsiveness of others. This occurs in almost pure form in some public meeting places. As one young woman was heard to remark to another, "Lets go to Joe's Place (a local bar) and look over the studs showing themselves off."

In sensual play each person indicates availability, suggests excitement, and perhaps attempts to entice the other. Yet each has the autonomy to withdraw from the transactions at any moment. Neither imposes on the other; instead each invites the other. On many occasions, sensual play at a distance goes on for some time. If the distance is closed too rapidly, it often brings the play to an abrupt end. When people play sensually each waits for the other to invite them before closing in.

Sensual play is often intertwined with other activities. A customer may flirt with the bartender as she orders her drink. Bosses sometimes initiate sensual play with their secretaries; secretaries sometimes initiate it with their bosses. Students flirt with fellow students. And on occasion, professors have been known to cast a wink at a good-looking student.

Sensual play is conducted largely in the universe of appearance. That is especially true during the opening stages of sensual play produced in public places. It can be conducted in touch or discourse. When sensual play is interwoven with other activities, as when two students study together, it is often conducted in touch and discourse. One may sit closer to the other than is required or make a teasing statement about the other's appearance or attractiveness. When sensual play is performed in touch or discourse, however, the touch is of short duration and the discourse is usually limited to curt statements.

Most sensual play does not have lasting consequences. Most such transactions momentarily spice up life. And, of course, many times sensual play is initiated, not with the intention of establishing a romantic relationship, but to locate an acceptable sex partner.

Sensual play is a highly ambiguous form of activity. Often one person cannot ascertain the intentions of the other. Sometimes the one who initiates sensual play does not know her own intentions. She may be looking for a little excitement if the right person comes along or if the right mood happens to develop. In the words of one woman, "Oh, sometimes I just throw out a flirt to see what will happen." Some people participate in it, not with the intention of finding a sex partner or establishing a relationship, but for the excitement generated by the activity itself.

The ambiguity of the activity sometimes has explosive results. Often one person has taken the suggestive eye contact, smiles, and posturing of another as a invitation. Sometimes, when one person responds to what she regards as an invitation for more intimate contact, she is rebuffed. Rebuffs produce bruised feelings, animosity, and sometimes explosions. Sensual play between strangers nearly always is contextualized by an audience. The sensual play between people in taverns is before an audience. An audience provides some protection from explosions (Traynowics 1986). Sometimes sensual play is contextualized by other relationships. When students, co-workers, or neighbors flirt with one another, their flirtations are encased by an established relationship. But even then, sensual play can get "out of hand."

Some sensual play is highly stylized. The prototype of stylized sensual play occurs between erotic dancers and their audiences. The dancers display themselves, suggest sexual involvement as a possibility, and attempt to indicate a personal interest in at least a few members of the audience. Some establishments with erotic dancers have explicit rules prohibiting touching between the erotic dancers and the audience; some also discourage conversations between patrons and performers. Some sensual play between individuals is almost as stylized as that between erotic dancers and their audiences.

Sensual play between strangers in public places sometimes consists of rapid-fire reciprocating acts; in contrast, sensual play between those with an established nonromantic relationship, for example, co-workers, is usually slower paced and may extend over weeks, months, or even years.

Sensual play is primarily a present-centered activity. Futures are hinted at, but no specific future is promised. It is one of the most complex forms of social activity that human beings produce that is not structured by a projected future. Sensual play is a "here and now" phenomenon.

The lack of a projected future and the self-exposure required for its production are two of the qualities that make sensual play an explosive form of activity. To do it well requires one to be very attentive and responsive. But one party may "turn off" and thereby publicly humiliate the other. That can be very stressful. Sensual play often has unanticipated and unintended consequences. It generates excitement, but not fulfillment.

The production of sensual play does not establish a romantic relationship. It is often the first step toward the establishment of a romantic relationship and sometimes continues to infuse romantic relationships. Yet it seems that sensual play tends to fade away as romantic relationships mature. Perhaps one reason is that as intimacy is established, the uncertainty that is an inherent part of playfulness is removed. Perhaps a second reason is that lovemaking is too intense an activity to allow for much playfulness.

Intimacy

Most people with a robust romantic relationship are both emotionally and physically intimate—although some lovers love from afar; they are emotionally intimate but not physically intimate. Other lovers are physically intimate, but not emotionally intimate. Sometimes a high level of emotional intimacy is established before any physical intimacy is initiated. At other times, people become physically intimate, including having sexual intercourse, without becoming emotionally intimate.

Intimacy is almost strictly a dyadic phenomenon. Sensual play is also dyadic. But sensual play is usually contextualized by either an audience or a nonromantic relationship. In contrast, the construction of intimacy requires creating situations that remove all factors except the two people who are becoming intimate. If the sensual play that precedes intimacy has been produced in front of an audience, those who wish to become intimate seclude themselves from the audience or render the presence of the audience inconsequential. Sometimes the audience cooperates and removes itself. Parents have been known to leave the scene so that young people can be by themselves. If the sensual play was contextualized by another relationship, that relationship is pushed to the background as those involved focus on each other and what transpires between them. When intimacy blossoms, each person becomes the center of attention for the other, and all other concerns recede into the background.

Movement toward intimacy validates the indications of mutual attractiveness that have been hinted at in sensual play. When people become intimate they indicate to each other that the other is worthy of serious attention.

Playfulness is replaced by seriousness. Of course, elements of playfulness may be interwoven with intimacy, but it is subordinated to a concern for the other.

As intimacy is established appearance recedes to the background; discourse and touch come to the fore. Sometimes the discourse precedes touch; at other times, touch precedes discourse. In either event a transformation in how evaluations of the other are made takes place. When people began talking and acquiring personal information about each other, the person who appeared very attractive and sparked one's interest may now be revealed as an overbearing, self-centered dolt. In a similar manner, when people begin touching each other, one may touch too aggressively and turn off the other (Traynowics 1986).

Both kinds of intimacy usually proceed from incidental intimacy to intense intimacy, although sometimes couples become either emotionally or physically intimate quite rapidly. The maturation of emotional intimacy occurs by each individual informing the other about personal interests, desires, phobias, and pasts. Sometimes it becomes established by the individuals telling one another all about themselves; at other times, it begins by one or both gently quizzing the other. Physical intimacy usually proceeds by individuals physically locating themselves next to each other, to incidental touching, to hand holding and kissing, to caressing.

In many cases, the maturation of the two forms of intimacy are closely intertwined. For example, two people might meet at a party, engage in a little sensual play followed by one asking the other to dance. Dancing establishes a mild form of physical intimacy. While dancing, they may exchange information about themselves. They may then sit next to each other, somewhat isolating themselves from others, and continue exchanging information about themselves. Before the evening is over, they may agree to date next week or maybe even go to bed with each other that night. In either event, they begin establishing themselves as a dyad and separate themselves from others.

Dating is an institution that facilitates the establishment and expansion of intimacy. When a couple convene and reconvene on dates, they usually move toward both greater emotional and physical intimacy — although to become emotionally intimate does not necessarily imply physical intimacy, nor does physical intimacy necessarily imply emotional intimacy.

Both kinds of intimacy carry risks. Whenever one person tells another about herself, she provides the other person with information that might later be embarrassing or might even be used against her if the budding relationship disintegrates. Reciprocally, by sharing information about themselves, the couple can establish if they are compatible, and each can also use the information to please the other. Self-exposure is a two-edged sword.

Physical intimacy obviously is risky. It has frequently lead to disasters. Many women have gone on a date, engaged in some petting with no intention of becoming sexually intimate, refused the advances of their partner, and been raped.

Intimate couples have their own little private world. They know things about each other and about what they have done that are not shared with the rest of the world. Dyadic privacy is a critical quality of all romantic relationships. If everything that occurs between two people is also shared with outsiders, it is impossible to maintain a robust romantic relationship. Perhaps one reason why robust romantic relationships are rare among small, primitive groups is that there are few secrets in such societies. Nearly everyone knows everything about everyone else.

Many romantic relationships have been shattered by one party making private information public. Lovers keep some of the information they have about each other and themselves as a unit from others.

Lovemaking

One quality that distinguishes human beings from all other animals is that they can intentionally sexually arouse themselves and each other. Other animals sexually display themselves and arouse the opposite sex, but the sexual displays and arousal of other animals are not under conscious control. The sexuality of other animals is physiological; it is not produced with the intention of providing oneself and another with a specific set of sensations. The sexuality of human beings also has physiological dimensions, but they are consciously controlled.

Mutual sexual arousal is one of the most intense, complex, delicate, and fulfilling of all social activities. Not all sexual encounters elicit intense sensations, but many do. The pleasures derived from satisfactory sexual encounters can be matched by few other experiences. The production of mutual sexual arousal is an exceedingly complex activity. Many never master the ability to sexually stimulate others; some become very adept at it. The production of mutually satisfying sexual experiences requires that both partners be sensitive to each other's and their own sensations while experiencing intense sensations. When these conditions are met, lovemaking can be the source of intense mutual satisfaction. When these conditions are not met, sexual encounters can be frustrating and painful.

Lovemaking is even more a dyadic event than is sensual play and intimacy. Each partner gives his entire attention to the other and to his own sensations; no attention is given to anything else. Each becomes entirely engrossed in each other's and his own feelings. The production of satisfying lovemaking sessions requires dyadic privacy. It occurs behind closed doors.

No telephones, no kids, no external distractions are allowed. If external distractions do occur they usually shatter the occasion.

Not all sexual encounters are lovemaking sessions; rape certainly is not lovemaking. Nor is lovemaking restricted to sexual activity. Kissing, caressing, expressions of mutual appreciation and many other activities are viable features of lovemaking sessions.

Not all lovemaking sessions are dyadic. Group orgies occur; and they are satisfying to some. But group orgies do not provide the experiences necessary for the validation of a romantic relationship. On occasion, three or more people have produced lovemaking sessions that were a part of a romantic relationship, but triadic and larger romantic relationships rarely endure.

Sensual play often is constructed primarily in appearance and intimacy is established by touch and discourse. In contrast, touching is the heart and soul of lovemaking. Some lovemaking sessions are restricted entirely to tactile contact and communication via touch. The tactile contact ranges from gentle touch to vigorous sexual intercourse. Appearance and discourse can be arousing, but tactile stimulation is more arousing for most.

It is necessary for both persons to make themselves highly available to each other as objects to achieve a high level of sensual arousal. They expose their unprotected bodies to each other to receive and provide sensual stimulation. They thereby increase their physical intimacy. They also usually become more emotionally intimate. Through lovemaking we come to know some of each other's deepest feelings and those stimulations that produce the most intense sensations.

Lovemaking is a complex social act. When making love, people simultaneously stimulate each other, expose themselves to receive stimulation, provide each other information about their ongoing sensations, and acquire information about each other. Sometimes all of these are accomplished entirely by communicating through touch. And the sensations are often very intense.

When contact is limited to the tactile mode, it is difficult to determine with any certainty the sensations of the other. About the only information communicated when contact is limited to the tactile mode is whether the contact is pleasant or painful. If the other person maintains close tactile contact it is assumed the stimulation is pleasant; if the person withdraws, that it is less than pleasant. Expressive vocal gestures, assertions, and facial gestures sometime are sources of information about the other's sensations.

One of the paradoxes of lovemaking is that while tactile stimulation is the primary means for producing high states of arousal, it is, comparatively speaking, a relatively ineffective means for informing the other of the specifics of one's sensations. Given the fact that lovemaking is heavily dependent on tactile stimulation, that the tactile mode is a relatively ineffective means of acquiring information about another person, and the intensity of the sensations elicited, it is understandable that lovemaking encounters do not always produce mutual satisfaction.

The high level of physical intimacy required for intense lovemaking also makes each person highly vulnerable to the other. An act intended to arouse deep and pleasant sensations sometimes is experienced as adverse impingement. The squeeze, pinch, kiss, or pelvic thrust intended to heighten sexual arousal may be too intense; an act intended to produce great excitation may produce pain.

Lovemaking is far more than merely providing and receiving tactile stimulation and experiencing intense sensations. The production of high levels of satisfactory sexual arousal requires each to note the indicators of the sensations of the other and to organize their actions to provide pleasureable stimulation for the other. If one partner is concerned only with personal sensations, or if one responds like a fencepost, high levels of mutual arousal are unlikely to be achieved. Intense and satisfactory sexual arousal requires sensitivity and thoughtfulness; it is not an automatic response to intense tactile stimulation.

The production of mutually satisfactory lovemaking is facilitated by each providing the other with indications of one's sensations. A groan of appreciation informs the other that what she has done or is doing is satisfying. Nonetheless, the display of these sensations is a two-edged sword. On the one hand, it provides the other with information that a given stimulation is pleasureable; on the other hand, it may lead to habitual lovemaking. In subsequent encounters, each may attempt to produce the same acts that elicited appreciation in the previous encounters. When that occurs, some of the spark that was present in earlier encounters may lessen.

Lovemaking, like all forms of social action, has several temporal dimensions. It occurs across time; lovers use their pasts to project futures, and they time their actions with each other. The encounter may begin with incidental touch, kissing, stroking, and caressing, leading to nude bodies becoming entangled, followed by vigorous intercourse. The movement across time from the beginning to the consummation of the sex act requires not only delicate and intense mutual stimulation but also each must note the other's state of arousal. One person may be more aroused than the other; to achieve equal levels of arousal, it may be necessary for one to withhold herself momentarily from the stimulations of the other.

Those who are sexually experienced use their pasts to organize their activity toward the other both to provide the other with pleasant sensations and to achieve pleasant sensations. Nonetheless, lovemaking is largely a present-centered activity. Pasts inform the activity and projected futures structure it, but to achieve high levels of mutual arousal, each must focus primarily on the immediate ongoing responses of the other. The only futures necessary are the proximal futures projected for each other's sensations. Each attempts to provide the other with a pleasant experience in the immediate future. It is not necessary to project a shared future to produce intense arousal. Of course, many lovers project the shared future of simultaneous orgasms, but that is not a necessary element for effective lovemaking. In fact, if too much attention is allocated to the shared future of simultaneous orgasms, it may lessen the level of arousal.

Turn-taking is not a necessary part of lovemaking. Of course, the activity can be performed in much the same way as people converse. One first can be primarily a stimulator, while the other is the recipient of the stimulation; then the other can be primarily a stimulator, while the other is the recipient. More commonly, lovers simultaneously stimulate and receive stimulation.

A common complaint of those who have been lovers for some time is that their lovemaking has lost its original spark. One of the reasons seems to be that the relationship has lost some of the ambiguity and uncertainty that pervades sensual play and the developmental stages of intimacy. As a romantic relationship becomes established, each person becomes more capable of anticipating the other's actions and responses. Playful and nonthreatening variation appear to be essential for the maintenance of highly satisfactory romantic relationships. One of the paradoxes of romantic relationships is how to continue the excitement of sensual play after the emotional and physical intimacy associated with lovemaking is established.

Mutual Satisfaction

A romantic relationship is validated when the partners acknowledge to each other that each satisfies the desires for sensate pleasure of the other. The cohesiveness of romantic relationships rests on the pleasure bond (Masters and Johnson 1974). Those with a purely romantic relationship have no other objectives than to receive pleasure from the other and provide pleasure for the other. The sources of pleasure are not necessarily restricted to sexual activity, although in some cases they are largely restricted to sexual pleasure.

The cohesiveness of purely romantic relationships is often very intense, but nonetheless fragile. Even relationships where both parties feel they could not live without the other often disintegrate. Sometimes the disintegration occurs as a result of external factors; at other times, one or both partners becomes bored with the other. Viable romantic relationships provide one of the most basic forms of pleasure that human beings experience. Nonetheless, mutual pleasure is a fragile foundation for an enduring association.

Romantic relationships are often intertwined with other relationships. Elements of solidarity often infuse romantic relationships. In many romantic relationships elements of solidarity are established before the relationship enters the lovemaking stage. When a couple do things together and find they have the same reactions to their activities, elements of solidarity are introduced. Additional elements of solidarity are often based on lovemaking itself. For example, when the lovemaking encounters are satisfactory to both, they are likely to elicit the response, "We are good for each other," from both.

Commitment

Romantic relationships often emerge in much the same way that solidary relationships do. Many begin by two people indicating their mutual attraction, beginning to do things together, becoming increasingly intimate, falling in love, and restricting their intimate heterosexual associations to each other. In the process the couple construct a private world that separates them from others and is to some extent based on emotional or physical intimacy or both. The shared pasts of romantic relationships are usually more private than the shared pasts of solidary relationships.

In many instances, as the shared past becomes elaborated and intimacy intensifies, both parties begin assuming that they will continue to reconvene in intimate and perhaps lovemaking encounters. Both begin presuming (or hoping) that the intimacy and pleasure each has with the other is restricted to them; that neither is intimate with others. Many intensely intimate romantic relationships develop without the couple explicitly committing themselves to each other. They begin dating only each other, having sexual relations only with each other, or living together. Each simply begins taking it for granted that theirs is an exclusive relationship.

Other couples explicitly commit themselves to an exclusive relationship; they agree that they will be intimate only with one another. Some couples become steadies; others live together; still others become engaged.

Whether the commitment implicitly emerges or is explicitly constructed, a new dimension is created. The two agree that they have a shared future that is exclusively theirs, that some aspects of their relationship are private, and that they will be "true to each other." Some couples explicitly construct an open relationship. They agree that each person can have sexual relationships with others but that their relationship will be the predominate one. Open romantic relationships, generally speaking, are more exciting, but provide less security than closed ones.

Marriage

Many believe the ideal marriage is based on romance. Those who subscribe to that ideal presume that when a couple mutually agree they are romantically attracted to each other, and believe their attraction will endure, they agree to marriage. Not all believe that romance is a sufficient foundation on which to build a marriage. Some take the position that romance and marriage are not necessarily linked to each other. Still others take the position that marriages should be based on such factors as similarities in family background and/or compatible personalities. Many who take the latter position hope that romance will blossom after marriage but that if it does not, so be it.

Some students of romance and marriage argue that the two relationships are inherently incompatible. Briefly their argument is that romance requires intense exciting variability in the here and now; that marriage is an intense form of accountability composed of constancy, obligations to each other, and obligations of the couple to the larger community. Further, they argue that romance is based on dyadic privacy and that marriage is a public relationship. When a couple marry, a third party—the community—becomes part of the relationship.

Romantic relationships and accountable relationships are composed of different elements of sociation. It seems that some elements that compose the two relationships are incompatible. The constancy and third-party elements of accountable relationships are inconsistent with the variability and dyadic privacy that are critical elements of romantic relationships.

A counterargument can be made, namely, that purely romantic relationships are so explosive and threatening that without the interjection of some elements of accountability, those who compose the relationships find it too threatening. To achieve the security necessary for an intense and mutually satisfying romance, it is necessary to encase the romantic relationship within an accountable relationship. At least some people seem to be able to construct a more robust romantic relationship within an accountable context than they can when no commitments are made. Of course, others regard the commitments of marriage as antithetical to romance. Still others simply do not wish to make the commitments associated with marriage.

Therapy

All social relationships have problems associated with them. Many of the subordinates in parental relationships think that their superordinates are holding them back, that they are not given the opportunity to mature as rapidly as they can. Members of solidary relationships sometimes find the relationship constraining. Accountable relationships are often thought of as being too demanding; the effort required to fulfill one's obligations is too great. Some authorities regard the responsibilities associated with the position as being overbearing; and subordinates of authority relationships often regard their authority as overbearing. The problems associated with romantic relationships seem to be more pervasive than those associated with parental, solidary, accountable, and authority relationships. Perhaps that seems to be the case simply because problems associated with romantic relationships are talked and written about more than problems associated with other relationships. In any event, many people specialize in offering treatment for messed-up romantic relationships.

One of the better known therapeutic traditions stems from the research of Masters and Johnson (1970, 1974). Two distinctive features of their therapy are that: (1) it is based on extensive research; and (2) the unit of analysis of the research is the couple (dyad).

The therapy procedures of Masters and Johnson derive from their research and is relationship focused; they do not treat individuals. One might argue that their therapy is directed to the resolution of sexual problems, not romantic problems. But when the therapy resolves sexual problems, it often allows couples to form a more robust romantic relationship than they had.

The typical therapeutic session lasts two weeks. Couples are required to remove themselves from their mundane, day-to-day world. Each couple leaves their community and rents a room in a hotel or a small apartment. They are instructed to free themselves from all other obligations. That procedure creates a context wherein the couple is more likely to focus on each other and on the therapists for the duration of the treatment. It attempts to create a situation where intimacy is given the opportunity to flourish.

The therapy is dyadic. One therapist works primarily with the woman, the other primarily with the man. Each person is first interviewed by a therapist of the same sex. On occasion, all four parties meet in group sessions. Also on occasion, the two therapists meet with only one partner. Each therapist is a supporter of the partner of the same sex. Both therapists offer instructions to the couple. The therapists avoid becoming mediators. They concentrate on determining and understanding the sensual problems of the couple and instructing the couple in sensate experiences.

The specific therapeutic procedures applied depend on the particular problems of the couple. In general, however, the treatment is sequenced to move from incidental or limited sexual stimulation to intense sexual activity. One procedure consists of instructing the couple how to stimulate each other. The couple is told to practice "sensate focus;" but not to attempt sexual intercourse. For example, the male may first stimulate the female with his hands while the female concentrates on her own sensations; then they reverse positions. They are told not to give each other a massage, but to find out what stimulation is especially pleasing to the other. The couple is instructed not to touch each other's breast, vagina, penis, or testicles during the first session or two.

The importance of touch as a means of communication is stressed. The person receiving the stimulation is told to guide the hands of the stimulator by his own hands. Discourse is kept to a minimum. These exercises "break up" lovemaking. Instead of both parties attempting to stimulate the other and receive stimulation, they take turns. The objectives are to make each person a more competent stimulater, to make each more aware of the other's sensations, and each more aware of his own sensations.

The sensate focus exercises proceed to more intense stimulation, but sexual intercourse is still forbidden. After the first session or two, the couple, depending on their progress, may be allowed to stimulate each other's genitals manually. They are instructed to concentrate on their own sensations and note what is pleasureable to the other. They are told to concentrate on the present. They are explicitly instructed not to concern themselves with achieving orgasms. They are to concentrate on the here and now.

The therapy attempts to free both parties of any sense of obligation, to remove all accountability from the relationship. "In a continuing relationship sex-as-service rarely leads to sustained pleasure" (Masters and Johnson 1974, 12). The therapy attempts to get the clients to focus on stimulations and sensations, not on the fulfillment of obligations.

The therapists attempt to remove any "third parties," real or imaginary, from the sensate focus exercises. Exercises and instructions are organized to focus attention on each other's sensation and each person on his or her own sensations. Clients are told that the problem is a dyadic or relationship problem, not the problem of one or the other.

The therapeutic procedures of Masters and Johnson are far more sensitive and complex than this brief overview indicates. They recognize that the resolution of romantic problems also requires creating conditions that facilitate the development of mutual trust. They observe that a "powerful sense of emotional well-being comes when each partner knows that at times of greatest vulnerability the other can be relied on to provide warmth, comfort and protection" (Masters and Johnson 1974, 56).

The therapy of Masters and Johnson is distinct from that of many others. It recognizes that sexual and romantic problems are properties of dyads, that many of the problems stem from incompetencies, and that lovemaking is a very complex and fragile form of social activity. To resolve problems, therefore, the therapy must be relationship focused, provide those who compose the relationship with the instructions necessary to complete the act successfully, and make lovers aware of the intensity and fragility of the activity.

Summary

Romantic relationships are not necessary for the survival of the human species, nor even for the continuation of societies. Robust romantic relationships are rarely, if ever, developed in some societies. Societies without them or with only poorly developed romantic relationships continue on. Many individual citizens of societies pervaded by romantic relationships go through life without becoming romantically involved. Some people have no interest in becoming romantically involved; some never have the opportunity; some attempt again and again to form romantic relationships, but either through bad luck, their own incompetencies, or the incompetencies of others never establish a lasting romantic relationship. Some establish a robust romantic relationship only to have it transform into a boring prison.

The intensity, durability, and extensiveness of romantic relationships are highly varied. Some are infused with sensual play; others contain almost no sensual play. Some are deeply intimate; others contain almost no emotional intimacy. Some lovers have thousands of intensely arousing lovemaking sessions; others none or almost none. Some are very satisfying to both parties, others to only one party, and some to neither.

Some dyads become physically intimate before they engage in sensual play. Others form romantic relationships with only little if any sensual play. In general, however, the sequential development of romantic relationships is from expressions of mutual attraction through sensual play, to emotional and/or physical intimacy, to lovemaking, to mutual satisfaction, and finally to commitment.

Romantic relationships are often complexly intertwined with other social relationships. They are inherently an egalitarian form, but many lovers establish and maintain an authority relationship that is intertwined with their romantic relationship.

Robust romantic relationships come closer to transforming two people into a single unit that any other relationship. In the extreme case, the two selves that compose the relationship almost become merged into a single self. The partners in such relationships sometimes literally find it impossible to live without each other.

Romantic relationships are but one form of social order. They provide us with emotional breadth, depth, and joy. But there is far more to human life than romantic relationships. Romantic relationships do not provide the foundation for the development of the ability to project and carry out long-range programs of action. Love, no matter how intense or enduring, is not sufficient for the construction of complex social structures.

Nonetheless, robust romantic relationships are far more than merely highly emotional encounters. They are mindful activities. Both their construction and continuation require not only sensitivity to the feelings of others but also thoughtful consideration of the other and the relationship between self and other.

Chapter 15 Exchange Relationships

Members of all societies must extract the necessities of life — food, clothing, and shelter — from their environment to survive. Some, for example, the young and infirm, are incapable of providing for themselves. Others must provide them with the necessities of life if they are to survive. Systems of production and distribution developed by human beings range in complexity from the simple food gathering and sharing procedures of nomadic bands to the complex technological production procedures and elaborate mass distribution processes of modern capitalist and communist societies. The distribution of goods is a social activity. At the minimum, one person supplies a service or good, and another receives it. One of the procedures for distributing goods and services in modern societies is through exchange relationships.

Human beings have developed and used many forms of social relationships to structure the distribution of goods and services. Systems of distribution range from those wherein all share with all others when food is available to those wherein the distribution of goods is structured by exchange relationships. In the idealized communist world, all contribute according to their ability and all receive according to their need. In the idealized capitalist world, all acquire goods and services at the market.

A close look at the distribution procedures of any society reveals that several procedures of distribution are practiced in most societies. Three of the most common procedures for distributing goods are sharing, centralized accumulation and dispersal, and exchange relationships. Other procedures that distribute goods include gift giving, charity, theft, looting and begging. Most of these forms of distribution can be observed in all human societies. In some societies, however, one form tends to be the dominate means for the distribution of goods.

In most primitive nomadic groups the predominate mode of distribution during times of plenty is sharing. In times of stress, members of primitive groups often fail to share with each other. Then individuals bargain for, beg for, and steal necessities (Holmberg 1969). Nor is the distribution of goods by sharing limited to primitive groups. In modern societies family members share with one another. When goods are shared, whether among a band of primitive food gatherers or within a family in modern society, the distribution of goods is structured by solidary relationships. Primitive bands normally share their goods only with other members of their band; in modern societies, most share only with family members.

In communist societies many goods and services are distributed by centralized accumulation and dispersal of resources. When goods and services are centrally accumulated and dispersed the distribution of goods is structured by a combination of solidary, accountable, and authority relationships.

In market-centered economies the predominate procedure for the distribution of goods is via exchange relationships. Exchange relationships are a major dimension of the social structure of Western societies. But societies with a market-centered system of distribution distribute many goods by other means. All modern capitalist societies also distribute some goods and services via centralized accumulation of wealth by taxation and the subsequent dispersal of goods and services. Reciprocally, despite the efforts of some communist nations to eradicate markets, the distribution of some goods within those societies is accomplished via exchange relationships.

The social structures of modern Western societies are so infused with exchange relationships that some have advanced the claim that they dominate all other social relationships. Polanyi (1957) developed the theory that before the industrial revolution, other relationships structured and constrained the distribution of goods. In contrast, according to Polanyi, in modern capitalist societies exchange relationships have come to dominate all other social relationships; other social relationships are only reflections of exchange relationships.

Exchange relationships occupy a central position in the lives of most adult citizens of Western societies. Nonetheless, the exchange relationship developed long before the industrial revolution. The evolutionary trajectory from primitive means of distribution to modern commercialism was from bargaining to exchange relationships to markets to industrial societies. In a parallel manner, as each individual becomes incorporated into the social fabric of modern societies, he first masters the intricacies of bargaining, acquires command of exchange relationships, and then becomes a participant in trade networks.

Nonetheless, Polanyi, who equates the arise of exchange relationships with the industrial revolution, does have a point. Not until after the industrial revolution was well under way did exchange relationships achieve a position of prominence in the social structure of societies. Exchange relationships and mercenary concerns infuse many human associations in modern societies. But in even the most highly industrialized societies, exchange relationships do not completely dominate human life (although at some markets nearly all other social relationships are relegated to a secondary position). But not all social encounters at markets are contextualized by the exchange relationship. Some social action produced by those who congregate at markets is contexualized by other social relationships. Reciprocally, exchange relationships are often activated at other locations besides markets.

An exchange relationship is activated when two people (1) establish contact for the purpose of acquiring a good or service in exchange for some other good or service; (2) establish congruent categorical indentities of buyer and seller; (3) attend primarily to one another's good or service during the encounter while giving little consideration to one another's welfare; (4) organize actions toward one another on the basis of a cost-benefit calculus; and (5) complete or fail to complete an exchange on the basis of their assessment of future benefit to self. Exchange relationships are activated for the explicit purpose of exchanging goods or services; they have no other objective.

The activation of the exchange relationship often collapses the act of bargaining. The making of offers and counteroffers often does not occur when an exchange relationship is activated. Instead goods are displayed at a set price by some, while others examine the goods and their prices. When that condition is established, shopping replaces bargaining. At some markets, people both shop and bargain.

Mercenary Contacts

The central feature of mercenary contacts is that one or both parties intentionally makes contact with the other for the purpose of acquiring some item in exchange for another item. Usually, mercenary contacts are item specific; those who initiate them are interested in acquiring a specific good or service. On occasion, individuals frequent markets to shop—to locate a good buy. The exchange relationship is activated when a "good buy" is located.

In modern societies we frequent stores, shops, and markets to obtain items of interest. But mercenary contacts are often initiated in other locations. Door-to-door salespersons go from home to home attempting to establish mercenary contacts; others call us on the telephone and attempt to activate an exchange relationship. In modern societies, when mercenary contacts are initiated outside stores, shops, and markets, it is usually sellers who initiate them. Only occasionally do buyers seek out others for a specific good or service.

Primitive bands do not have marketplaces. Keill (1977) provides an insightful description of how groups without markets establish mercenary contacts. Individuals from two of these groups meet and negotiate a time and place for a meeting of the two groups for the purpose of acquiring each other's products. These groups live in the same general area, but do not have routinized contact with each other. At the designated time and place, the two groups meet and display their goods and examine the goods offered by the other group. The value of the products displayed and traded is limited, but nonetheless the contacts are strictly mercenary. "The relationship between the parties to the exchanges seem to consist of nothing more than the transfer of goods itself" (Keill 1977, 259).

All the members of one group presume that all the goods displayed by members of the other group are for sale. All the bargaining is intergroup; no one bargains with fellow tribesmen. Each person makes contact with members of the other group solely for the purpose of acquiring the goods on display by offering something in return.

Each time a citizen of a modern society goes to the store or to a market to acquire goods and services, he establishes contact with others on the same basis. Potential buyers go to where the goods and services are offered and make contact with others solely for the purpose of acquiring possession of a good or service by offering another good or service in return.

Congruent Categorical Identities

When a mercenary contact is established at a marketplace, the congruent categorical identities of seller and buyer are usually activated the moment contact is made. When a person approaches goods on display, the person displaying the goods assumes that the one approaching is interested in purchasing the goods; the one approaching the display assumes that the person displaying the goods is interested in selling the goods. When the assumptions of both are correct, a mercenary contact and congruent categorical identities (as buyer and seller) are activated simultaneously. Congruent categorical identities of buyer and seller are often activated via communication in the universe of appearance. A seller who notes a potential buyer examining a good might attempt to activate congruent functional identities of bargainers by asking, "Are you interested?". The seller may be successful or may elicit the response of, "No thanks, I'm just looking."

If congruent functional identities of bargainers are established an offer-counteroffer sequence may follow. Bargaining is pervasive at primitive markets. But shopping has largely replaced bargaining as the means of completing exchanges in modern societies. Shoppers go from outlet to outlet examining goods and their prices and making decisions to purchase or not on the basis of the relative worth and cost of items.

In modern societies most of the routine purchases for food and clothing are made by shopping. The consummation of major economic exchanges usually includes some bargaining. When an automobile or home is purchased, most people both shop and bargain.

When an exchange relationship is activated, no other identities than those of buyer and seller are relevant. Of course, in many mercenary encounters, other identities are activated. Sellers of used cars usually are not content with establishing only their identity as seller; they usually also attempt to establish the identity of "honest person."

The categorical identities of buyer and seller can be established at locations other than markets. For example, a man may find out that his friend plans to sell his motorcycle. The man may then attempt to activate the identities of buyer and seller. The potential seller may indicate that while he is interested in selling his motorcycle, he prefers not to sell it to his friend. He may inform his friend that the motorcycle has hidden defects. In such instances, other relationships contextualize the encounter and prevent the activation of the identities of buyer and seller.

Pure exchange relationships are not contextualized by either a shared past or a shared future. Each person takes the other into account in the here and now solely on the basis of their categorical identities as buyer and seller. Both bring to the encounter common pasts that allow them to identify each other correctly as buyer and seller, and they organize their actions toward each other solely on the basis of those identities. The only extended temporal dimensions activated in exchange relationships are those of common pasts and contingent futures. A pure exchange relationships is established when two strangers consensually identify each other as buyer and seller and have no intention of having any contact with each other after their mercenary encounter is completed. When a buyer and seller consummate a transaction contextualized by an exchange relationship and anticipate that they will have further contact with each other, then an element of accountability may become part of the exchange relationship.

Bargaining is not limited to encounters contextualized by the categorical identities of buyer and seller. Friends sometimes bargain with each other; and spouses often make deals with each other. When that occurs, however, the transactions are constrained by other considerations; they are not strictly mercenary encounters (although some spouses seem to have largely an exchange relationship.) In some marriages, each maintains the marriage largely on the basis of anticipated payoff. In general, however, when friends, lovers, and spouses bargain, they usually are sensitive to the consequences an exchange will have for their solidary or romantic relationship. One distinctive feature of social encounters framed by the congruent categorical identities of buyer and seller is the absence of any concern for the welfare of the other; mercenary encounters are populated by self-centered individuals.

Focus on Goods

Potential buyers roam through stores and markets and leaf through catalogs assessing the goods displayed. Attention is focused on the goods offered; no attention is given the other; each party views the other simply as a means for acquiring items of interest. Each party assesses the items offered and compares them with similar items offered by others. Each party is simply an instrument for the other. Despite the instrumental nature of mercenary encounters, they are complex social endeavors. At the minimum, both parties attend to what can be obtained for what. In addition, in most mercenary encounters the items offered by the other are compared to similar items that can be obtained from other sellers.

When the exchange relationship is established between experienced traders, each is aware of the orientation of the other. Each attempts to make his items as attractive as possible and that often leads to false advertisement. Sometimes, goods are doctored to make them appear of greater worth than they are; other times, claims are made that are not authentic. Sellers frequently misinform buyers. The dictum "buyer beware" informs the behavior of many traders.

Consequently, mercenary encounters, especially those activated at a market where there are several sellers in competition with one another are often explosive. Romantic encounters are also explosive, but the explosive nature of the two forms of encounters stems from different factors. The explosive nature of romantic encounters stems from the high level of vulnerability and the intense sensations that are inherent features of romantic encounters. In contrast, the explosions that occur at markets usually stem from some combination of deception, the lack of temporal depth of the relationship, and the mixed motives that are inherent features of bargaining.

The focus on goods and the lack of attention to the other person in encounters contextualized by the exchange relationship make them more open than many relationships. During the formative periods of solidary, accountable, authority, and romantic relationships, the attention of each is primarily focused on the other person. People with undesirable characteristics are often excluded from those relationships on the basis of their personal characteristics. In contrast, when the focus is primarily on the items offered by the other, then social contact is often established with people who would be avoided in other circumstances.

Cost-Benefit Calculus

Those who make their living as traders do not become embedded with or obliged to others. The level of involvement with others by professional traders in encounters contextualized by an exchange relationship tends to be shallow. Sophisticated traders are almost walking calculators. Each time they examine items offered by another person they compare them with items offered by others, calculate the benefit that might be derived by making an exchange, and make assessments of future developments. Professional traders are neither altruistic nor responsible persons; but they are rational.

Some encounters contextualized by an exchange relationship are structured by one party projecting a distal future and by the other party projecting a proximal future. Many people buy or sell impulsively; however, in the long run, impulsive buyers and sellers lose out. They do not become professional traders. Those who are most rationalistic, who decide to sell and buy solely on the basis of a long range cost-benefit calculus, tend to succeed. It is they who dominate markets, not the impulsive buyers and sellers.

Professional traders become informed people as a consequence of participation in a multitude of mercenary encounters. Markets are not merely clusters of exchange relationships; they are also the focal points of communication networks. Valuable information flows through markets. Traders usually are better informed than those who only infrequently participate in mercenary encounters. Professional traders often use their information to take advantage of amateurs.

Personal Benefit

When individuals activate an exchange relationship, each anticipates that he will benefit from the encounter. For example, when a man with more green beans than he wishes to consume contacts a man with more tomatoes than he wishes to consume, and each desires the other's vegetable, an exchange will benefit both. Nonetheless, the fulfillment of the other's anticipation of deriving benefit is of no concern to either party in a pure exchange relationship. Each person structures action on the basis of anticipations of the consequences of making an exchange for himself. Often, of course, both do benefit, but that outcome does not structure their action. The objectives that structure exchange relationships are personal, not collective.

Most social encounters contextualized by social relationships are informed by a shared past and structured by a shared distal future. In contrast, mercenary encounters contextualized by an exchange relationship require neither a shared past nor a shared distal future. All that is necessary are common pasts that allow each to identify the other as a buyer or seller with each projecting a personal future of acquiring benefit from the encounter.

When the exchange is effected in face-to-face encounters, it is necessary for the participants to project a proximal future of the possibility of effecting an exchange. The mass distribution systems of modern societies make it possible to effect exchanges without even a proximal shared future. Those who mass produce goods project a future that some people will be interested in their product, produce the items, and put them on display. Potential buyers shop and examine the items on display. Many goods are distributed in modern societies without the sellers and buyers establishing contact with one another. The prototype of this particular distribution is the vending machine. Some people place items of interest to consumers in vending machines, and others extract the items from the machines; the seller and buyer never establish contact with each other.

Neither a collective concern nor a concern with the other need be activated in mercenary encounters. In fact, concern with the other or with a collectivity places an individual at a disadvantage in mercenary encounters. The most successful individuals are those who are solely concerned with themselves. The self-centered (selfish) individual has an advantage over the altruistic person at the marketplace. Greedy people advance and altruistic ones fall by the wayside at markets.

Markets

Markets take many forms. Ancient and primitive markets simply consisted of recognized locations where pluralities of individuals congregated for the purpose of selling and buying goods (Couch 1984a, Chpt 6). They emerged out of exchange relationships and consisted of clusters of exchange relationships. Modern industrial societies contain many different markets. Some of them, like shopping malls, are similar to the ancient primitive markets; others are highly specialized. Some are legal; others operate underground. Whatever their content and form, they all share the characteristic of a plurality of people knowing where and with whom they can establish contact to acquire a good or service.

One distinctive feature of markets is that they consist of clusters of relatively open relationships. Anyone with the necessary resources is free to enter the market. On entering a market, however, every man is on his own. If he succeeds, well and good; if he fails and starves to death, that is his problem. The coldness and impersonal nature of exchange relationships at markets renders each person vulnerable to rapid and catastrophic changes. Those who enter markets with limited resources at their command usually fall by the wayside. They become beggars or hangers-on, and some starve. Few professional traders shed a tear for those who fall by the wayside.

Not only is the success of each person subject to rapid changes but markets themselves are highly volatile. They are so volatile that it is almost impossible to maintain a market based solely on exchange relationships.

Most markets also contain elements of solidarity, accountability, and authority. Professional traders form associations on the basis of their common interests. They thereby construct a degree of solidarity. They then collectively endow some individuals with the responsibility of policing the market and resolving disputes. The function of these specialists are similar to those of the Securities and Exchange Commission (SEC) which is empowered to oversee the stock market in the United States. The deception generated when people interact solely for the purpose of obtaining goods and the mixed-motive nature of bargaining usually produce so much hostility and interpersonal antagonism that it is impossible to maintain a large market based entirely on clusters of exchange relationships.

In open markets there are a plurality of both buyers and sellers. No one has complete control of any given service or good. Each buyer shops as well as bargains; and each seller offers goods to a plurality of potential buyers. The clusters of exchange relationships that are the heart and soul of markets make them "one of the most viable, volatile, attractive, and yet one of the ugliest institutions ever invented" (Couch 1984a, 110-111). Markets generate wealth, creativity, personal autonomy, and civility. They also generate indifference and exploitation.

Markets extend social contacts. They make all more interdependent, but in the process they transform our social worlds into a world of strangers (Lofland 1973). Each is dependent on others; yet no one cares about the welfare of other buyers and sellers. It is a heterogeneous world with little constancy. Diversity and change are the hallmarks of markets.

One of the spinoffs of markets is wagelabor. Those with no resources are required, if they are to participate in the world of the market, to sell their labor. They prostitute themselves. They make their bodies available as instruments to those with greater material resources.

Nonetheless, mercenary encounters, exchange relationships, and markets rest on a foundation of mutual benefit. More individuals have access to greater amounts of material wealth than would be possible if exchange relationships had never been developed and markets never established.

Competition is inherent in open markets. When there is a plurality of both sellers and buyers of a given item, the sellers are in competition with one another and the buyers are in competition with one another. Each attempts to get an advantage over the other. Each seller and buyer recognizes that if the competition can be eliminated, then his welfare will be enhanced. Consequently, many attempt to minimize competition. Sometimes, one party acquires a monopoly; then he no longer has to compete with other sellers.

If a seller is successful in eliminating all other sellers, the buyers suffer. They have no choice but to buy from the one with a corner on the market.

When that occurs, the egalitarian nature of exchange relationships moves toward asymmetry. In extreme cases, those with a monopoly of a given good establish a tyrannical relationship with those who desire the good. The buyers must meet the price of the seller or do without.

Summary

Many claim that all of modern life is contaminated by a mercenary mentality. Each person supposedly makes and maintains relationships solely for personal benefit. That human beings are sometimes self- centered and hedonistic cannot be denied. It also seems that citizens of modern societies are more self-centered than members of traditional societies. Contemporary critics of the mercenary mentality generated in markets are not the first to offer negative assessments of markets. Markets and those who populate them have long been the target of criticisms. In the Old Testament markets are characterized as pits of inequity. Among the ancient Greeks, traders were scorned. Aristotle regarded trading as hucksterism written large (Finley 1973).

Markets have also had their advocates. In 1776, Adam Smith published *The Wealth of Nations*. Smith laid the foundation for classical economics. He argued that exchange relationships, especially when clustered together to form markets, create communal wealth and are the source of many benefits. Smith did not argue that exchange relationships and markets enticed individuals intentionally to act to promote the welfare of the community. Instead, he argued that by creating social arrangements where all could pursue their selfish interests without hindrance, communal opulence would follow. He believed that by allowing all to be self-centered, the community as a whole would benefit.

Many economists continue to advocate Smith's theory. Other analysts of modern societies argue that exchange relationships and markets need to be replaced by other social arrangements or if not replaced, at least placed under the control of more humane relationships. Some Marxists would eradicate the exchange relationship. They would substitute in its place nationwide communal solidarity and the centralized accumulation and distribution of goods.

Whether one agrees with the position of classical economists or with Marxists, nearly all agree that the exchange relationship has become a significant social form in all modern societies. Most would also agree that the emergence of exchange relationships as a common social form has been accompanied by a decline in the significance of some other social forms, especially a decline in the extensiveness and intensity of solidary relationships.

Exchange relationships, especially those that come to the fore when all restrictions on trade are removed, do erode, if they do not destroy, other social relationships. Polyani's (1957) thesis that a great transformation has occurred in Western societies as the consequence of the expansion of markets and manufacturing has merit. The distribution of the necessities of life was achieved primarily within other social relationships before the industrial revolution. Now the distribution of goods is achieved, if not primarily, at least in large part through the activation of an exchange relationship. Futhermore, other social relationships have become infused with mercenary elements.

This transformation has made the distribution of goods more efficient, extended human interdependence, and enhanced our material wellbeing. It has also generated selfishness and greed, and has undermined communal solidarity and personal accountability.

Chapter 16 Charismatic Relationships

Max Weber (1964) developed the concept *charisma* in his analysis of asymmetrical relationships. Weber specified three forms of asymmetrical relationships: traditional authority, bureaucratic (rational) authority, and charismatic authority. Traditional authority, for Weber, consisted of responsibilities and prerogatives legitimated by cultural tradition. The prototype of traditional authority is the male head of the family in a patriarchal society. Bureaucratic authority is established when responsibilities and prerogatives are assigned to individuals on the basis of formal criteria. An example of that form of authority is the search for and selection of a person to occupy an administrative position in a formal organization.

Weber recognized that these two forms of asymmetry did not characterize all asymmetrical relationships. He noted that some individuals achieved positions of influence not based on either tradition or formal criteria. He used the concept *charismatic authority* to designate asymmetrical relationships that emerged in transactions between a person and his followers that were not legitimated by cultural tradition nor formal criteria.

Weber used the concept charismatic authority in two similar, but somewhat different, ways. Sometimes, he used the term to refer to extraordinary qualities that some individuals possess that command the attention of others. Other times, he used the term to refer to the assignment of extraordinary qualities to an individual by others. When the concept is used in the latter manner, it directs attention to the characteristics of an individual or to characteristics assigned to an individual by others; it does not focus on the relatedness between people.

In contrast, the concept charismatic relationship focuses on the elements of sociation mutually established by a leader and his followers. A charismatic relationship is established when one person becomes the focal point for a number of people by uttering statements that elicit agreement from others. A charismatic relationship is not established by an individual's claiming extraordinary qualities nor by a plurality of others assigning extraordinary qualities to an individual. Instead a charismatic relationship emerges from dynamic transactions between an individual offering himself as a focal point and others attending to and positively responding to the person who offers a definition of a situation. The imputation of extra-

204

ordinary qualities to a charismatic leader is a consequence of the charismatic relationship. It is not the foundation for a charismatic relationship.

Charismatic relationships are not a form of authority. The focal point of a charismatic relationship does not have the prerogative to issue directives to others. Instead the charismatic leader articulates definitions and others validate the definitions offered. The charismatic leader and his followers establish new solidarities, new consensual realities, and formulate programs of action for instituting or resisting changes. Some authority and tyrannical relationships are infused with elements of charisma. Nonetheless, the purely charismatic relationship is neither authoritarian nor tyrannical.

Authority relationships are constructed by established collectivities endowing individuals with prerogatives and responsibilities on the basis of existing solidarities. Tyrannical relationships are established by pluralities of individuals agreeing that one person has the ability and willingness to use coercion to elicit compliance from others. In contrast, a charismatic relationship emerges when an individual articulates commonly held sentiments and elicits solidary responsiveness from others. The solidarity that emerges within charismatic relationships is asymmetrical; it is not egalitarian. The solidarity is focused on the individual serving as the focal point, the definitions of the situation offered, and the programs of action for the future offered.

Charismatic relationships tend to emerge when there is widespread dissatisfaction within a population. They are formed either to bring about change in the established structure or to resist changes that are occurring within the established structure. The solidarities that emerge in conjunction with the formation of a charismatic relationship usually conflict with existing solidary, accountable, and authority relationships.

The core of many social movements is provided by a charismatic relationship. The objective of most charismatic movements is to institute or revalidate a particular social arrangement. Charismatic movements that succeed usually transform into either authority or tyrannical relationship and replace established asymmetrical relationships. Successful charismatic movements also transform taken-for-granted realities.

Some charismatic movements are of limited scope. They are composed of only a few people and call for only minor and local changes. A charismatic relationship might be formed within a group of workers by one of the workers becoming the spokesperson for common dissatisfactions and have only the objective of changing local working conditions. Other charismatic movements are dedicated to sweeping changes.

All charismatic movements have modest beginnings. In the early days they consist of only a leader and a few followers. For example, the Nazi movement emerged from a small discussion group that called itself the German Workers Party. Hitler held membership card number seven in the organization (Abel 1968, 59). In return for joining the group, Hitler was granted a free hand in propaganda (Abel 1968, 59). Hitler rapidly asserted himself and became the primary spokesman of the group.

Many individuals offer themselves as leader of a movement to right wrongs and bring about changes only to have their offer rejected. But a few would-be leaders acquire a following and initiate sweeping social changes. Well-known examples of movements that had at their core a vibrant charismatic relationship are Hitler and the Nazi party, Martin Luther King, Jr. and the civil rights movement, and Jim Jones and the People's Temple. Hitler and his followers acquired control of the political system of Germany and brought about worldwide havoc, but in the end the movement was destroyed in World War II. The civil rights movement wrought many changes in the social structure of the United States. The civil rights movement has transformed from a structure that rested primarily on the charismatic relationship focused on Dr. King into an organization that rests on solidary, accountable, and authority relationships. Jim Jones achieved a modicum of short-lived success after he and his followers founded the People's Temple. The People's Temple achieved a membership of several thousand. The movement came to an end in 1978 when over nine hundred members committed collective suicide in Guyana. The episode was a major news event for a few weeks, but the movement had no significant consequences for the social structure of the United States.

Charismatic movements range widely in both the size of their membership and the scope of their programs. Some consist of only a few people; others achieve memberships that reach into the millions. Some have only limited objectives; others attempt to transform the nature of human existence. Whatever the size and scope of the movement, charismatic relationships contain the following elements of sociation: (1) One person articulates commonly held dissatisfactions; (2) a plurality of individuals are solidarily responsive to the definitions offered; (3) new consensual definitions of reality are established within the collectivity; and (4) a program of action is formulated that calls for the modification, overthrow, or preservation of some social arrangement.

Articulating Dissatisfaction

Whenever dissatisfaction is widespread, people attempt to express it and locate its causes. Many have difficulty articulating their dissatisfactions, and many diverse factors are put forward to explain unhappy situations. When that happens, nothing more than diffuse grumbling is likely to occur. But when someone articulates common dissatisfactions and offers an explanation for them and others begin agreeing with the statements put forth, the first step toward the formation of a charismatic relationship is taken.

Before a charismatic relationship can emerge, a significant percentage of a population must be disenchanted with current conditions. But widespread dissatisfaction does not automatically lead to a charismatic relationship. Before a charismatic relationship can emerge, dissatisfactions must become focused; someone must give voice to commonly held sentiments. Often a charismatic relationship fails to emerge because all are fearful of giving voice to commonly held sentiments; at others times, no one capable of articulating common sentiments emerges as a spokesperson. At still other times, several individuals compete to establish themselves as the focal point of a charismatic relationship.

When several persons attempt to establish themselves as the spokesperson and compete with one another for a following, several new collectivities may be formed. Sometimes the leaders and followers of these collectivities conflict so intensely that a viable movement does not emerge. On occasion, two or more emerging movements have merged into a single entity. If a charismatic movement is to become a viable instrument of change, a single person must become consensually identified as the one most capable of articulating the dissatisfactions of others. Other would-be leaders fall by the wayside.

The articulation of common sentiments by a single person does not create a charismatic relationship. Others must publicly indicate their approval of the statements made by the would-be charismatic leader. Often many regard the situation as hopeless and are indifferent; they resign themselves to live with current conditions. Some who are frustrated fail to agree publicly with statements that criticize current conditions. They are often fearful of reprisals from established authorities and tyrants.

Would-be charismatic leaders often must overcome both apathy and fear before a viable charismatic relationship can be established. The effective charismatic leader transforms private and common dissatisfactions into public and shared dissatisfactions. For example, only seven people attended the first meeting called by Hitler (Abel 1968, 62). Several months later, nearly two thousand attended a rally he organized. As Hitler became known for his ability to articulate the frustrations of German citizens, attendance at his rallies increased by leaps and bounds. The public expression of private dissatisfactions is a major source of vitality for charismatic movements. Vague dissatisfactions and diffuse anger coalesce and become focused on the leader.

During the emergence of the civil rights movements, Afro-American citizens became aware of the definitions of the situation offered by Martin Luther King, Jr. They also became aware that many others experienced the same frustrations. Conditions regarded as annoyances were transformed into intense public dissatisfactions. Before the civil rights movement emerged, many Afro-Americans regarded segregated seating as an arrangement they had to tolerate. But as Dr. King and others advanced the definition of the situation that segregation was immoral, many began sharing their personal frustrations with one another. A new social unity emerged based on sentiments articulated by a charismatic leader.

The establishment of consensual public dissatisfactions is not simply the accomplishment of the charismatic leader; it is social accomplishment. Many would-be charismatic leaders attempt to articulate the dissatisfactions of others only to have their definition of the situation ignored. In such instances, a charismatic relationship is not established. The would-be charismatic leader becomes merely a prophet crying in the wilderness.

When dissatisfaction is widespread, some individuals strive for leadership; but friends and acquaintances of an articulate person often encourage that person to speak out and assume leadership. And, of course, in some instances, individuals seek leadership and are encouraged by others to seek it. Occasionally, individuals have become the focal point of a charismatic relationship unintentionally.

Martin Luther King, Jr., did not seek leadership, nor was he explicitly encouraged by others to do so during the early stages of the civil rights movement. Before the Montgomery, Alabama bus boycott, he was a relatively unknown young minister. He did not play a major role in formulating the plan for the boycott. After the plan for the boycott was formulated, he was selected by fellow ministers to go fiom church meeting to church meeting to explain the boycott and call for its support. Two reasons why fellow ministers selected him for the task were that he was relatively unknown and was articulate. He soon became well known in the Afro-American community as he carried out his assignment. It was during the boycott that he became consensually identified as spokesperson for the movement. Others began to think of him as the leader of the movement and he began to think of himself as the leader. The establishment of publicly shared dissatisfactions and the emergence of a charismatic leader are twin born; they emerge simultaneously.

Sometimes, publicly shared dissatisfactions and a charismatic leader are established rapidly; other times, their establishment is drawn out over a period of years. The emergence of charismatic leaders often appears to be an "overnight" affair. Their seemingly sudden appearance reflects the fact that outsiders often are relatively unaware of activities that occur among disenchanted populations. Other times, the apparent sudden appearance of a charismatic relationship is related to the fact that those who compose the relationship are secretive. Members of such movements often think, and usually with just cause, that if outsiders became aware of an emerging charismatic relationship, action would be taken to stamp out the budding social movement. Many of those most active during the early stages attempt to prevent outsiders from becoming aware of developments within the disenchanted population until after the movement has reached a size and level of solidarity deemed adequate for confronting the establishment.

New Solidarities

Charismatic relationships emerge when old solidarities are ebbing, when there is widespread disenchantment with at least some facets of the current social structure. When people began to solidarily respond to the statements of an emerging spokesperson, the second step toward constructing new solidarities is taken. The solidary responsiveness elicited during the early phases is diffuse and limited to small numbers. It is usually produced within small collectivities with one person speaking to a few others. Typically the speaker negatively characterizes current conditions and may indicate that a particular program of action is necessary. When others positively respond to the speaker's statements, elements of solidary responsiveness are established.

If and when a speaker acquires a reputation for articulating current dissatisfactions and perhaps offering viable alternatives, early followers begin recruiting friends and family members to come listen to the speaker. As the leader's reputation as a spokesperson increases, meetings and rallies are scheduled. Appeals are issued for all who are interested to attend. The early meetings are usually open to anyone interested.

During the early stages many come to meetings to hear the speaker and assess what is said. Those who attend the early meetings usually have diverse and vague dissatisfactions. Some have specific frustrations; others are diffusely dissatisfied; and some are bored. Some attend rallies merely for the excitement. Many early members of the Nazi party stated that they first attended a Nazi rally because a friend or family member asked them to, or out of curiosity. For example, one early joiner of the Nazi party reported that he had never concerned himself with politics but that after attending a rally he "went home deeply moved" (Abel 1968, 120). He subsequently decided to devote his life to the Nazi party.

The would-be charismatic leader must determine with some accuracy the diverse dissatisfactions of those who attend rallies and formulate a theme that appeals to many of those in attendance. A successful leader transforms private dissatisfactions into solidary responsiveness. The effective charismatic leader is a catalyst, creating unity out of diversity.

Some speakers have experienced the same frustrations as many of those in attendance at the meetings. Thus the speakers can transform private dissatisfactions into public dissatisfactions when they give voice to personal frustrations. Other speakers make assessments of the dissatisfactions that are most common among the audience and attempt to articulate them. In most cases, some combination of voicing personal dissatisfactions shared by members of the audience and deliberately forming a message that has wide appeal is involved. Hitler often claimed that he had experienced the same frustrations as his listeners. He also was aware of the fact that it was necessary for him carefully to select the content of his speeches to appeal to a given audience. Furthermore, while delivering a speech, he carefully noted the responses of the audience and elaborated on statements that elicited approval from the audience. He self-consciously attempted to establish a vibrant responsiveness between himself and his audience.

The production of a solidary relationship between speaker and audience requires the speaker to establish in discourse shared foci that elicit uniform responsiveness from the audience. Charismatic speeches are not orations; instead a dynamic mutual responsiveness between speaker and audience is intertwined with solidary responsiveness. Members of the audience are not passive listeners; they contribute to the encounter. Audience contributions are largely restricted to expressive gestures, however. Members of the audience rarely contribute much discourse content. In a typical case, the speaker offers statements such as, "You, the law abiding citizens of the nation, know (the dissatisfaction). Right?" Then the speaker pauses and provides the audience with the opportunity to validate the assertion.

By providing the audience with opportunities to validate assertions, the speaker allows for the emergence of a vibrant solidary responsiveness. If a speaker merely lectures to them, the audience would not have the opportunity to respond in unison. When members of the audience respond in unison to assertions of the speaker, they take the first step toward constructing a new solidary relationship with the speaker as the focal point of the relationship.

In charismatic speeches the flow of influence is not unilateral from speaker to audience, but bilateral. The audience influences the speaker, as well as the speaker influencing the audience. Hitler has been described as playing "the crowd like a giant organ, pulling all the stops, permitting the listeners to rave and roar, laugh and cry. But inevitably the stream flowed back, until a fairly alternating current welded speaker and listeners into one" (Dobert 1940, 166).

The production of a vibrant charismatic encounter is sometimes facilitated by a leader and close followers orchestrating the meetings. Not only do most charismatic speakers self-consciously select statements that have wide appeal, but they also make other arrangements they think will elicit intense solidary responsiveness from those in attendance. For example, the rallies of Hitler were carefully programmed so that the auditorium or stadium was filled to capacity. Precautions were taken to avoid any distractions. In addition, Hitler effectively used marching music to create the desired ethos at his rallies. One of Hitler's early supporters reports, "I played him some of the Sousa marches and then my own 'Falarah,' to show how it could be done by adopting German tunes" (Hanfslaengl 1957, 52). Hitler immediately saw how these marches could be used to enhance the responsiveness of audiences. "I had Hitler fairly shouting with enthusiasm" (Hanfslaengl 1957, 53). Afterward, Hitler's mass rallies were contextualized by bands playing stirring marches.

The relationship between speaker and audience is reciprocal, but it is not symmetrical. The speaker frames the encounter and has the task of keeping the audience's attention and formulating statements that the audience's understands and approves. The speaker is onstage and accountable. Members of the audience are for the most part anonymous and not accountable. Many members of the audience, especially when a charismatic leader is building a reputation, come to meetings with the attitude of "we are interested, convince us." Charismatic speakers attempting to establish a charismatic relationship are well aware that they are accountable whereas the members of the audience are not. The speaker is in a one-down position and must appeal to them. To establish a charismatic relationship the speaker must subordinate personal interests to the interests of the audience. Members of the audience, especially in the early stages, often are critical of the speaker. In contrast, in the early stages, the speaker is accepting of all who attend.

Not only is a particular relationship generated between speaker and audience, but in addition a special relationship is generated among members of the audience. Members of the audience glance at one another and hear one another's verbal approvals of the speaker's statements. The speaker has the objective of eliciting uniform verbal and nonverbal responses from the audience. A successful speaker serves as the catalyst for the establishment of a solidary relationship among members of the audience, as well as between speaker and audience.

The expression of contradictory or divergent ideas from any members of the audience inhibits the generation of solidary responsiveness among members of the audience. If divergent ideas are expressed, it is likely that some members of the audience will be reflective about the ideas offered by the speaker. Therefore, members of the audience must be inhibited from expressing divergent ideas if an intense charismatic relationship is to emerge. After a charismatic relationship has matured, many charismatic speakers employ henchmen who remove any in attendance who express divergent ideas.

The assumption of the position of speaker by a would-be charismatic leader is a risky endeavor. Many would-be charismatic leaders have been humiliated by their audiences. Charismatic leaders have been beaten; some even have been killed. Attendance at a meeting is sometimes risky, but generally speaking, it is far less risky to be a member of the audience than to occupy center stage.

During the early stages, the speaker is faced with the task of making himself appear to be identical with members of the audience and at the same time clearly differentiating himself by occupying center stage. He is speaking; they are listening. Most speakers attempt to overcome this differentiation by offering utterances that emphasize what they share with members of the audience.

Attendance at, and participation in, rallies is critical during the early stages of a charismatic movement. In his study of the early joiners of the Nazi party, Abel (1968, 117) concluded, "Irrespective of the nature of the first contact, our contributors are unanimous in the contention that it was their attendance at the meetings that induced them to join the movement."

New Consensualities

Successful charismatic leaders redefine reality. The articulation of dissatisfactions is a past-centered activity; the references are to what has been. As a charismatic relationship matures, less attention is given to the taken-for-granted past and new definitions of reality come to the fore. Usually, the definitions of reality that come to the fore are ideas previously accepted by only a few people. Definitions previously held by only a few are articulated by the charismatic leader and become established as the prevailing definition of reality within the movement.

Before the emergence of the civil rights movement, some held the opinion that blacks were equal to whites, but that was not the prevailing definition of reality. The idea that blacks were equal to whites became a viable part of the definition of reality among the followers and supporters of the civil rights movement. In time, that definition of reality became the official definition of reality as federal and state judical and legislative bodies formulated new laws. In a similar manner, prior to the emergence of Hitler and the Nazi party, Germany's defeat in World War I was more or less consensually defined as the fault of Germans. Hitler was able to transform that definition of reality into one that specified that the fault lay with the Jews.

New definitions of reality that emerge are linked to the asymmetrical solidarity established and provide a new morality. The followers and supporters of the movement develop a sense of righteousness. Many of the followers conclude that they are moral and that all who oppose them are immoral.

The definitions of reality advocated by charismatic leaders are nearly always regarded as irrational by those opposed to the movement. Most supporters of the establishment who opposed the civil rights movement regarded the claim that blacks had as much right as whites to participate in political affairs as irrational. During the early years of the development of the Congress of Industrial Organizations (CIO), many leading economists claimed that the formation of industrial-based labor unions was irrational; it either could not be done, or if done, it would wreck havoc on the economic structure of the United States.

One arena of conflict between charismatic movements and the establishment is a battle of words that center on whose definition of reality is to be the prevailing one. These conflicts often escalate into physical confrontations. Those who oppose charismatic movements often raid, beat up, and even kill members of charismatic movements; in turn, followers of charismatic leaders often assault and even kill supporters of the establishment. Many charismatic movements disintegrate under the assault from outsiders. Occasionally, charismatic movements are successful and either modify or overthrow established structures and institute social structures that reflect their definitions of reality.

The sense of righteousness, reciprocal fear, and mutual suspicion that often emerges between members of charismatic movements and supporters of the establishment tends to erode, if not completely destroy, any significant communication between them. Often the only contact between members of charismatic movements and others is antagonistic. Negotiation between members of the movement and outsiders often becomes impossible. Violent conflict between members of charismatic movements and outsiders is a frequent consequence. Many charismatic movements have led to civil wars. Then one side defeats and annihilates or subordinates the other.

Programs of Action

Many are adept at articulating dissatisfactions and offering new definitions of reality, but are relatively inept at formulating programs of action necessary for instituting and maintaining alternative social arrangements. If a movement is to have a significant impact on existing social structures it is necessary for the leader of the movement or top lieutenants to formulate programs of action to bring the projected new arrangements into being. The effective charismatic leader must project a viable future as well as articulate causes of dissatisfaction and offer new definitions of reality.

As charismatic movements mature, a utopian future is formulated. How the utopian future is to be achieved often is not clearly specified. The overthrow of existing social structures and the establishment of new structures require the formulation of a division of labor. Not all charismatic movements undergo that transformation. Some, after confronting the establishment, turn inward and develop into separatist movements. Those movements do not bring about major changes in social structures.

Nor do all movements that project a utopian future of transforming the existing social structure succeed. Many are destroyed. But the projection of an alternative social arrangement is necessary if the existing social structure is to be transformed. Hitler projected a future of a thousand-year reich with Germany assuming its rightful place as the leading nation and all good Germans living the good life. Martin Luther King, Jr., projected a future wherein all would have equal opportunity to participate in the economic and political systems, and all would be judged by their character instead of their skin color. Unless a future that is attractive to followers is projected, a movement will have few consequences for the established social structure.

I Am God

The so-called extraordinary qualities of charismatic leaders are a consequence of the development of a charismatic relationship; they are not the foundation for charismatic relationships. As the charismatic relationship matures, the leader often becomes thought of as something special by followers—and many charismatic leaders begin to think of themselves as special. The generation of the belief that the leader has extraordinary qualities often results in the "I am God" syndrome.

Not even Hitler thought of himself as possessing extraordinary qualities in the early days of the Nazi movement. Abel (1968, 68) notes that it is doubtful Hitler had aspirations to become dictator in the early years of the Nazi movement. Hitler wrote, "I considered myself at the time the drummer of the cause against marxism. I was not looking for the title of a minister" (as quoted in Abel 1968, 68).

When the "I am God" syndrome emerges, the charismatic leader assumes and is allowed prerogatives denied rank-and-file members of the movement. Charismatic leaders have often been worshipped by followers, and many charismatic leaders have treated followers as something less than human. Many charismatics have been elevated to the status of a god, if not God. Many of those elevated have in turn regarded their followers as merely instruments to be used for the leader's personal satisfaction.

In the early years, Jim Jones was very sensitive to the personal problems of his followers. He went out of his way to help those in need and asked nothing in return. He insisted that his followers call him by his first name. After he became widely known and adored by his followers, however, he insisted that his followers call him Father, admit their most important relationship was the one each of them had with him, claimed the right to determine who was to have sex with whom, and a host of other prerogatives. He came to think himself a god and was regarded as a god by some of his followers. The movement collapsed when he called on all his followers to commit collective suicide. Many acted as he ordered. Some parents killed their children before killing themselves. Over nine hundred of his followers died.

The emergence of the "I am God" syndrome has enticed many charismatic leaders to advocate programs that have wrecked havoc on members of the movement and outsiders. Many charismatic leaders come to believe that they are not subject to any constraints; they are free to do whatever they wish.

The "I am God" syndrome is usually accompanied by a transformation of the charismatic relationship into a tyrannical relationship. Whereas during the early stages of a charismatic relationship leaders are usually sensitive and responsive to followers, in the later stages, leaders often become insensitive and indifferent to followers as they seek personal agrandizement.

The tyrannical elements that often emerge within charismatic movements stem from a combination of the "I am God" syndrome and the practical problems of establishing new social structures. When the leaders of charismatic movements acquire power and attempt to institute the promised changes, often the future does not unfold as promised and anticipated. Failures must be explained. Often the blame falls on some of the followers. Some followers are accused of violating the dictates of the leader. Purges are a common result. Many loyal followers of charismatic leaders have been executed once the leader has acquired a position of power. The unity and excitement of the early days are often replaced with hierarchy, threats, and fear.

The emergence of tyranny is usually "the unintended result of the leader's failure to modify his charismatic self-image in keeping with the realities of his new position" (Dow 1968, 335). The solidary unity and monolithic definition of reality that are integral facets of charismatic movements tend to preclude debate, dissent, and public expression of differences (Dow 1968, 336). Those features of charismatic relationships provide a fertile seedbed for the growth of tyrannical relationships. Some successful charismatic movements become even more repressive and exploitive than the social structures they replace. The seeds are sown for the emergence of another charismatic movement. Charismatic relationships are more volatile than other asymmetrical relationships such as parental and authority ones. Their volatility stems from the intense asymmetrical solidarity generated, the imputation of god-like qualities to charismatic leaders, and the fact the projected utopia is never achieved.

Summary

Charismatic relationships, like all social relationships, are mutually constructed. They do not simply flow from the activities of a single person. They are the product of dynamic and constantly evolving alignments between the focal point of the relationship and followers. The relationship rests on a distinctive type of solidarity, namely, an asymmetrical solidarity. The relationship is paradoxical. On the one hand, all, the leader and followers, have the same objectives; on the other hand, to achieve the objectives, it is necessary for one person to be differentiated from all others.

Superficially, charismatic relationships project equality. A closer look demonstrates that the relationship is asymmetrical. In the typical charismatic relationship, one of the themes is that we, the members, are all the same. But at the same time it is apparent that we are not all the same. Some speak; others listen. The speaker initiates; the listeners respond. The speakers create; the listeners accept what is created.

Vibrant charismatic relationships are a distinctive dyadic form. The leader is one half of the dyad; the followers the other half. The leader articulates dissatisfaction, defines reality, and formulates programs of action for the future; the followers attend and respond to the leader. The successful leader establishes a consensual and monolithic shared standpoint. The monolithic standpoint generated within vibrant charismatic relationships is the source of security for the followers, but it also provides a foundation for the leader to repress any who might disagree with the definitions of reality and programs of action the leader offers. Those with divergent and minority thoughts must either keep their opinions to themselves or risk becoming targets of repression.

In purely charismatic relations, the focal person does not have the prerogative of issuing directives. The leader is definer, not a director. Of course, as the movement matures and attempts to institute its programs, the leader or top lieutenants must coordinate the activity of the collectivity. When that occurs, the relationship becomes something less than an ideal charismatic relationship. Many charismatic relationships transform into tyrannical relationships wherein the leader is accountable to no one and the followers are mere instruments of the leader.

The charismatic relationship is a transitional form. Therefore, charismatic relationships tend to be somewhat more unstable than some other social relationships. If a charismatic relationship is successful, it is necessary for it to transform. Unity can be generated by speeches, but speeches alone are not sufficient to plant the crops, build the roads, and run the factories. In order to accomplish the latter, it is necessary for a division of labor and accountability to be established. The establishment of these forms of social relationships inherently detracts from the unity generated in charismatic relationships.

Elements of charisma infuse many asymmetrical relationships. The teacher who captures the rapt attention of her students with each of them hanging on to her every word infuses the parental relationship with elements of charisma. The authority or tyrant who stirs the emotions of his subordinates and entices them to make an extra effort to fulfill their obligations infuses the authority or tyrannical relationship with elements of charisma. Parents, teachers, bosses, politicians, and dictators who capture the attention of their subordinates and interject elements of asymmetrical solidarity into the relationships are regarded as effective leaders. Their effectiveness as leaders stems from their ability to elicit a pseudo-charismatic relationship.

Chapter **17** Tyrannical Relationships

Tyrannical relationships have some of the same features as authority relationships. In both, one person programs, directs, and coordinates the behavior of others — the subordinates. Nonetheless, the two sets of relationships rest on different foundations. Authority relationships rest on solidary relationships; tyrannical relationships are based upon coercion. The division of labor of authority relationships is either mutually constructed or there is a preexisting hierarchical division of labor and individuals are recruited to assume identities within the preexisting structure. Both superordinates and subordinates willingly enter authority relationships. In contrast, tyrannical relationships are imposed; one party imposes his will on another. A tyrannical relationship is established when two parties mutually recognize that one party has greater ability to do violence to the other and is willing to do violence to the other, but the more powerful party indicates a willingness to withhold violence as long as the other party complies with the directives issued. Tyrannical relationships are an extension of the chase. One party is a predator and captures the prey; but instead of destroying the prey, the predator demands subordination of the prey to the will of the predator. The victim is transformed into an instrument. The superordinate indicates that violence will not be directed at the subordinate as long as the subordinate obeys.

Tyrannical relationships are instituted in several ways. Sometimes, authority and charismatic relationships transform into tyrannical relationships. At least some authority and charismatic relationships become infused with elements of tyranny. On other occasions, individuals or groups intrude on others, capture them, and offer them the alternative of being subordinates in a tyrannical relationship or suffering the consequences. On occasion, groups and societies have elected to establish a tyranny. Usually that has occurred when there is widespread dissatisfaction and it is believed that a rigid and highly centralized order is necessary to resolve the situation.

Tyranny is an extremely asymmetrical relationship. Subordinates are merely instruments for the extension of the tyrant's will. Only the tyrant exercises initiative; subordinates have only the choice of complying with the dictates of the tyrant or becoming targets of violence. In pure tyrannical relations there are no moral constraints. The tyrant does whatever he

218

wishes, within limits of his ability, toward his subordinates. The subordinate's welfare is controlled by the tyrant.

Some tyrannies endure but for a short time; others endure indefinitely. When a thug points a knife at a citizen and asserts, "Your wallet or your life," he attempts to establish a short-lived tyranny. If the citizen complies, a minor tyranny has been established. The slaver who captures people and sells them attempts to impose a lifelong tyrannical relationship on victims.

A tyrannical relationship is established when (1) both parties acknowledge that one party can do violence to the other without the target's being able to reciprocate in kind; (2) the more powerful party indicates a willingness to do violence to the other if compliance is not forthcoming; (3) both parties recognize that the more powerful party has the ability to keep the weaker party under surveillance; and (4) the superordinate programs the future and organizes the behavior of the subordinate.

Tyrannical relationships are uncommitted relationships. Tyrannical relationships rest on agreements; both parties agree that one is more powerful than the other. But members of a tyrannical relationship do not construct commitments and obligations. Tyrannical relationships are instrumental; they are not moral.

Despite the fact that tyrannical relationships rest on violence, in one sense, they are mutually constructed. If the victim refuses to agree that the would-be tyrant has the ability to do violence to him, a tyranny cannot be established. Even if the target agrees that the would-be tyrant has the ability to do violence to him, if the target refuses to comply, a tyranny will not be established. Of course, in such situations, the would-be tyrant might kill the target, but as long as the target withholds compliance, a tyranny is not established. Many targets of would-be tyrants have chosen martyrdom over becoming subordinates in tyrannical relationships (Leichty 1975).

Imposing Asymmetrical Vulnerability

Tyrannical relationships are infused with violence, but the violence of tyrannical relationships is contextualized entirely differently from the violence of conflict. Combatants relate as equals; each combatant presumes that he can inflict violence on the other. In contrast, in tyrannical relationships the subordinate recognizes that the other can inflict more violence on him than he can on the other. The subordinate regards himself as vulnerable to violence.

Tyrannical relationships have been established in different ways. On many occasions, they were established by one society invading another and defeating them. Sometimes, the survivors of the defeat were then enslaved. The survivors had the alternative of abiding by the dictates of their conquerors or being killed. On other occasions, those with the more powerful instruments of violence have raided and captured members of enemy societies. On still other occasions, individuals have sold themselves, or been sold by members of their family, into slavery. Many authority and charismatic relationships have transformed into tyrannies. For example, the relationship between Hitler and his followers originally was primarily a charismatic relationship, but when the Nazi party became the ruling party in Germany, the relationship between Hitler and the citizens of Germany became largely tyrannical. Some parents have imposed a tyranny on their children.

After a tyranny is in place, then those born into the system are encased by the relationship from the beginning. The offspring of slaves usually are also slaves. The children of slaves are socialized into the preexisting system; they learn early in life that they are vulnerable to violence.

Whether a tyranny is imposed following violent conflict, voluntarily established, or preexistent, one of the necessary elements is the mutual recognition by the tyrant and subordinates is that the subordinates are more vulnerable to violence than the superordinate. The subordinates must also recognized that the superordinate is willing to use violence to elicit compliance.

The continuation of tyrannical relationships requires the tyrant to demonstrate from time to time the ability to inflict violence on subordinates, to reaffirm the condition of asymmetrical vulnerability. Access to instruments of violence has to be controlled if a stable tyrannical relationship is to endure. If subordinates acquire access to instruments of violence they are likely to attempt to transform the tyrannical relationship into conflict. "If the superordinate is as available to the subordinates as the subordinate is to the superordinate a tyrannical relation cannot be maintained" (Miller, Weiland, and Couch 1978, 272).

Enforced Compliance

After it is agreed that one has greater coercive power than the other, members of tyrannical relationships must also agree that the one with the greater coercive power will direct the behavior of the subordinates. The tyrant specifies objectives and programs of action for achieving objectives. The subordinate has no autonomy and is not allowed to initiate action. Subordinates have only the choice of complying or suffering the consequences. When those conditions are mutually recognized and accepted, tyrant and subordinates have established congruent categorical identities.

Compliance is not always automatic. Sometimes, subordinates are not capable of acting as directed. Parents sometimes attempt to institute a tyrannical relationship with infants and young children. If the child is not capable of acting as directed, a tyrannical relationship is not established. Often, child abuse is the consequence. Sometimes, subordinates misunderstand the directives; at other times, they refuse to comply.

From the point of view of the tyrant the ideal subordinate understands directives, is competent to act as directed, and does not think. Then, on completion of the called-for activity, the subordinate makes himself available to the tyrant for the next directive. Tyrants create that relationship by making their subordinates fearful of the consequences of non-compliance. Those who are well socialized into their subordinate position within tyrannical relationships are very attentive and responsive to their tyrant.

Within enduring tyrannical relationships, how and when the subordinate may approach the superordinate is clearly specified. The subordinate is denied the prerogative of casting claims on the superordinate. The superordinate establishes and maintains the prerogative of dismissing the subordinate at any time (Miller, Weiland and Couch 1978, 273).

In the ideal tyrannical relationship, the only future projected by the subordinate is continued availability and responsiveness to the tyrant. The subordinate projects no other future than that of compliance. Reciprocally, the tyrant indicates willingness to continue to structure the activities of the subordinates. The tyrant programs the future; subordinates attempt to bring it to fruition. The division of labor is complete; the tyrant uses his mind, and the subordinates perform the called-for activity.

Of course, it is impossible to eradicate thought completely. Even in the most extreme form of tyranny, subordinates assess and evaluate the context. Whenever subordinates have the opportunity to think, it is likely that disruptive elements will be interjected into the relationship. Thoughtful subordinates are to be avoided if the tyrannical relationship is to be preserved. It is necessary to keep subordinates busy. If they cannot be kept busy, then it is necessary either to confine them or keep them under close surveillance. An accepted cliche of tyrants is "Idle hands are the devil's workshop."

Tyrant and subordinates are categorically and hierarchically differentiated. Nearly all tyrants categorically regard their subordinates as inferior to them, but it is difficult to convince completely subordinates that they are categorically inferior to their tyrants. Slaves often regard their relationship with their masters as unjust.

The categorical classification of subordinates as inferior nearly always has a degree of tentativeness to it from the point of view of the subordinates. Most tyrants recognize that their subordinates do not always agree that they deserve to be treated as instruments. The construction of complex and enduring tyrannical relationships is difficult. Typically, it requires that the tyrant from time to time punish the subordinates to remind them of their inferiority (Miller, Weiland, and Couch 1978, 275).

Asymmetrical Surveillance

When the opportunity occurs, slaves and other victims of tyrannical relationships often take flight. The continuation of the relationship requires not only asymmetrical control of instruments of violence but also effective restrictions on the mobility of the subordinates. Victims of tyrannical relationships are sometimes immobilized. Slaves are placed in irons, confined in holding pens, or their ability to flee is lessened by violent surgery. These techniques, of course, render them less useful as instruments.

Tyrannical governments construct walls to prevent the flight of citizens. The maintenance of the tyrannical relationship over fully mobile people requires that they be under constant surveillance or be made fearful of flight. It is difficult to maintain constant surveillance. The person who maintains constant surveillance over another has little time for anything else. Therefore, tyrants often attempt to maintain the relationship by making subordinates fearful of flight. Those who escape are relentlessly hunted down, brought back and subjected to public torture.

Tyrants often expend more effort in capturing and bringing back runaway subordinates than they are worth. When runaways are returned, they are then publicly tortured or killed to inform others of what is in store for them if they attempt to escape. Of course, not all runaways are recaptured. An alternative is to punish those who remain. To be effective, the punishment need not be administered to those responsible for the escape. All that is necessary is that those who remain be assured that violence will be unleashed whenever anyone escapes. The threat of punishment inhibits others from attempting to escape or aiding those planning to escape.

The maintenance of the surveillance necessary to prevent flight and assure compliance places a tyrant in a bind. A tyrant who keeps subordinates under constant surveillance exposes himself to subordinates. They can then monitor his behavior when he is monitoring them. That provides them with opportunities to acquire information about the tyrant; they can better anticipate his actions. Experienced tyrants are well aware of this. Most minimize their appearances before their subordinates and carefully orchestrate the appearances they do make.

The ideal condition, from the point of view of the tyrant, is when actions of subordinates can be carefully monitored, but they cannot monitor the tyrant's actions. Many tyrants employ lieutenants to oversee their victims. For example, owners of large plantations manned by slaves hired overseers to supervise the work and coordinate the activity of the slaves (Genovese 1976). But the use of overseers has its risks. It is only effective when the lieutenants are trustworthy and thorough.

One factor compounding the problems of tyrants is that subordinates attempt to minimize their exposure to their tyrant. Subordinates usually hide from their tyrants whenever they can. The tyrant has to minimize the opportunities of subordinates to avoid surveillance or take measures that render their efforts to avoid surveillance inconsequential.

Random terror has often been employed to maintain order within tyrannical relationships. It not only inhibits escape attempts but also minimizes rebellious acts by subordinates. The administration of random terror from time to time powerfully informs all that they are vulnerable to the violence of the tyrant. In addition, it creates a context where the subordinates become extremely anxious if any of their fellow subordinates deviate from the wishes of the tyrant. Some will inform on their fellow subordinates to lessen the likelihood of unleashing random terror.

Most large-scale tyrannies use secret police and informers to keep the subordinates under surveillance. Some subordinates inform on other subordinates to curry favor from the tyrant. When subordinates are unable to identify the police and informers, they are fearful of committing any acts that deviate from the wishes of the tyrant.

Contingent Futures

Contingent, not shared, futures structure tyrannical relationships. The welfare of the subordinates depends on the tyrant's withholding violence; the interests of the tyrant are served by subordinates' continuing to abide by the directives issued by the tyrant. Personal, not social, objectives structure social encounters contextualized by tyrannical relationships. Both the objectives to be achieved and the programs to be implemented to achieve the objectives are formulated by the tyrant. The tyrant specifies the sequences of activities that are to be taken.

Tyrants project distal futures and then program the action to be taken between the present and the distal future. The tyrant's actions and the actions of subordinates are assessed by the tyrant on the basis of their contribution toward the achievement of the tyrant's objectives. In extreme tyrannical relationships, subordinates live from moment to moment. They do not project futures beyond the immediate encounter. They only project a future of being attentive and responsive to the tyrant. Tyrannical subordinates become concerned with immediate gratifications.

If the tyrant can maintain a focus on distal futures while subordinates are concerned with immediate gratification, it makes the tyrant's position more secure. The construction of a rebellion requires subordinates to project a distal future. If the subordinates are not given the opportunity to think of distal futures, they are less likely to rebel.

The continuation of a smooth tyrannical relationship requires that the subordinates be competent. They must be capable of performing the tasks called for by their tyrant. That, of course, requires that they receive some training. Even the completion of mundane tasks, such as harvesting fields, requires some instruction. Whenever subordinates are exposed to ideas, it is a threat to the continuation of the relationship. Even learning how to harvest a crop provides subordinates with a skill that might have some value in other situations, if they manage to escape.

The tyrant is faced with a paradoxical situation. On the one hand, if subordinates are to be competent, they must have some knowledge. On the other hand, any information made available to them at least implicitly threatens the stability of the relationship. The paradox is usually resolved by providing subordinates with only the information essential for the effective performance of their assignments and minimizing their exposure to any other information. The more information they have at their command, the more likely subordinates are to flee or rebel.

While the establishment and maintenance of the tyrannical relationship rests on asymmetrical vulnerability, the continuation of an enduring and stable tyrannical relationship is facilitated by the tyrant's maintaining as nearly as possible a complete monopoly of knowledge (Innis 1951, 1972). Ignorant subordinates are easier to control than informed ones. Of course, it is almost impossible to maintain a complete monopoly of knowledge. As long as the subordinates have some contact with others, they are likely to have access to information. When they have access to information, the relationship is rendered somewhat unstable.

In the extreme tyrannical relationship, tyrant and subordinate have no shared futures. They have only contingent futures based on reciprocal dependence. The subordinates' objectives are to avoid punishment and to survive; the tyrant's objectives are personal benefits extracted from subordinates. For them to coordinate their actions, however, they must establish a series of objectives. The tyrant specifies those objectives. If the tyrant loses the ability to control either his or the subordinates' future, the relationship will disintegrate.

Standpoints

In the extreme tyrannical relationship, there is no sharing of standpoints. Tyrant and subordinates are neither mutually nor solidarily responsive. Each attends to the other, and they attend to shared foci. But they are only bilaterally responsive. They attend and respond to each other, but they do not act with each other. The tyrant notes the ongoing and projected activity of subordinates, but not to act with them. Instead, the tyrant keeps them under surveillance to control and direct them effectively. Reciprocally, subordinates give primary attention to the tyrant and whatever the tyrant directs them to attend to.

The responsiveness of the tyrant to subordinates is similar to that of the predator to the prey; the responsiveness of subordinates is similar to that of the prey. Subordinates minimize contact, and if that is not possible, they attempt to minimize the likelihood of unleashing violence.

When human beings jointly produce coordinated action and achieve social objectives, they are commonly solidarily responsive when they achieve their objectives. Whenever a tyrant and subordinates achieve an objective specified by the tyrant, it tends to elicit solidary responsiveness. If a pure tyrannical relationship is to be maintained, however, the tyrant does not celebrate with subordinates. A tyrant who does so tends to become embedded with them, thereby attenuating the asymmetrical relationship. Of course, in some instances, tyrants have adopted the standpoints of their subordinates. When that occurs, to an extent it lessens the severity of the tyrannical relationship.

Tyrants and their subordinates sometimes adopt the same standpoint. For the most part, however, that comes about by subordinates adopting the standpoint of the tyrant. Many subordinates come to view events from the point of view of tyrants. As a consequence, a pseudo solidary relationship sometimes infuses tyrannical relationships. The shared standpoint is not mutually constructed, but comes about by the subordinates adopting the standpoint of their tyrant. In the extreme form, the subordinates adopt the same standpoint toward themselves as does their tyrant. They come to see themselves as nothing more than instruments of their tyrant. When that standpoint is adopted by subordinates, they are relatively easy to control.

When that occurs, or to the extent it occurs, only a single standpoint is viable within the relationship—that of the tyrant. The subordinates do not have a standpoint that is distinctive from their tyrant. Nor is a third-party standpoint a viable part of tyrannical relationships. Authority relationships rest on a solidary foundation that contains a third-party standpoint. Both the authority and the subordinates have their own distinctive standpoints, but in addition, they share a standpoint provided by their solidary relationship. An authority and a subordinate may not be in complete agreement on the standpoint derived from their solidary relationship, but at least they agree that there is another perspective that is relevant when they assess their relationship. In contrast, the only standpoint that is viable in the tyrannical relationship is that of the tyrant. There is no basis for negotiation. One either complies, flees, rebels, or suffers the consequences.

Bettelheim's Observations

Many think that tyrannical relationships are something that existed in the distant past. Yet tyrannical relationships of considerable complexity still pervade many modern societies. They are not merely historical phenomena. One of the relatively recent social structures infused with tyranny was that of Nazi Germany. The social structure of Nazi Germany was composed of many intertwined social relationships (Abel 1968); at its core, however, was a complexly intertwined set of authority and tyrannical relationships. At one extreme of that set of relationships were the relationships that existed between guards of the concentration camps and inmates of the camps. That relationship approached pure tyranny (Weiland 1975).

Many scholars have offered their interpretations of the events that occurred within these camps (Arendt 1973; Hilberg 1961; Kogon 1950). The following account is derived largely from the observations of Burno Bettelheim (1943). Bettelheim was an inmate of Dachau and Buchenwald in 1937-38. Bettelheim stated his primary reason for studying the relationships between the guards and prisoners was to keep from going insane. "It (the study) was developed to protect this individual against a disintegration of his personality" (Bettelheim 1943, 421). His analysis was framed by a effort to understand "the concentration camp as a means of producing changes in prisoners which will make them more useful subjects of the Nazi state" (Bettelheim 1943, 419).

The first obvious fact was that the inmates were violently captured and forcibly transported to the camps. Many of them were brutally beaten and tortured; some were killed before they arrived at the camps. They were in a state of shock when they arrived at the camps, and were then exposed to additional brutalities. The prisoners were a diverse lot. Among the inmates were social democrats, communists, other political activists, former members of the French Foreign Legion, Jehovah's Witnesses, Jewish prisoners, former members of Nazi groups who had fallen from grace, and a few who were targets of revenge by powerful Nazis. Despite the variation in their social backgrounds there were many similarities in their response to the tyrannical relationship.

The typical victim was retained for several days in prison before being transported to a camp. Most were first exposed to torture after arriving at the camp. The initial torture was referred to by the Gestapo as "the prisoner's welcome" (Bettelheim 1943, 424). The prisoners were whipped, kicked, shot, and wounded with bayonets. The specifics of the torture varied. Some were required to stare for hours at glaring lights, or kneel for hours; now and then a prisoner was killed. The physical torture alternated with forcing the prisoners to accuse themselves of vile crimes, accuse their wives of adultery, and sundry self-humiliations. "The purpose of the tortures was to break the resistance of the prisoners, and to assure the guards that they were really superior to them" (Bettelhiem, 1942:429). Most of those who resisted the torture and humiliation were killed by the Gestapo guards.

Bettelheim states that he was able to endure because he became convinced that these horrible experiences "did not happen to 'him' as a subject, but only to 'him' as on object" (Bettelheim 1943, 431). Other inmates developed the same attitude.

The violence that implements a tyrannical relationship must be controlled violence. If the torture is too great, it is not effective. In one instance the prisoners were forced to stand at attention in the winter without overcoats because two prisoners had escaped. "After about 20 prisoners had died from exposure the discipline broke down. The threats of the guards became ineffective" (Bettelheim 1943, 434). When the torture was too violent and sustained, the prisoners became indifferent to threats. The guards were no longer able to elicit compliance.

When victims first entered the camps, they were primarily concerned with maintaining their personality intact. Those who survived and became old-timers became primarily concerned with "how to live as well as possible within the camp" (Bettelheim 1943, 437). Once that state was reached the earlier separation between self as object and self as subject disappeared. Then things that happened to them were regarded as real. They accepted the position of subordinate in a tyrannical relationship. There was variation in how long it took the prisoners to adopt that standpoint, and some never adopted it; nearly all who did not were killed. A few escaped, and a few others avoided becoming ideal subordinates by establishing underground affiliations with other victims.

Once the prisoners accepted their subordinate position within the tyrannical relationship, they discontinued being concerned with distal futures. "When the author expressed to some of the old prisoners his astonishment that they seemed not to be interested in discussing their future life outside the camp, they frequently admitted they no longer could visualize themselves living outside the camp" (Bettelheim 1943, 439). "The prisoners lived only in the immediate present; they lost the feeling for the sequence of time, they became unable to plan for the future" (Bettelheim 1943, 445).

Bettelheim notes that the prisoners had reached the final stage of adjustment when they accepted the values of the Gestapo; or the prisoners became subordinates in a stable tyrannical relationship when they adopted the standpoint of their tyrants. Some of the prisoners began using the same words the guards used in describing themselves and other prisoners. "Practically all prisoners who had spent a long time in the camp took over the Gestapo's attitude toward the so-called unfit prisoners" (Bettelheim 1943,

448). Some attempted to acquire bits of the Gestapo uniform despite the fact that the Gestapo would punish them for their efforts if they were caught. One of the games the Gestapo guards played was to take turns hitting each other in the chest with their fists. The one who quit lost the game. "This game was copied by the old prisoners" (Bettelheim 1943, 450).

Many other things occurred within these camps. Some prisoners helped one another escape. Some elements of solidarity emerged among the prisoners. The emphasis in the above account is on the tyrannical relationship and its consequences. Studies of other tyrannical relationships reveal many of the same consequences. Most of us would respond in much the same way as these prisoners did if forced to occupy a subordinate position within an extremely tyrannical relationship.

The tyrannical relationship that prevailed between the Gestapo and inmates of the concentration camps of Germany is but one example of complex tyrannical relationships constructed in modern nations. Tyrannical relationships are pervasive in many contemporary societies. Most of these tyrannies, like that of Nazi Germany, are rationalized as necessary for the collective welfare. Hitler claimed he was acting in the interests of the German people; and many supported him. All contemporary tyrannies are rationalized in much the same way.

Recently, a president of the United States attempted to infuse his office with elements of tyranny. Richard Nixon attempted to get the Internal Revenue Service to audit the tax returns of citizens who opposed his policies. He also attempted to withhold information from citizens on the grounds that it would threaten the security of the nation. Of course, what was threatened was Nixon's occupancy of the office. Nixon attempted to interject elements of coercion into the relationship between the office of the presidency and citizens.

Consequences

Acts toward others tend to elicit a response in kind. The infliction of violence on another tends to elicit a violent response. Tyrants are well aware of that. If they are not, they will not long retain their position. They know that many of their subordinates would do them violence if they had the opportunity. To rule through terror is to live in terror. Tyrants surround themselves with protective devices and bodyguards. These provide some security. But no one can remain constantly alert to all dangers, and many tyrants have been killed by those hired to protect them. Tyrants who survive for any length of time learn to trust no one.

Tyrannical relationships rest on violence. That makes the tyrant the focal point of a web of complex fragile relations. Tyrants must continually be on their toes. Their life is neither dull nor secure. All tyrants must prevent other members of the relationship from acquiring the knowledge, material resources, and following that would allow a challenge to them.

Tyrants of large-scale tyrannies need lieutentants. Yet those who are the closest to the tyrant are the ones the tyrant can trust least. They are the ones who are most likely to depose him. The lowly members of tyrannical relationships seldom have the resources to challenge the tyrant — although tyrants have been killed by rank-and-file members of tyrannical relationships. More commonly, tyrants are deposed by their closest lieutenants. The lieutenants are most likely to have the knowledge, command of instruments of violence, and following necessary to challenge the tyrant. Furthermore, the lieutenants recognize that if they attempt to depose the tyrant, it is unlikely that many will come to the defense of the tyrant under attack. From the point of view of the rank-and-file, one tyrant is as good or bad as another. Most of the rank-and-file are indifferent to, if not antagonistic to, the incumbent tyrant.

Many lieutenants of tyrants become disenchanted with their tyrant. Some become alienated because they fear they may be destroyed by their tyrant. Others become disenchanted with the policies of the tyrant. Hitler's right-hand man, Alfred Speer, plotted to kill Hitler (Speer 1970). Nearly all who attempt to depose tyrants rationalize their actions on the grounds that the tyrant has became corrupt and vicious. Most insurgents promise to institute a more humane and stable social order. That rationalization has been offered at least from the time of Julius Caesar.

All tyrants who have retained their position for any length of time recognize that they are the targets of animosity. They know that many, including their lieutenants, have become disenchanted with them. Yet to maintain a large-scale and enduring tyranny, tyrants must rely on their lieutenants. As a consequence, the tyrant must maintain a delicate balance between relying on lieutenants and keeping them dependent. Some have successfully maintained that balance for decades, but many have been killed by their closest advisers.

When social structures become interlaced with tyranny, social order is maintained by fear and intimidation. Corruption and egoism come to the fore as each person becomes primarily concerned with himself. Tyranny atomizes people; each person tends to withdraw into a personal world. Selfish concerns predominate; in extreme tyranny, compassion for others and altruistic behavior become uncommon, if present at all. Each individual, including the tyrant, becomes primarily concerned with self-survival.

One of the paradoxes of tyranny is that while the institution of tyranny is rationalized as necessary to establish or maintain social order, its continuation creates disorder. Tyrannical systems create strong antagonisms and animosities. The lack of attachment to and embeddedness with others erodes the social foundation necessary for personal and social stability. All, including the tyrant, become more erratic as a tyranny endures. Many tyrants have been famous for erratic behavior. One Roman dictator conferred upon his favorite horse membership in the Roman senate. The behavior of the subordinates of tyrannical system also tends to become erratic. Many subordinates are ambivalent. On the one hand, they tend to identify with their tyrants; on the other hand, they hate their tyrants. How each person will behave becomes highly dependent on the immediate situation. A slave may one moment express awe and gratitude toward the tyrant, and the next moment, if the opportunity presents itself, attempt to kill the tyrant.

Tyrannical systems produce irresponsible persons. Solidarity and accountability, which provide the foundation for compassion and obligations, are replaced by fear. Consequently, individuals do not regard themselves as responsible for their own actions. They do whatever is demanded of them, but as the relationship strips them of the ability to make choices, they no longer regard themselves as responsible for the consequences of their actions. Responsibility is vested in the tyrant, but the tyrant is not accountable. Reciprocally, subordinates are highly accountable to their tyrant, but have no responsibility for the consequences of their actions. The actions of subordinates reflect only the will of the tyrant; they do not reflect their personal will.

Tyranny also produces ignorant people. The stability of a tyrannical systems is enhanced if subordinates can be kept ignorant. Most tyrants recognize that; they "keep private what should be public — the knowledge and competence needed for planning and carrying out the future of a community" (Miller, Weiland, and Couch 1978, 282). The subordinates lack the knowledge necessary to program long-range and complex futures. That lack of knowledge is often used by tyrants to justify the continuation of tyranny. Nearly all tyrants claim their subordinates are incapable of looking after their own welfare; they need a strongman to order their personal lives.

Many who call for the replacement of a tyrant locate the source of the current difficulties in the personality of the tyrant. They presume that if a different person were the focal point, all would be well. The evils of tyranny are not located in the person, but are located in the relationship between the tyrant and subordinates and the relationships among the subordinates. When one tyrant is replaced by another, the level of corruption and selfishness often diminishes for a short time, only to reemerge as the new tyranny matures. Tyrannical relationships cannot be reformed by replacing one tyrant with another. The only reasonable alternative is to replace a tyrannical relationship with another relationship.

Summary

Tyranny is one social form that human beings have devised to construct and maintain social order. It is a rather sad commentary on humanity, but many social structures of ancient and modern civilization were (are) infused with tyranny. Nor does the evidence indicate that tyranny is disappearing. The tyranny present in Nazi Germany, Stalin's USSR, and contemporary Iran seems to compare favorably with that of the Roman Empire, ancient Egypt, and ancient China. And, of course, classrooms, work groups, bureaucracies, and therapy centers are sometimes infused with elements of tyranny. When elements of tyranny are established in such groups, it is done with "good intentions;" coercion is deemed necessary to deal with a difficult situation.

Many tyrannies emerge from authority relationships. Authorities often find themselves frustrated by a lack of compliance from their subordinates. One way of managing the situation is to interject violence, or at least the threat of violence. The interjection of threats and violence sometimes solves the immediate problem. The long-range consequences are seldom, if ever, satisfactory. At least they are not satisfactory to the subordinates — although some tyrants are at least temporarily pleased with the results.

Small tyrannies are common in many custodial institutions of democratic societies. Most of them do not flow from the viciousness and meanness of employees of these institutions; they emerge as a consequence of the frustrations of employees.

For example, prison guards often establish, if not a tyrannical relationship, at least a relationship infused with tyranny toward the prisoners. The guards have an obligation to manage the prisoners and prevent their escape. Very few prisoners have any commitment to the system that has placed them in prison. Therefore, it is difficult to maintain order on the basis of an authority relationship. Compliance often is not forthcoming unless a threat is issued. To make threats effective, it is necessary from time to time to wreck a little violence on the prisoners.

The guards are hypothetically accountable to their superiors. But guards often are not under surveillance by their superiors; even when they are, their superiors are likely to regard a little violence as necessary for maintaining order. That combination almost invites tyranny. One consequence is that those committed to these institutions often become subordinates in a complex set of hierarchical relationships infused with tyranny.

The transformation of misfits and incompetents into adjusted and competent social beings is seldom achieved by making them subordinates in tyrannical relationships. Sometimes the transformation is accomplished via parental, solidary, and accountable relationships. These relationships are often conspicuously absent in therapeutic and correctional institutions.

Chapter 18 Representation

Representative relationships, like parental, authority, charismatic, and tyrannical relationships, are asymmetrical. But representative relationships are profoundly different from other asymmetric relationships. The focal point of the other asymmetric relationships is the dominate person. The flow of influence is primarily from parent, authority, charismatic leader, or tyrant to other members of these relationships. Generally speaking, the person who serves as focal point in other asymmetrical relationships exerts greater influence on each of the other members than does each member on the focal point. In contrast, the focal point of representative relationships — the representative — does not necessarily exercise any greater influence than other members of the relationship. Representatives frequently complain that they are at the beck and call of their constituents.

The representative is the focal point of representative relationships, but is not superordinate to constituents. Constituents evaluate and issue directives to representatives. In parental relationships, the superordinate instructs the subordinate; in authority and tyrannical relationships, the superordinate directs and supervises activities of subordinates; and in charismatic relationships, the leader defines the world for followers. In contrast, in representative relationships both the representative and constituents program the actions of the representative, and reality is a collective construction. Representatives neither instruct their constituents, direct their actions, nor define their world for them. Furthermore, representatives are beholden to their constituents; constituents are not beholden to their representatives.

Two distinctive features of representative relationships are that (1) one person is authorized to act in behalf of others in dealings with members of other collectivities; and (2) the representative is accountable to constituents, while the constituents are only minimally accountable to the representative. The representative relationship is not universal. Some primitive groups do not seem to have developed this particular social form. According to Lee (1959), some American Indian groups never authorized one person to act in behalf of others; nor did individual members of these groups presume to act in behalf of others when dealing with outsiders. Other primitive groups on occasion activated a quasi-representative relationship when dealing with outsiders. In most instances, however, the representative relationships

232

established in primitive societies were of short duration and limited significance.

A few primitive groups developed enduring representative relationships. For example, the Iroquois Indians had a system of interconnecting tribal councils and a grand council that united all the Iroguois tribes (Wallace 1972). Each member of the council represented a clan. Each council member was accountable to his clan; on occasion, a council member was deposed when his clan became displeased with his performance.

In many ancient civilizations, the kings, tyrants, and leaders of societies negotiated with other kings, tyrants, and leaders. In most of these instances, however, the person who negotiated with outside groups had an authority or tyrannical relationship with other members of his society. His actions were not programmed by the collectivity, nor was he accountable to .rank and file members of his society for his actions while negotiating with outsiders.

On many occasions, intergroup relationships were formulated and modified by persons delegated by authorities or tyrants. These delegates implemented the wishes of the authority or tyrant by meeting with the delegates, authorities, or tyrants of other societies. But these delegates were not selected by rank-and-file members of their societies, nor were they accountable to them. They were selected by the authorities or tyrants of their society and accountable to them. This same form of managing intergroup relationships still prevails in most international negotiations. Presidents, prime ministers, and kings of societies select ambassadors; the ambassadors meet and attempt to resolve conflicts and formulate intergroup policies. These delegates are not accountable to a collectivity.

The representative relationship as a distinct social form seems to have emerged among the ancient Greeks. Some of the Greek city- states selected citizens to act in behalf of the city. The selection of the representatives was accomplished in a number of ways. Some were elected, others were selected by lot, still others were selected by a combination of elections and lotteries. Those selected were authorized to act in behalf of the city; and those selected were accountable to all other citizens. A nebulous form of the representative relationship was established in a number of societies. But clearly defined and robust representative relationships were first established during the American Revolution. Those who drafted the Constitution of the United States articulated a system of social relationships that had at its core the representative relationship. They called the system they proposed a republic, to distinguish it from participatory democracy. Perhaps, a better term would be *representative democracy*. The proposed system of relationships called for the election of persons to act in behalf of others. Those selected were accountable to the people who had elected them. The objective of the proposed system was to maintain social unity among large collectivities with a minimal degree of authority and to prohibit the establishment of a tyranny (Epstein 1984).

The representative relationship emerged as an alternative to tyranny, charismatic leadership, and authority. It provides the means for a number of collectivities with different interests to maintain peaceful intergroup relationships. Representatives are selected to negotiate differences and formulate principles of action that all, including the representatives, must follow. The representative, unlike the tyrant or authority, does not have the prerogative of directing the behavior of other members of the collectivity. The representative is authorized only to act in their behalf when dealing with outsiders and is accountable to constituents for actions when dealing with outsiders.

The logistics of human interaction are such that it is impossible for all members of two large collectivities to interact peacefully with each other. Two large collectivities can conflict in the form of hurling insults at each other, going to war, diffusely intermingling with each other, or avoiding each other. If two large collectivities are to formulate stable intergroup relationships, it is necessary for a single person or a few people from each group to meet and formulate programs of actions. Two large collectivities cannot formulate programs of intergroup relationships by all members of each collectivity interacting with all members of the other collectivity. The formulation of intergroup relationships requires that a few be authorized to act in behalf of others.

A mature representative relationship is established when (1) one member of a collectivity is authorized to act in behalf of the collectivity; (2) criteria for who can serve as representative and participate in the selection of the representative are formulated; (3) the representative is given some autonomy in dealings with other collectivities; (4) the constituents maintain some surveillance of their representative's action when acting in their behalf; and (5) it is consensually acknowledged that the representative is accountable to constituents. Representatives are selected by the collectivity, evaluated by the collectivity, and can be replaced by their constituents.

The emergence and maintenance of a representative relationship rests on a foundation of a solidary relationship. Members of the collectivity, including the representative, acknowledge that the collectivity has interests that are distinct from the interests of other collectivities, yet project a future of peaceful relationships with other collectivities. The members of a labor union recognize that their interests are distinct from and somewhat incompatible with the interests of management, but project a future of peacefully relating to management. Reciprocally, members of management recognize that their interests are distinct from and somewhat incompatible with the interests of labor and project a future of peacefully relating to labor. The members of both collectivities also project a future of resolving differences and formulating programs of action for future intergroup relationships by having representatives of each collectivity meet and negotiate their differences.

Authorization

The categorical identities of representative and constituents emerge from a solidary base. Those with shared interests authorize one among them to act in behalf of the collectivity in confrontations with other collectivities. It is understood that someone from the competing collectivity will act in behalf of the opposing collectivity. The authorization of a person to act in behalf of others is contextualized by mutual recognition of competing interests and the projection of a distal future of interdependence between the collectivities.

Representatives are authorized to "re" "present" the interests of their collectivities when meeting with representatives of the opposing collectivity. They are categorically differentiated from other members of their collectivity for a limited duration. The duration of the categorical differentiation may be for only a single encounter with the opposition or may be for a specified period of time — say, two years. Whatever the duration of the assignment, for the time being the representative is authorized to present the interests of the collectivity in encounters with other collectivities. Only the representative, not the constituents, is authorized to offer proposals to the opposition.

Newly forming protest groups sometimes fail to recognize the necessity of authorizing individuals to act in behalf of the collectivity. Sometimes, members of newly forming protest groups, especially those with a robust solidarity, insist that all members of the collectivity meet with the opposition (Weiland and Couch 1975). When more than two individuals interact to resolve differences, the complexity of the interaction renders the encounters chaotic. The completion of intergroup negotiation sessions almost demands that the interaction between collectivities be structured so that they consist of two individuals offering proposals and responding to each other's proposals.

More than two individuals may be present at intergroup sessions, but even then, if the sessions are to culminate in agreements, it is necessary for the interaction to take the form of two spokespersons offering proposals, listening to each other's proposals and responding to each other's proposals. If more than a single individual from each side becomes involved in the negotiations, it is very likely the sessions will become so chaotic that no programs for future relatedness between the two collectivities will be established. Sometimes, two or more people are authorized to act in behalf of each collectivity, but even then, as the intergroup sessions unfold, one person for each side usually becomes the spokesperson.

Some representatives are only authorized to address a single issue when meeting with the opposition; others, like the members of state legislatures, are authorized to act in behalf of their constituents when addressing a wide range of issues. In all cases, it is understood by both the representative and the constituents that the representative is obliged to advance the interests of constituents.

The specification of the obligations of a representative is a collective endeavor. Theoretically, all constituents have the prerogative of instructing their representative. In practice, some constituents contribute more than others; the interests of some become obligations of the representative more than do the interests of others. Some constituents remain relatively silent when the actions of the representative are programmed; others are vociferous. In large collectivities such as those that select state representatives, two or more persons offer themselves as would-be representatives and indicate the standpoint they will adopt and the lines of action they will pursue if elected representative. The constituents select one of the would-be representatives as their representative.

Constituents are not subordinate to their representatives. In fact, the opposite is the case. The representative is subordinate to her constituents. Constituents routinely issue directives to their representative. They tell the representative how to behave when meeting with the opposition. The representative-to-be may contribute to the program formulated, but it is not the representative's program. It is the program of the collectivity. The representative-to-be does not dominate the constituents. The interaction between representatives tends to be egalitarian with the representative attempting to articulate the interests of all in meetings with other collectivities. Representatives are the focal point of interaction within their collectivities, but they are not superior to their constituents.

Nonetheless, the authorization of a person to act in behalf of a collectivity's interests requires internal differentiation. Only one or a few can be designated as representatives. That act implicitly places the representative in a superior position. At the minimum, the selection of a person to act in behalf of others implies that the person selected is more capable of representing the interests of the collectivity than are other members of the collectivity.

Criteria for Participation

On occasion, a short lived representative relationship is constructed on the basis of informal and unspecified criteria. For example, the members of two youthful gangs might make contact with each other with a short-lived representative relationship emerging. One person from each group may emerge as spokesperson for the two gangs, meet, and negotiate. Within such encounters, the criteria for who can participate in the selection of the representative and who can serve as the representative may not be specified. But nearly all enduring collectivities that maintain a representative relationship formulate explicit criteria specifying who can take part in the selection of representatives, who can serve as representatives, how the representatives are to be selected, and the duration of the representatives' terms of office.

Often, all who meet the formal criteria for membership in voluntary organizations are eligible to participate in the selection. All dues-paying union members have the right to take part in the selection of those who will represent the interests of labor when negotiating with management. All citizens eighteen years of age or older have the prerogative of voting in elections that select legislators in some states.

Within established collectivities, the criteria for participating in the selection of representatives are usually so well established that they are taken for granted. With emerging special interest groups, however, the criteria are not precisely formulated. Usually, only after an emerging interest group has become recognized as a viable collectivity does the issue of who can participate in the selection of representatives come to the fore. Then criteria for membership are usually specified, and all who meet the criteria have the right to participate in the selection of their representative.

Generally speaking, anyone who meets the criteria for taking part in the selection of a representative is also eligible to serve as representative—although in some cases the criteria specifying eligibility for serving as representative are more restrictive than those specifying who can take part in the selection of the representative. For example, the constitution of the United States specifies that only those twenty-five years of age or older are eligible to serve as federal legislators. In some states, those eighteen years of age or older can take part in the selection of federal legislators.

The selection of the representative of emerging groups is often achieved by internal negotiation. Once an interest group becomes established, however, election procedures are usually formulated. The most common procedure for selecting representatives is that each member is authorized to cast a vote. Other procedures have been used. For example, among the ancient Greeks, the selection of some representatives was accomplished by lot. The names of all eligible persons were placed in a container; the person whose name was drawn from the container was designated representative.

One distinctive feature of the representative relationship is that occupancy of the position of representative is for a limited duration. U.S. senators serve for six years; members of the House of Representatives serve for two years. Established collectivities commonly select representatives for one, two, three, or four years. The specification of a time limit assures that all representatives will be accountable to their constituents.

Autonomy

The activity of each representative when meeting with the opposition is at least partially programmed by constituents. Sometimes the programming of the representative's action is only implicit. That is typically the case when citizens of a region select legislatures. In order to act as a representative, however, it is also necessary for the representative to have some autonomy. If the activity of the person designated to meet with the opposition is completely specified by constituents, the person is merely a messenger, not a representative. Yet it is implicitly recognized by all—the representative, constituents, and members of competing collectivities—that the actions of the representative are constrained. The parameters constraining some representatives are very restrictive; others are allowed to exercise considerable autonomy during intergroup negotiations.

The mixed-motive nature of the relationships between collectivities that work out their differences through representation requires that the representative be allocated some autonomy. Members of competing collectivities, implicitly at least, if not explicitly, recognize that their representative will not be able to achieve all the objectives desired; some compromises will be necessary. Of course, some groups adopt a nonnegotiable position in their confrontations. They send representatives to "make demands" of the opposing collectivity. When that standpoint is adopted, a representative relationship has not been constructed. The spokesperson in such cases is merely a messenger.

When a representative relationship is constructed, the representative is authorized to make proposals, respond to proposals of the other representative and make agreements with the opposing representative. The representative may or may not be authorized to forge commitments that are binding on constituents. The representatives of labor usually are not authorized to forge commitments with management. The representatives of the two sides meet, make proposals, evaluate each other's proposals, and sometimes reach agreements. In most instances, however, the agreements are not binding on either labor or management until they have been submitted to the constituents. The constituents in these instances retain the prerogative of validating or repudiating agreements reached by representatives. In other instances, such as negotiations between state legislators, the representatives are authorized to make commitments that are binding on their constituents without the constituents having the opportunity to validate or reject the agreements.

Surveillance

Constituents must have access to some information about their representative's actions during intergroup negotiating sessions if a viable representative relationship is to be maintained. If the constituents have no access to information about their representative's action or have only the information provided them by their representative, the representative relationship tends to evolve toward an authority or tyrannical relationship (Katovich, Weiland, and Couch 1981).

The nature and amount of information available to constituents are highly varied. In some instances, say in confrontations between small and local collectivities, information about the representative's actions is available to all. Interested parties attend negotiating sessions and directly observe the actions of the representatives and spread the word to other members of the community. When members of the school board of a small community meet with representatives of the teachers to negotiate next year's contract, many members of the community and other teachers may be in attendance. Then many, if not all, of the constituents of both sides have detailed information about the negotiating sessions. In contrast, when some members of the U.S. House of Representatives meet in private to work out a compromise on a piece of legislation, almost no one except the representatives concerned knows what transpires in the meetings.

Information about a representative's action can come from a variety of sources: direct observation of intergroup negotiations, media accounts of the event, accounts provided by opposing representatives, and accounts provided by representatives to their constituents. If the only source of information available to the constituents is reports provided by representatives, the information acquired will usually be inadequate for calling the representative into account. Most representatives minimize their failures and usually provide information that reflects favorably on their performance.

The representative who can control the information available to constituents has a monopoly of knowledge (Innis 1950, 1972). Then the representative relationship is likely to transform into an authority or tyrannical relationship. Unless information derived from direct observation or from an independent source is available to constituents, it is almost impossible to maintain a representative relationship. The First Amendment to the Constitution of the United States explicitly recognizes the necessity of an independent source of information for the maintenance of a viable representative relationship.

One major paradox of the representative relationship is that when the intergroup negotiating sessions are public, readily observable to all, it is almost impossible for representatives to resolve differences and reach agreements. When the actions of representatives are highly observable, each representative tends to adopt a rigid position, and compromises are difficult to achieve. If the representative's actions are *not* observable, and if the relationship endures for some time, representatives tend to become corrupt. They have the opportunity to make private deals with opposing representatives that benefit the representatives but do not benefit the constituents.

One of the delicate problems associated with the representative relationship is creating the context necessary for the representatives to reach agreements yet providing the constituents with sufficient information to make the representatives accountable to the constituents. If representatives are under intense surveillance, the intergroup sessions are likely to be deadlocked and perhaps result in an escalation of conflict between the two collectivities. If surveillance is minimal, a common long range development is that the representatives sell out their constituents.

Accountability

Perhaps the most distinguishing feature of the representative relationship is that the focal point of the relationship is highly accountable to others, whereas others are minimally, if at all, accountable to the focal point. The representative relationship is the opposite of the tyrannical relationship on this dimension. The activities of representatives are under more or less continual surveillance, and their actions are almost continually evaluated by the constituents. Representatives are expected to provide accounts of their actions to their constituents. If their actions are unsatisfactory to their constituents, the constituents have the prerogative of replacing the representative. Constituents, in contrast, are hardly, if ever, accountable to their representatives. Constituents have interests; and the representative is obliged to advance those interests. In sharp contrast, in the tyrannical relationship, the tyrant is not accountable to subordinates. The tyrant is subject to some surveillance, but as long as the tyrant controls the powers of coercion, subordinates' assessments have little, if any, import. Reciprocally, the tyrant's subordinates are intensely accountable to the tyrant. Subordinates who deviate can be punished, banished, or killed.

Representatives retain their position by satisfying constituents; the subordinates of a tyrant retain their position by satisfying the tyrant. The only accountability of the typical constituent is a diffuse one of the "duties of a citizen" or the "duties of a good union member." Constituents are no more accountable to the representative than they are to fellow constituents.

A presumption of a unity of interest among members of the collectivity underlies all representative relationships. That solidary foundation provides a base for making the representative accountable to all. In all but the smallest collectivities, however, there is less than complete unity within collectivities. Some want their representative to advance the cause of wheat farmers; others call for the construction of better transportation systems; still others desire improvements in the educational system. The typical representative is subjected to calls for accounts that stem from different foundations. It is nearly always impossible to act in a manner that is satisfactory to all.

That condition, in conjunction with the fact that most representatives occupy a critical position in the flow of information, entices many representative to become less than completely open when providing their constituents with information. Some naive representatives do attempt to be as open as possible with their constituents, but as representatives acquire experience, most learn to withhold certain bits of information and to give wide circulation to other bits of information. Experienced representatives also learn that if they carefully orchestrate their appearances before their constituents, they can lessen the likelihood of calls for account.

The presumption of a uniform solidary foundation, the focus of accountability on the representative, and the central position the representative typically occupies in the flow of information often result in representatives' becoming disenchanted with their constituents. Many conclude they are not sufficiently appreciated by their constituents. When that belief emerges, some representatives take advantage of their special position. Many representatives have opportunities to act to achieve personal benefit as well as to advance the interests of their constituents. Experienced representatives may take bribes and accrue personal wealth by taking advantage of opportunities associated with the position.

Practical difficulties often make it almost impossible for constituents to maintain the level of surveillance necessary to effectively call their representatives into account. This is especially true when representatives meet, interact with, and negotiate with several other representatives. The constituents of federal legislators, for example, often have a difficult time determining and evaluating the actions their representatives take in their behalf. And these representatives sometimes become corrupt. A partial correction for this problem comes from other representatives. Representatives can easily monitor one another. On occasion, the corrupt practices of a representative have been exposed by fellow representatives. The partisan interests of representatives and their close contact with one another can supplement the surveillance and accountability of each representative's constituents (Epstein 1984).

Summary

The representative relationship is an asymmetrical form. Unlike all other asymmetrical social relationships, the focal point of the relationship is not superior to other members of the relationship. Individuals assigned the categorical identity of representative are obliged to others, but they have few prerogatives with respect to other members of the relationship. The only prerogative they have is to negotiate with other collectivities. In those meetings, they remain obliged to their constituents. Furthermore, subsequent to the intergroup negotiations, they are accountable to their constituents. The representative epitomizes the interests of a collectivity and is the focal point of interaction within a collectivity. The identity of representative is burdensome. The obligations are many and the prerogatives few. But it is a prestigious identity. Each representative stands for collectivity and is the center of attention.

The centrality of the identity provides the representative with opportunities to acquire more information relevant to the interests of the collectivity than that acquired by most constituents. The obligations of representatives in conjunction with the special information and contacts they make, often entice them to take advantage of the situation and advance their personal interests at the cost of the interests of their constituents.

Each representative relationship is inherently unstable. The intense accountability associated with the representative identity entices some representatives to attempt to transform the relationship into an authority or tyrannical relationship. Some representatives become disenchanted with the position and return to the ranks.

Generally speaking, efforts on the part of representatives to transform the relationship into an authority relationship are resisted by constituents. Nonetheless, many representatives have been able to make the transformation. Representatives usually have more resources and information at their command than do most of the constituents and therefore are sometimes able to entice and/or coerce constituents to become subordinates.

The representative relationship, in contrast to authority, charismatic, and tyrannical relationships, presumes that all are competent to contribute to the formation of collective objectives. It presumes people are intelligent enough to know their own best interests. In short, the representative relationship presumes an informed populace capable of looking after their own welfare and structuring their own future.

The charismatic relationship and representative relationship are often intertwined in political affairs. Political candidates offer to serve as representatives. Each candidate competes with other candidates by attempting to establish a charismatic relationship with the electors. The candidates, like charismatic leaders, attempt to articulate widespread dissatisfactions and formulate programs of action that have wide appeal to the electors. Often, the political candidate who is most successful in constructing a charismatic relationship with the electors is the one authorized to assume the identity of representative. When the identity of representative is acquired, however, the individual becomes highly accountable to the electors. Representatives then find that constituents no longer evaluate them on their ability to articulate dissatisfactions, but on their ability to advance the constituents' interests when meeting with other representatives.

Chapter **19** Macrostructures

Complex worldwide social structures encase all of us. As a consequence, the future welfare of every person is contingent on the actions of others. Opportunities to obtain necessities and luxuries are dependent on the complexly entangled and ever changing relationships that compose international trade. That network is consequential. Who goes hungry and who does not is partially a consequence of that macrostructure. In a similar manner, the security of our lives is contingent on networks of relationships that compose governmental structures and international relations.

The sets of social relationships that constitute the macrostructures of modern societies and international relations have become far more complex and consequential than ever before. They allow human beings to undertake endeavors that were not possible in the past. The intertwined social relationships that link nations together allow citizens of wealthy nations to render aid and assistance to citizens of the less wealthy. Conversely, the authority relationships that are the heart of national armies are exceedingly threatening, not only to the less powerful, but also to one another. These complex sets of relationships allow the more powerful nations to unleash forces of destruction that can cause death and suffering for millions.

Macrostructures provide opportunities, but they are accompanied by constraints and risks. Even the welfare of the hermit living in a mountain retreat depends on the actions of others. If the Soviet Union and the United States begin a nuclear war, the hermit will suffer the consequences. The hermit, like each of us, has some control over his own life. But the life of the hermit, like each of our lives, is also contingent on the actions of others far removed from his everyday life. The multitude of social relationships and their interlinkages create a condition where the lives of all are contingent on the actions of others. Some of the complex macrostructures that human beings have invented allow multitudes of people to produce complex social endeavors that have improved the human condition; other structures have allowed some to wreck unmeasureable suffering on multitudes.

Therefore, if we are to obtain greater understanding of human conduct, and thus greater control of future developments, we need to analyze social action, social relationships, and macrostructures. We focused on the nature and consequences of forms of social action and forms of social relationships in the preceding chapters. But the development of a comprehensive explanation of human conduct requires giving attention to macrostructures as well as forms of social action and social relationships.

If we direct attention only to transactions produced within immediate encounters, the negotiating sessions of a married couple attempting to resolve their marital conflicts seem to contain the same elements of sociation as transactions produced by two ambassadors attempting to forge an international treaty. In both social encounters, two parties offer proposals, evaluate them, attempt to reach agreements and forge commitments that will structure the futures of the negotiating parties. A superficial analysis of the two negotiations might lead one to conclude that they are but two instances of the same form of social action. In one sense, they are; in another sense, they are not the same.

The negotiations of the husband and wife are an instance of interpersonal negotiations; the negotiations of the two ambassadors are an instance of intergroup negotiations. The actions within the two encounters have many similarities. Nonetheless, the consequences that flow from the two encounters are apt to be entirely different.

The resolution of a marital conflict is not likely to have sweeping consequences. If the couple are parents, then a failure to resolve their conflicts will have consequences for their children. Even if they do not have children, a failure to resolve their differences will probably have some consequences for their families and friends. Whether or not a particular marital conflict is resolved, however, usually does not have a resounding impact on the lives of a multitude of others.

The failure of the ambassadors of two superpowers to resolve differences is likely to have significant consequences for millions. The negotiations of ambassadors are contextualized by exceedingly complex sets of social relationships. The differences in consequences that flow from successful or unsuccessful negotiations of these two kinds of negotiations flow from the differences in how the negotiators are linked to the macrostructure.

Both encounters are contextualized. The negotiating sessions of the married couples are contextualized by their romantic, solidary, and accountable relationships and the relationships that each of them has with members of their extended families, their work associates, and their friends. Nonetheless, the extensiveness of their relationships with others is far less than the extensiveness of the relationships of international ambassadors. The negotiations of the ambassadors are encased by a far more complex set of social relationships than are the negotiations of married couples.

Therefore, to develop a comprehensive explanation of social life, it is necessary to simultaneously attend to the transactions produced by human beings when they convene, the relationships they activate when they convene, and the macrostructures that contextualize their encounters. An explanation of the consequences of social action cannot be achieved by attending only to the action produced within social encounters. The formulation of a comprehensive explanation of the difference in the consequences that flow from a marital versus an international negotiating session must attend to both the microprocesses produced in the encounters and the macrostructures that encase the negotiating sessions.

The consequences that may flow from these two kinds of negotiations are neither simply the result of the action produced by the negotiators nor simply the result of the macrostructure. The consequences are a function of both the actions of the negotiators and the macrostructures that encase the actions.

Despite the fact that there is great variation in the consequences flowing from the two kinds of negotiations, the interaction in both negotiations has many structural similarities. In both, if a successful resolution of differences is to be achieved, the negotiators must subordinate their mutually recognized differences to the social objective of formulating programs of action for the future that are mutually acceptable and that will control conflict.

There are complex interactive linkages for both sets of negotiators between their positions within their social structures and the transactions they produce. The specific set of relationships activated by each set of negotiators informs and constrains their actions within the encounters; in turn, the impact of their actions on the lives of others and on existing structures is contingent on their positions in the macrostructures. A failure of the married couple to resolve their differences will have consequences for a few others. In contrast, a failure of the international ambassadors to resolve the differences between their nations may result in the destruction of millions.

We have so far focused on elementary social processes and relationships. The presumption has been that if a set of concepts and frame of thought can be developed that is adequate for understanding basic social processes and relationships, these concepts and the frame of thought can be elaborated and applied to macrostructures. Social processes and relationships are the building blocks of social structures. Once complex social structures have emerged, however, these social structures in turn interface with elementary social processes and relationships. The development of understandings of that interface requires attending to both microprocesses and relationships and macroprocesses and relationships. Perhaps some insight into how that might be accomplished can be obtained by an examination of how complex social structures evolved.

The Evolutionary Trajectory

The development of complex macrostructures has greatly expanded the breadth of human life. Most members of modern societies interact with a large number of other people each day. Our lives are much more varied and more stimulating than the lives of those who live within social structures composed of only elementary social relationships. Few of us would trade our way of life, despite its risks and uncertainty, for that of nomadic food gatherers. At least we have the opportunities to expose ourselves to a far greater variety of experiences and to participate in a much wider range of activities than do most nomadic food gatherers; and for the most part, we can do that within a relatively peaceful context.

One of the obvious differences between the lives of members of primitive bands and the lives of citizens of modern nations is the complexity of the macrostructures that encase their actions. Our ancient ancestors lived out their lives within relatively simple macrostructures. Before the establishment of sedentary communities, which probably first occurred about twelve thousand years ago, everyone lived in small nomadic bands. Currently, very few live out their lives in such bands. Even the few who do are affected by the macrostructures of industrial societies. No contemporary band, tribe, or nation is free from the consequences of actions taken by citizens of complex societies.

The evolutionary trajectory of human societies has taken somewhat the same form as that of how each human being becomes incorporated into modern macrostructures. The ability of each human being to produce forms of social action precedes the emergence of the ability to use social relationships to structure social encounters; the simpler forms of social relationships are mastered before the more complex ones are; and recognition of the linkages between forms of social relationships is not acquired until at least two forms of social relationships have been mastered.

The general evolutionary trajectory of human societies has been from simple macrostructures to more complex ones. But the evolutionary trajectory has not been linear. Many different kinds of macrostructures have been constructed. Even today, there is considerable cross-nation variation in the macrostructures of complex societies. For example, the representative relationship is a significant dimension of the macrostructures of some modern nations; in other modern nations, the representative relationship is present only minimally, if at all. Tyrannical relationships infuse the social structure of some societies; other societies are relatively free of tyrannical relationships.

We will never know the exact sequence of the transformations that resulted in the establishment of modern social structures. But studies of contemporary primitive societies allow us to infer with a fair degree of certainty the order of some of the major developments. Members of all societies conflict, compete, accommodate to, and cooperate with one another. In some internal conflict is rare, in others it is common, but the members of all human societies cooperate with each other. If there is no cooperation among members of a society, the society disintegrates. Cooperation is *the* form of social action that is the foundation stone on which all human societies rest.

Parental and solidary relationships structure some actions of members of all societies except those undergoing complete disintegration. This suggests that the first social relationships developed by our ancient ancestors were parental and solidary. Elements of accountable and romantic relationships have been observed in nearly all primitive societies. These two social relationships also probably have an ancient past. Nearly all contemporary primitive groups also have command of the exchange relationship, although command of this relationship by these groups is often the consequence of members of primitive groups having established repetitive peaceful contacts with members of more complex societies. Tyrannical and authority relationships may not extend much farther back into history than five thousand years ago. It was about 3000 B.C. that city-states emerged in Mesopotamia and the Egyptian nation emerged in the Nile valley. Charismatic and representative relationships seem to be relatively recent inventions.

The emergence of complex macrostructures was contingent on the development and refinement of several different forms of social relationships. As each social relationship was developed, it became intertwined with preexisting social relationships. Sometimes, when a new relationship developed, it partially replaced an old relationship. For example, when mature representative relationships developed, they partially replaced authority and tyrannical relationships.

It may seem reasonable to expect that societies with large populations and complex macrostructures emerged directly from small and simple societies. But this does not seem to have been the case. Ethnographic studies of contemporary primitive groups indicate that nomadic hunting and gathering groups seldom reach a population of more than thirty people. When they approach that size, they fragment—divide into two smaller groups. It is reasonable to assume that the nomadic food-gathering societies of the ancient past also fragmented when the bands achieved populations in excess of thirty to fifty persons. Contemporary hunting and gathering societies have been squeezed into the less productive natural habitats. Therefore, it is possible that some ancient nomadic groups, living in the richer environments, achieved somewhat larger populations than contemporary nomadic societies. Nonetheless, it is doubtful that any achieved populations much greater than contemporary nomadic bands. The establishment of societies with large populations and complex macrostructures required that sedentary communities be established. Therefore, one of the central questions is: How did sedentary communities become established? A subsidiary question is: What was the nature of the most ancient sedentary communities?

Intergroup Relationships

The traditional explanation for the emergence of complex societies is that they rest on a foundation of agriculture. The presumption is that agricultural production enticed some groups to become sedentary. These sedentary communities in turn developed complex social structures. Yet archaeological evidence indicates that the most ancient sedentary communities were not populated by farmers. There is no evidence of domesticated plants or animals at the sites of the most ancient sedentary communities (Mellaart 1967).

In the ancient past, when all human beings lived in small autonomous nomadic groups, each band sought out the necessities of life independent of other bands. On occasion, two groups made contact with each other. Some of the bands had repeated contacts with each other. Sometimes members of the two groups intermingled in a friendly manner. Some contemporary nomadic bands routinely intermingle with other bands; other bands actively avoid one another. In any event, it seems that thousands of years ago, some nomadic groups had repeated contacts with others. Individuals from the different groups bargained and traded with one another. In some cases, trade became common. Exchange relationships emerged out of the bargaining encounters. When bands had repeated friendly contacts with each other and exchanged goods, members of the bands could then intentionally establish contact with each other for the purpose of trade. The invention and elaboration of the exchange relationship probably preceded the establishment of sedentary communities and provided one of the foundation stones for the emergence of sedentary communities.

The exchange relationship did not emerge from members of nomadic bands bargaining with other members of their own bands. First, the members of these bands had few possessions, and of the few they had, most members of each particular band possessed the same items. Second, the solidary relationship of nomadic bands operates to promote sharing, not bargaining. During times of stress, members of nomadic bands sometimes fail to share with one another. Then members of a band often compete and conflict for the necessities of life. Internal conflict over the necessities of life promotes fragmentation, not the elaboration of social relationships.

Many groups, both ancient and contemporary, have acquired some goods from other groups by raiding and looting. But intergroup contacts infused with hostility could not have provided the foundation for the elaboration of social relationships or the establishment of sedentary communities. The elaboration of social relationships that accompanied the establishment of sedentary communities rested upon the expansion of peaceful intergroup contacts. Neither internal conflict nor conflict between nomadic groups could have provided the foundation for the first sedentary communities.

Therefore, it seems likely that intergroup trade provided the foundation for the emergence of the exchange relationship, which in turn enticed some groups to become sedentary. After groups had repeated trade contacts with each other, when members of two bands who had a past of trading with each other met, they could activate an exchange relationship. Some individuals and groups became sedentary as they became more involved in intergroup trade. These developments spanned thousands of years.

The development of sustained intergroup exchange relationships was interlaced with intergroup hostilities. Groups as diverse as the simplest nomadic bands to the most powerful and complex modern civilizations often simultaneously maintain both hostile and peaceful relationships. For example, groups of Australian aborigines sometimes convened to trade with one another. Sometimes these meetings erupted into conflict. Both before and after World War II, Japan and the United States had extensive trade contacts. Similarly, the United States and the Soviet Union have both peaceful trade relations and almost routinely threaten each other.

Exactly how more elaborate social relationships and sedentary communities were achieved is unknown. But it seems likely that the transformation was brought about as some bands acquired access to a valued resource and traded that resource to other bands. The transformation from a nomadic life to a sedentary life seems to have first occurred in western Asia. The earliest sedentary communities seem to have been established when some individuals or groups settled in a region where a valued resource was plentiful (Couch 1984b, Chpts. 6 and 7). The transformation did not occur rapidly; nor did all societies become sedentary. Only a few sedentary communities were established; most remained nomadic. Finally, primitive markets were established. These markets became locations where several nomadic groups came to acquire valued goods.

Once sedentary communities were established, exchange relationships came to occupy a more central position in the lives of those living the sedentary life. Several communities of considerable size emerged before farming communities were established (Mellaart 1967; Couch 1984b). One item widely traded in western Asia was obsidian. Obsidian, in comparison to flint, is like steel compared to pig iron. Sharper and longer-lasting instruments can be made from obsidian than from any other common stone.

Obsidian probably was one resource that contributed to the extension of intergroup mercenary contacts and the emergence of the exchange relationship.

During the development and expansion of the ancient primitive markets, many other developments also took place. These centers became the targets of raiders and looters. Those who established the first sedentary communities had no greater wealth than did those who continued to live in nomadic bands. As the residents of these communities became sophisticated in trade, however, the residents of the trade centers acquired greater wealth than the members of nomadic bands. Their sedentary life allowed the traders to accumulated more items of value than could members of nomadic bands. Members of nomadic bands cannot accumulate many possessions. They must carry their possessions as they move from location to location. Any items not regularly used are discarded.

The greater wealth of the residents of the sedentary community acted as a magnate to the surrounding nomadic groups. In bountiful times, nomadic groups trekked to these ancient markets to acquire goods via trade. In stressful times, some went to the sedentary communities in search of the necessities of life. They had little to offer residents of the sedentary communities in exchange. They were not able to acquire the necessities of life by trade. Sometimes, the nomadic groups stole from and raided the sedentary communities. Warfare between sedentary and nomadic groups became common. Many of the sedentary communities were destroyed. It has been estimated that the settlement at Jordan, one of the most ancient sedentary communities, was destroyed at least sixteen times.

One of the consequences of conflicts between sedentary communities and nomadic groups was that residents of the sedentary communities built walls to defend themselves. For example, it seems that the first two communities established at Jordan did not have walls. The communities emerged and existed for several hundred years and then collapsed; they may have been destroyed by raiders. The third time a community emerged at that location, the residents built a wall. In order for a community to become sufficiently organized to construct a defensive wall it is necessary for the community to establish accountable relationships and probably some authority or tyrannical relationships.

Agricultural communities emerged from the early primitive markets and trade centers. The domestication of plants, especially wheat and barley, provided an additional resource that allowed these communities to achieve larger populations. These agricultural communities in turn expanded and provided the foundation for the emergence of city-states and nations. Some of these communities became infused with authority and tyrannical relationships. Some of them in turn warred on others. Sometimes, these wars resulted in the destruction of one or both nations. At other times, the victorious nation established a tyrannical relationship with the loser and extracted tribute. In a few instances, as with the Roman Empire, millions of people became encased in macrostructures infused with tyranny.

The first nations appear to have emerged about 3000 B.C. Their emergence seems to have been coterminous with the emergence of complex and multitiered authority/tyrannical relationships. The first complex and multitiered hierarchical relationships seem to have been developed by the Sumerians in Mesopotamia about 3,000 B. C. (Adams 1966; Couch 1984b; Wright 1977; Wright and Johnson 1975). At that time, a new kind of specialist was established in some Sumerian city-states—the *sanga*. The *sanga* were the first administrators; they were in charge of the economic wealth of their communities. Originally, the *sanga* maintained records of community resources and.were accountable to the citizens of their communities. As the administrative apparatus enlarged and military operations became more common, the elite members of the administration and military became less accountable to the rank-and-file members of their communities. Complex, rigid, and multitiered hierarchical relationships emerged. The elite of these communities systematically exploited the rank and file. Social unity was maintained on the basis of asymmetrical accountability, coercion, and monopoly of knowledge. Totalitarian societies became established in several regions.

The citizens of these ancient civilizations were encased by a much more complex macrostructure than were the members of nomadic bands and residents of primitive markets. The solidary relationships that prevailed in primitive bands and the exchange relationships that prevailed at the primitive markets were supplemented and to an extent replaced by asymmetrical relationships. The citizens of these societies lived an entirely different life than did members of food gathering bands and members of small trade centers and simple agricultural communities. Subsequently, other forms of social relationships developed, but these social forms were largely the consequence of internal processes.

Internal Developments

The coordinated actions necessary for survival in nomadic groups are usually achieved by members of the band being attentive and responsive to each other as they undertake activities contextualized by parental and solidary relationships. Some members of nomadic bands establish reputations as good hunters; they provide leadership, but usually they do not have the prerogative of directing the actions of others. A member of a nomadic band who has the reputation of a good hunter does not thereby become an authority. All who have studied nomadic bands agree that authority relationships are seldom part of the social structures of nomadic bands. The members of nomadic groups usually reject any efforts to establish authority relationships. Sometimes, one of the members of these groups attempts to establish an authority or tyrannical relationship; more often than not, this results in group fragmentation. Other members of the band simply reject the effort to establish an authority relationship.

The nomadic bands that existed before the establishment of sedentary communities, like contemporary nomadic groups, probably had macrostructures that included at least parental and solidary relationships. Elements of accountable and romantic relationships may have been present. But ethnographic studies indicate that accountable and romantic relationships are present only minimally, if at all, in many contemporary bands of hunters and gatherers.

Accountable relationships are such a taken-for-granted part of our lives that it is difficult to imagine a society without them. Yet some nomadic groups seem to have endured without them. In some nomadic groups, one individual seldom calls another into account; nor do members of these societies make themselves accountable to one another. They do not feel obliged to each other. Among the Dakota Indians, "Autonomy was a prerogative of all, young and old, men and women" (Lee 1959, 65). Members of these societies had affection and compassion for each other and assumed responsibility for each other's welfare, but they were not accountable to each other. "The Dakota were responsible, but were accountable to no one for their conduct. Responsibility and accountability had nothing in common for them" (Lee 1959, 65).

The members of some primitive groups actively avoid becoming obliged. For example, a saying among some Eskimo groups is "Gifts make slaves; like whips make dogs" (Carpenter 1973). They do not wish to become obliged to others by taking a gift. Members of societies without accountable relationships have affection for, hostility toward, and an embeddedness with others, but they are not obliged to one another.

If viable accountable relationships are not present in a society, authority relationships cannot be established. Several contemporary nomadic groups established procedures that inhibited the emergence of authority relationships. The Mesquakie Indians, for example, did not seem to have developed authority relationships before their contact with Western Europeans. The Mesquakie, on occasion, raided other groups. It would seem that before they could undertake raids, they would have to have activated an authority relationship. If they did, it was only a nebulous form of authority. Raids were undertaken by one young man indicating that he was going to go raid another group and calling for others to join him. If others indicated a willingness to join the undertaking, a raid was mounted. Yet those who agreed to go did not become subordinates of the one who initiated the raid. The relationship between the organizer and others was that of the leader and the led. It seems to have had greater similarity to a charismatic relationship than to an authority relationship. Anyone who joined the raid and became disenchanted with the enterprise felt free to leave the raiding party without providing an account (W. Miller 1955).

Furthermore, if by chance the raid was successful, the members of the raiding party had to complete a purification ritual before they were allowed to rejoin the tribe (W. Miller 1955). If the raid was unsuccessful, it was not necessary to complete the purification ritual. Apparently, this tribe wanted to prevent any authority relationship from becoming established on the basis of a reputation acquired by military exploits.

Exactly when and how accountable and authority relationships emerged and became established within societies will probably never be known. Furthermore, it is likely that accountable and authority relationships emerged at many times in many different groups. Some of these groups endured; others disintegrated.

It seems some elements of accountable and authority relationships emerged as kinship systems were elaborated. All known human societies have a kinship system (Murdock 1949). A feature of all kinship systems is the specification of who is obliged to care for infants and young children. When these duties are specified the parental relationships are infused with elements of accountability—although the degree of accountability is often minimal. In some societies, if the adult male who is responsible for providing the necessities of life for an infant or child fails to do so, he may be the target of gossip, but he is not necessarily called into account.

In many primitive societies nebulous authority relationships are part of the kinship system. In a patriarchical society, the eldest male of each family occupies a focal position and in some nomadic societies has the prerogative of giving orders to other members of his family and expecting obedience. The emergence of authority relationships as part of the kinship system may be limited to sedentary primitive groups. In some nomadic groups, neither the father nor the mother nor anyone else necessarily has an authority relationship with young children. Obedience is not a universal feature of family structures. Among the Wintu Indians, when a child asked, "Can I," he was not asking for permission but "for information of the rules of the structure; for instance, they may be seeking clarification about a religious taboo or a social custom" (Lee 1959, 6). Among the Wintu, parents did not give permission to their children, "because it was not theirs to give" (Lee 1959, 6).

The development of enduring accountable and authority relationships probably was not intentional; enduring accountable, authority, and tyrannical relationships probably emerged as the consequence of action taken by citizens of sedentary communities to protect themselves from attacks by other communities. For example, among the ancient Sumerians when a community was under threat of attack, the community appointed one man as war leader. He was given the title *luga*. The ancient Sumerians established a temporary authority relationship in which the person vested with authority was accountable to the community. That temporary relationship transformed first into an enduring authority relationship and then became tyrannical. In subsequent generations, the title *luga* came to mean "king."

Much the same seems to have occurred in many other ancient sedentary societies. When the person who is the temporary focal point of an asymmetrical relationship becomes the permanent occupant of the position and is not accountable, the subordinates lose control of their own lives. In some of the ancient groups, however, when asymmetrical relationships emerged, they provided a means for larger numbers of people to act in unison and at least in some instances contributed to the survival of the groups. Some of these civilizations then conquered and subordinated less powerful groups.

The transformation of human life from that of small solidary groups to that of complex structures suffered from many fits and starts and went down many different paths. Some of the paths were dead ends; they did not contribute to the emergence of large macrostructures. Other developments contributed to the expansion of macrostructures but also resulted in much human suffering. Some contributed to both the expansion of macrostructures and human welfare.

The emergence of each new social form has transformed human existence. Each of these transformations was achieved by human beings developing new social relationships. Some of the social relationships have given human beings new opportunities, but with each new opportunity, new constraints also emerged.

The movement of human beings from a world of nomadic bands to that of contemporary civilizations has involved a dynamic and continual interplay between the social actions of human beings and the macrostructures they have invented. The emergence, modification and devolution of social relationships continues. No social structure is static.

The Micro-Macro Dichotomy

Most social activity is essentially dyadic, yet most social encounters are contextualized by intertwined social relationships. That feature of human conduct is probably responsible for the emergence within social science of micro- and macroanalyses of social life. The dichotomy between micro-and macroanalyses has become taken for granted by many social scientists. It is generally accepted that students of interpersonal processes examine microprocesses, and institutional sociologists examine the structures of large organizations and societies. In general (there are exceptions), the two sets of specialists have given little attention to the other. Each has proceeded quite independently of the other. One might say that each set of specialists has regarded the work of the other as irrelevant to their own work.

The dichotomy between micro- and macroanalysis is justified for some purposes, but has had some unfortunate consequences. It has enticed some microanalysts to ignore the context that encases the microprocesses they study. Many studies of microprocesses have been completed without giving any attention to the macrostructures that contextualize the microprocesses investigated.

Conversely, many who have made analyses of macrostructures have proceeded by giving little, if any, attention to social action. Many who adopt the macroposition stress the importance of the structures of human institutions and ignore the fact that human life exists only in movement. Unless human beings act with each other, there is no society. Social structures emerge out of social action and in turn provide a structure for social action. The boss and worker interact within a context provided by their conceptions of the authority relationship. They do not merely have a formal relationship but also act toward, for, against, and with each other within the context provided by their particular relationship. Each encounter between a boss and a worker is contextualized by both a generic social relationship and the particular social relationship that have created as they have acted in unison in the past. A comprehensive analysis of the interaction of bosses and workers requires that attention be given to both macro (generic) factors and micro (particular) factors.

In recent years some students of human conduct have attended to both microprocesses and structures and macrostructures. For example, Strauss and his associates have attended to both processes and structures in their studies of negotiations and awareness contexts (Glaser and Strauss 1964, 1967; Strauss 1978, 1985). Farberman (1975) in his study of the automobile industry and Denzin (1977b) in his study of the liquor industry attended to both process and structure. And there are others.

An Alternative

Some social scientists have called for a merger of the two kinds of analyses. The most promising line of attack for acquiring greater understanding of human affairs is what has been called the "bottom up" approach (Collins 1981; Couch 1984a). Briefly, the argument is that if attention is first focused on simple units of social action, greater understanding will be achieved than if attention is originally focused on the formal properties of large structures. The organization of this book has been from the bottom up. Attention was first focused on the microprocesses of how newborn human infants become incorporated into the social structure that surrounds them, how they acquire the ability to communicate with others, how they then acquire the ability to construct various forms of social action with others. Attention was then given to how human beings develop, use, and are constrained by social relationships.

The two modes of analysis are not inherently contradictory. Each has and will continue to expand our understanding of social life. Nonetheless, if microanalysts would attempt to incorporate a concern with macrostructures into their research endeavors and theorizing, and if macroanalysts would recognize that all macrostructures are human inventions maintained and modified by human beings aligning their actions with each other, greater understanding of the social life would be acquired.

Human beings produce social processes every time they establish copresence and act with respect to each other. After they have acquired command of forms of social relationships, the processes they produce are contextualized by mutually activated social relationships. On occasion, people fail to establish a mutually recognized social relationship. Sometimes they do not understand one another; other times they have incongruent intentions; and other times one or both are incapable of activating a social relationship. Then they must turn their attention to the establishment of a social relationship before they can complete a complex unit of social action.

To understand any given social transaction requires giving attention to the activity produced in the immediate situation, the social relationship(s) activated, and the marcostructure that contextualizes the activity. The significance of an act is not derived solely from the act and the relationship(s) activated. The significance of a social act also stems from the macrostructure that encases the act. Students of human life must simultaneously attend to both process and structure.

CONCLUSIONS

It is obvious that macrostructures both free and constrain human beings. Those who live in complex societies have both less freedom and more opportunities than those who live in simple societies. Some of the social forms developed and used by human beings have generated much suffering; others have generated joy; some have been responsible for both. Some have provided security, others excitement. All the forms of social relationships that human beings have developed, imposed, adopted, and discarded have provided both freedom and constraints.

Perhaps if we acquire more knowledge of how the various forms of social activity and social relationships are produced, and more knowledge of the consequences of various social relationships, some of the pitfalls of the past can be avoided. Also, perhaps if we use our imaginations to invent new forms, we will be able to structure our future actions more wisely than has sometimes been the case. The primary obligation of social scientists is to contribute to that development.

GLOSSARY

ACCOUNT. An explanation and/or an apology for disturbing another person.

ADVERSE IMPINGEMENT. An act that is stressful to another.

ASYMMETRICAL RELATIONSHIP. The unequal distribution of power, responsibilities or prerogatives between people that endures across encounters.

AUTHORIZATION. The collective assignment of responsibilities and/or prerogatives to a person or a social unit.

BILATERAL RESPONSIVENESS. A condition created when two people are reciprocally attentive and take each other into account in the organization of their conduct but do not act with each other.

CATEGORICAL IDENTITY. The social identification and classification of a person as having an attribute shared with some others.

COLLECTIVE IDENTITY. Recognition that a plurality of persons share a significant characteristic that differentiates them from others.

COLLECTIVITY. Any plurality of individuals who are copresent and/or act with each other.

COMMON FOCUS. An event or object attended to by two (or more) people, but those attending the event or object are unaware of the focus of attention of the other.

COMMON PAST. The condition established when two (or more) people recognize that they have previously performed activity similar to that called for in the immediate situation, but those composing the encounter have not previously acted with each other.

COMMUNICATION. The sharing of symbolic information.

COMPATIBLE INTERESTS. Mutual recognition by two (or more) people that the interests of each person are different but agreeable.

CONGRUENT FUNCTIONAL IDENTITIES. The display and detection of compatible lines of forthcoming activity by two (or more) people.

CONTINGENT FUTURES. A condition created when two (or more) people mutually recognize that each of their futures depends on the actions of the other(s).

COPRESENCE. Mutual awareness by two (or more) people that each is part of the perceptual field of the other.

259

DISJUNCTIVE ACT. An act by one person that interferes with or prevents the achievement of an objective.

DISTAL FUTURE. An event that is anticipated but that will not occur until after some other event has occurred.

DIVISION OF LABOR. A mutual agreement between two (or more) people about who is responsible for the completion of specific tasks to achieve one or more social objectives.

DYAD. Two people capable of independent action, engaged in interdependent action.

x EXCHANGE ACT. The reciprocating transfer of goods and/or the reciprocating providing of services.

FUNCTIONAL IDENTITY. A line of action intentionally undertaken by one person that is noted by another person.

HONORING AN ACCOUNT. The acceptance of an explanation and/or apology offered by another for a disruption.

INCONGRUENT FUNCTIONAL IDENTITIES. The projection of future lines of action by two (or more) people that are incompatible; one projected future deflects or blocks the other projected future.

INSTRUMENTAL IDENTITY. Mutual recognition by two (or more) people of a task performed or to be performed outside the immediate situation.

INTERACTION. Simultaneous reciprocal influence.

INTIMACY. The mutual sharing of self or parts of self with another that are not shared with all others.

⊀ INTRUSIVE ACT. An act that disrupts the experiences and/or activity of another person.

MONOPOLY OF KNOWLEDGE. The control of information by one party that is relevant to the interest or welfare of others.

MUTUAL RESPONSIVENESS. A condition created when two (or more) are reciprocally attentive and each indicates to the other a willingness to relate to and act with the other.

MUTUALITY. Reciprocal pleasurable excitation.

MUTUALLY RECOGNIZED DIFFERENCES. Mutual understanding by two (or more) people that they disagree on some issue or that they have different standpoints.

OFFER-COUNTEROFFER SEQUENCE. The reciprocating set of offers made by bargainers as they attempt to formulate an agreement to effect an exchange.

PARALLEL ALIGNMENT. A condition created when two (or more) people are reciprocally attentive and produce identical or similar lines of action.

PROPOSAL-RESPONSE SEQUENCE. The reciprocating set of statements offered by negotiators in search of an alternative to resolve their differences.

PROXIMAL FUTURE. An event or accomplishment anticipated to occur in the immediate situation.

RECIPROCAL ALIGNMENT. A condition created when two (or more) people are reciprocally attentive and produce different, but congruent, lines of action.

RECIPROCAL ATTENTIVENESS. The condition created when two (or more) people direct their attention to each other.

RECIPROCALLY ACKNOWLEDGED ATTENTION. A condition created when two people indicate to each other that they have noted each other's attention.

REFLEXIVE ROLE-TAKING. The adoption of another person's standpoint toward oneself.

SHARED FOCUS. An event or object simultaneously attended to by two (or more) people with both aware that they are attending to the same event or object.

SHARED FUTURE. The mutual projection of a future that will have similar consequences for two (or more) people.

SHARED PAST. Mutual awareness by two (or more) people that they have acted with each other prior to the immediate situation.

SIGNIFICANT GESTURE. An act produced with the intention of eliciting a specific response from another.

SIGNIFICANT SYMBOL. An act produced with the intention of eliciting a shared sensation, shared standpoint, and/or co-orientation.

SOCIAL COMMITMENT. An agreement between two (or more) people that obliges one or both of them to act in a specific manner in the future.

SOCIAL OBJECTIVE. A potential future accomplishment projected by two (or more) people that structures their activity.

SOCIAL RESPONSIVENESS. A condition created when two (or more) people are reciprocally attentive and indicate that the presence and/or activity of the other is taken into account in the organization of each person's behavior.

SOLIDARY RESPONSIVENESS. A condition created when two (or more) people indicate to each other that they have a shared focus and respond in unison to the shared focus.

STANDPOINT. A position or point of view adopted toward an event or object or a series of events and objects.

STRUCTURALLY SITUATED. The condition created when two (or more) people mutually acknowledge a categorical identity of each of them as relevant to their activity in the immediate encounter that is also linked to the external macrostructure.

BIBLIOGRAPHY

Abel, Theodore. 1968. *The Nazi Movement.* New York: Prentice-Hall. Originally published in 1938 as *Why Hitler Came to Power.*

Adams, Robert McC. 1966. *The Evolution of Urban Society.* Chicago: Aldine.

_____ 1981. *Heartland of Cities.* Chicago: University of Chicago Press.

Allee, Randel D. 1982. "Is Bargaining Alive in Salvage Yards and Salebarns?" Manuscript.

Altheide, David, and John Johnson. 1980. *Bureaucratic Propaganda.* Boston: Allyn and Bacon.

Althusser, Louis and Elienne Babbar. 1970. *Reading Capital.* New York: Panthion Books.

Arendt, Hannah. 1973. *The Origins of Totalitarianism.* New York: Harcourt Brace Jovanovich.

_____ 1976. *Eichmann in Jerusalem: A Report on the Banality of Evil.* New York: Penguin Books.

Ball, Donald W. 1981. "Sarcasm as Sociation: The Rhetoric of Interaction." In Gregory P. Stone and Harvey A. Farberman, eds., *Social Psychology through Symbolic Interaction,* 147-53. New York: Wiley.

Bettelheim, Bruno. 1943. "Individual and Mass Behavior in Extreme Situations." *Journal of Abnormal and Social Psychology* October):417-52.

Birch, A. H. 1971. *Representation.* New York: Preager.

Blake, Robert E., and Jane S. Mouton. 1961. "Loyalty of Representatives to In-group Position during Inter-group Competition." *Sociometry* 24:177-83.

Blumer, Herbert. 1969. *Symbolic Interactionism.* Englewood Cliffs, NJ: Prentice-Hall.

_____ 1980. "Mead and Blumer: The Convergent Methodological Perspectives of Social Behaviorism and Symbolic Interactionism." *American Sociological Review* (June):409-19.

Buban, Steven L. 1976. "Focus Control and Prominence in Triads." *Sociometry* 39 (September):281-88.

Byrne, Patricia. 1982. "Can Interpersonal Accounting between Different Sites and Groups be Compared." Manuscript.

Carpenter, Edmund. 1973. *Oh, What a Blow That Phanton Gave Me!* New York: Holt, Rinehart and Winston.

Collins, Randall. 1981. "The Microfoundations of Macro Sociology." *American Journal of Sociology* 85:984-1004.

Couch, Carl J. 1982. "Temporality and Paradigms of Thought." In Norman K. Denzin, ed., *Studies in Symbolic Interaction,* 4:1-24. Greenwich, CT: JAI Press.

_____ 1984a. "Symbolic Interaction and Generic Sociological Principles." *Symbolic Interaction* (Spring):1-13.

_____ 1984b. *Constructing Civilizations.* Greenwich, CT: JAI Press.

_____ 1986a. "Questionnaires, Naturalistic Observation and Recordings." In Carl J. Couch, Stanley L. Saxton, and Michael A. Katovich, eds., *Studies in Symbolic Interaction: The Iowa School,* 45-60. Greenwich, CT: JAI Press.

_____ 1986b. "Elementary Forms of Social Activity." In Carl J. Couch, Stanley L. Saxton, and Michael A. Katovich, eds., *Studies in Symbolic Interaction: The Iowa School,* 113-30. Greenwich, CT: JAI Press.

262

Couch, Carl J., and Robert A. Hintz, Jr. 1975. *Constructing Social Life*. Champaign, IL: Stipes.

Couch, Carl J., Stanley L. Saxton, and Michael A. Katovich. 1986. *Studies in Symbolic Interaction: The Iowa School*. Greenwich, CT: JAI Press.

Couch, Carl J. and Marion W. Weiland. 1986. "A Study of the Representative-Constituent Relationship." In Carl J. Couch, Stanley L. Saxton, and Michael A. Katovich, eds., *Studies in Symbolic Interaction: The Iowa School*, 375-92. Greenwich, CT: JAI Press.

Darley, John, and Bib Latane. 1968. "Bystander Intervention in Emergencies: Diffusion of Responsibility." *Journal of Personality and Social Psychology* 8:377-83.

Denzin, Norman K. 1977a. *Childhood Socialization*. San Francisco: Jossey-Bass.

_____ 1977b. "A Case Study of the American Liquor Industry: Notes on the Criminogenic Hypothesis." *American Sociological Review* 43:905-20.

_____ 1978. *The Research Act*. 2nd ed. New York: McGraw-Hill.

Dittman, Allent. 1972. "Developmental Factors in Conversational Behavior." *Journal of Communication*. 22:404-23.

Dobert, Eitel. 1940. *Convert to Freedom*. Translated by Heinz and Ruth Norden. New York: Putman's.

Dow, Thomas E., Jr. 1968. "The Role of Charisma in Modern African Development." *Social Forces* 46 (March):328-38.

Eiseley, Loren. 1961. *Darwin's Century*. Garden City, NY: Doubleday.

Epstein, David F. 1984. *The Political Theory of the Federalist*. Chicago: University of Chicago Press.

Farberman, Harvey A. 1975. "A Criminogenic Market Structure: The Automobile Industry." *Sociological Quarterly* 16:438-57.

Finley, Moses I. 1973. *The Ancient Economy*. Berkeley: University of California Press.

Genovese, Eugene. 1976. *Roll Jordon, Roll*. New York: Random House.

Glaser, Barney G., and Anselm L. Strauss. 1964. "Awareness Contexts and Social Interaction." *American Sociological Review*, 29 (October):669-79.

_____ 1967. *The Discovery of Grounded Theory*. Chicago: Aldine.

Gross, Edward, and Gregory P. Stone. 1964. "Embarrassment and the Analysis of Role Requirements." *American Journal of Sociology* 70:1-15.

Gulliver, P. H. 1979. *Disputes and Negotiations*. New York: Academic Press.

Hanfslaengl, Ernst F. S. 1957. *Hitler: The Missing Years*. Edited by Brain Connell. London: Eyre and Spotteswoods.

Hardesty, Monica J.. 1986. "The Formal Analysis of Processual Data." In Carl J. Couch, Stanley L. Saxton, and Michael A. Katovich, eds., *Studies in Symbolic Interaction: The Iowa School*, 89-105. Greenwich, CT: JAI Press.

Hardesty, Monica J. and Michael A. Katovich. 1986. "Two Triadic Interaction Contexts of Socialization." In Carl J. Couch, Stanley L. Saxton, and Michael A. Katovich, eds., *Studies in Symbolic Interaction: The Iowa School*, 269-94 Greenwich, CT: JAI Press.

Hewitt, John P., and Randall Stokes. 1975. "Disclaimers." *American Sociological Review* 38 (February):1-11.

Hilberg, Raul. 1961. *The Destruction of the European Jews*. New York: Harper & Row.

Hintz, Robert A., Jr. 1975. "Foundations of Social Action." In Carl J. Couch and Robert A. Hintz, Jr., eds., *Constructing Social Life*, 47-64. Champaign, IL: Stipes.

Hintz, Robert A., Jr., and Carl J. Couch. 1975. "Time, Intention and Social Behavior." In Carl J. Couch and Robert A. Hintz, Jr., eds., *Constructing Social Life*, 27-46. Champaign, IL: Stipes.

Holmberg, Allan R. 1969. *Nomads of the Long Bow*. Garden City, NY: The Natural History Press.

Homans, George C. 1974. *Social Behavior: Its Elementary Forms*. New York: Harcourt, Brace and World.

Ikle, Fred C. 1964 *How Nations Negotiate*. New York: Harper & Row.

Innis, Harold A. 1951. *The Bias of Communication*. Toronto: University of Toronto Press.

_____ 1972. *Empire and Communication*. Revised by Mary Q. Innis. Toronto: University of Toronto Press.

Katovich, Michael A. 1984. "Symbolic Interactionism and Experimentation: The Laboratory as a Provocative Stage." In Norman K. Denzin, ed., *Studies in Symbolic Interaction, 5*, 49-67. Greenwich, CT: JAI Press.

_____ 1986 "Temporal Stages of Situated Activity and Identity Activation." In Carl J. Couch, Stanley L. Saxton, and Michael A. Katovich, eds., *Studies in Symbolic Interaction: The Iowa School*, 329-52. Greenwich, CT: JAI Press.

Katovich, Michael A., Marion W. Weiland, and Carl J. Couch. 1981. "Access to Information and Internal Structures of Partisan Groups: Some Notes on the Iron Law of Oligarchy." *Sociological Quarterly* (Summer):431-46.

Keil, Dana. 1977. "Markets in Melanesia?" *Journal of Anthropological Research* (Fall):258-276.

Kogon, Eugene. 1950. *The Theory and Practice of Hell*. Translated by Heinz Norden. New York: Berkley.

Kuhn, Manford H. 1964. "Major Trends in Symbolic Interaction Theory in the Past Twenty-Five Years." *Sociological Quarterly*, 5:61-84.

Labov, William. 1973. "Rules and Ritual Insults." In David Sudnow, ed., *Studies in Social Interaction*, 120-69. New York: Free Press.

Lee, Dorothy. 1959. *Freedom and Culture*. New York: Prentice-Hall.

Leichty, Marilyn G. 1975. "Sensory Modes, Social Action and the Universe of Touch." In Carl J. Couch and Robert A. Hintz, Jr., eds., *Constructing Social Life*, 65-79. Champaign, IL: Stipes.

_____ 1986. "Social Closings." In Carl J. Couch, Stanley L. Saxton, and Michael A. Katovich, eds., *Studies in Symbolic Interaction: The Iowa School*, 231-48. Greenwich, CT: JAI Press.

Lemert, Edwin M. 1981. "Paranoia and the Dynamics of Exclusion." In Gregory P. Stone and Harvey A. Farberman (eds.), *Social Psychology through Symbolic Interaction*, 415-28. New York: Wiley.

Lofland, Lynn. 1973. *World of Strangers*. New York: Basic Books.

Luckenbill, David F. 1980. "Criminal Homicide as a Situated Transaction." In Delos H. Kelly, ed., *Criminal Behavior*, 275-90. New York: St. Martin's Press.

Lutfiyya, May Nawal, and Dan E. Miller. 1986. "Disjunctures and the Process of Interpersonal Accounting." In Carl J. Couch, Stanley L. Saxton, and Michael A. Katovich, eds., *Studies in Symbolic Interaction: The Iowa School*, 131-48. Greenwich, CT: JAI Press.

Maines, David R. 1977. "Social Organization and Social Structure in Symbolic Interaction Thought." *Annual Review of Sociology*, 235-59.

_____ 1981. "Recent Developments in Symbolic Interaction." In Gregory P. Stone and Harvey A. Farberman (eds.), *Social Psychology Through Symbolic Interaction*, 461-86. New York: Wiley.

Markey, John F. 1928. *The Symbolic Process*. New York: Harcourt, Brace.

Marshack, Alexander. 1972. *The Roots of Civilization*. New York: McGraw-Hill.

Masters, William H., and Virginia E. Johnson. 1970. *Human Sexual Inadequacy*. Boston: Little, Brown.

Masters, William H., and Virginia E. Johnson, in association with Robert J. Levin. 1974. *The Pleasure Bond*. Boston: Little, Brown.

McPhail, Clark. 1979. "Experimental Research is Convergent with Symbolic Interaction." *Symbolic Interaction* (Spring):89-94.

Mead, George Herbert. 1932. *Philosophy of the Present*. LaSalle, IL: Open Court Press.

_____ 1934. *Mind, Self and Society.* Chicago: University of Chicago Press.

_____ 1938. *The Philosophy of the Act.* Edited by Charles W. Morris. Chicago: University of Chicago Press.

Mellaart, James. 1967. *Catal Huyuk: A Neolithic Town in Anotolia.* London: Thomas and Hudson.

Milgram, Stanley. 1963. "Behavioral Study of Obedience." *Journal of Abnormal and Social Psychology* 76:371-378.

_____ 1965. "Some Conditions of Obedience and Disobedience to Authority." *Human Relations* 18:57-75

_____ 1968. *Obedience.* A film.

_____ 1974. *Obedience and Authority.* New York: Harper & Row.

Miller, Dan E. 1986a. "Milgram Redux: Obedience and Disobedience in Authority Relations." In Norman K. Denzin, ed., *Studies in Symbolic Interaction,* 7, 77-106. Greenwich, CT: JAI Press.

_____ 1986b,. "Hypnosis as Asymmetric Interaction" In Carl J. Couch, Stanley L. Saxton, and Michael A. Katovich, eds., *Studies in Symbolic Interaction: The Iowa School,* 167-94. Greenwich, CT: JAI Press.

Miller, Dan E., Robert A. Hintz, Jr., and Carl J. Couch. 1975. "The Elements and Structure of Openings." In Carl J. Couch and Robert A. Hintz, Jr., eds., *Constructing Social Life,* 1-24. Champaign, IL: Stipes.

Miller, Dan E., Marion W. Weiland, and Carl J. Couch. 1978. "Tyranny." In Norman K. Denzin, ed., *Studies in Symbolic Interaction,* 1, 267-88. Greenwich, CT: JAI Press.

Miller, Walter. 1955. "Two Concepts of Authority." *American Anthropologist* (April):271-89.

Miyamoto, S. Frank. 1970. "The Social Act: Re-examination of the Concept." In Gregory P. Stone and Harvey Farberman, eds., *Social Psychology Through Symbolic Interaction,* 293-99. Waltham, MA: Ginn-Blaisdell.

Molseed, Mari O. 1986. "Time and Form in Triadic Interaction." In Carl J. Couch, Stanley L. Saxton, and Michael A. Katovich, eds., *Studies in Symbolic Interaction: The Iowa School,* 255-68. Green, CT: JAI Press.

Morley, Ian E. and Geoffery M. Stephenson. 1977. *The Social Psychology of Bargaining.* London: Allen and Unwin.

Moser, Mark G. 1982. "A Look at Interpersonal Accounting." Manuscript.

Murdock, George P. 1949. *Social Structure.* New York: Macmillan.

Neff, Ronald. 1975. "Toward an Interactionist Theory of Social Structure." In Carl J. Couch and Robert A. Hintz Jr., eds., *Constructing Social Life,* 183-93 Champaign, IL: Stipes.

Philby, Gregory. 1983. "Decisions, Decisions, Decisions: A Study of Two Forms of Authority." Manuscript.

Piliavin, I. M., J. A. Piliavin, and J. Rodin. 1969. "Good Samaritanism: An Underground Phenomenon?" *Journal of Personality and Social Psychology* 13:289-299.

_____ 1975. "Costs, Diffusion, and the Stigmatized Victim." *Journal of Personality and Social Psychology* 32:429-38.

Pitkin, Hanna E. 1967. *The Concept of Representation.* Berkeley: University of California Press.

_____ 1968. "Commentary: The Paradox of Representation." In J. Roland Pennock and John W. Chapman, eds., *Representation,* 38-42. New York: Atherton Press.

Polanyi, Karl. 1957. *The Great Transformation.* Boston: Beacon Press.

Powell, Joel O. 1986. "Diffusion and Social Relations." In Carl J. Couch, Stanley L. Saxton, and Michael A. Katovich, eds., *Studies in Symbolic Interaction: The Iowa School,* 295-308. Greenwich, CT: JAI Press.

Rosenthal, A. M. 1964. *Thirty-eight Witnesses.* New York: McGraw-Hill.

Rubin, Jeffrey Z., and Bert R. Brown. 1975. *The Social Psychology of Bargaining and Negotiation.* New York: Academic Press.

Saxton, Stanley L., and Carl J. Couch. 1975. "Recording Social Interaction." In Carl J. Couch and Robert A. Hintz, Jr., eds., *Constructing Social Life,* 255-62. Champaign, IL: Stipes.

Scheff, Thomas J. 1970. "Negotiating Reality: Notes on Power in the Assessment of Responsibility." *Social Problems* 16:3-17.

Schegloff, Emanuel A. 1968 "Sequencing of Conversational Openings." *American Anthropologist,* 70(December):1075-95

Schegloff, Emanuel A., and Harvey Sacks. 1973. "Opening Up Closings." *Semiotica VII* 4:290-327.

Schreibman, Laura, and Robert L. Koegel. 1975. "Autism: A Defeatable Horror." *Psychology Today* (March):61-67.

Scott, Marvin B., and Stanford M. Lyman. 1968. "Accounts." *American Sociological Review* 33 (February):46-62.

Sehested, Glenda J. 1975. "The Evolution of Solidarity." In Carl J. Couch and Robert A. Hintz, Jr., eds., *Constructing Social Life,* 99-118. Champaign, IL: Stipes.

Sehested, Glenda J., and Carl J. Couch. 1986. "The Problem of Authoritarianism and Laboratory Research." In Carl J. Couch, Stanley L. Saxton, and Michael A. Katovich, eds., *Studies in Symbolic Interaction: The Iowa School,* 61-78. Greenwich, CT: JAI Press.

Simmel, Georg. 1949. "The Sociology of Sociability." *The American Journal of Sociology,* 55 (3).

_____ 1950. *The Sociology of Georg Simmel.* Translated and edited by Kurt Wolff. New York: Free Press.

_____ 1971. *On Individuality and Social Forms.* Edited by Donald N. Levine. Chicago: University of Chicago Press.

_____ 1981. "On Visual Interaction." In Gregory P. Stone and Harvey A. Farberman, eds., *Social Psychology Through Symbolic Interaction,* 97-106. New York: Wiley.

Sink, Barbara Burger, and Carl J. Couch. 1986. "The Construction of Interpersonal Negotiations." In Carl J. Couch, Stanley L. Saxton, and Michael A. Katovich, eds., *Studies in Symbolic Interaction: The Iowa School,* 149-66. Greenwich, CT: JAI Press.

Smith, Adam. 1937. *The Wealth of Nations.* New York: Modern Library.

Speer, Albert. 1970. *Inside the Third Reich.* Translated by Richard and Clara Winston. New York: Macmillan.

Spindler, George D., and Louise Spindler. 1971. *Dreamers without Power: The Menomini Indians.* New York: Holt, Rinehart and Winston.

Stone, Gregory P. 1981a. "Appearance." In Gregory P. Stone and Harvey A. Farberman, eds., *Social Psychology Through Symbolic Interaction,* 107-14. New York: Wiley.

Stone, Gregory P. 1981b. "Appearance and the Self: A Slightly Revised Version." In Gregory P. Stone and Harvey A. Farberman, eds., *Social Psychology Through Symbolic Interaction,* 187-202. Boston: Houghton-Mifflin.

Strauss, Anselm, L. 1978. *Negotiations: Varieties, Contexts, Processes and Social Order.* San Francisco: Jossey-Bass.

_____ 1985. "Work and the Division of Labor." *Sociological Quarterly* (Spring):1-20.

Travisano, Richard V. 1975. "Comments on a Research Paradigm for Symbolic Interaction." In Carl J. Couch and Robert A. Hintz, Jr., eds., *Constructing Social Life,* 272-280. Champaign, IL: Stipes.

Traynowics, Laurel. 1986. "Establishing Intimacy." In Carl J. Couch, Stanley L. Saxton, and Michael A. Katovich, eds., *Studies in Symbolic Interaction: The Iowa School,* 195-208. Greenwich, CT: JAI Press.

Turner, Ralph H. 1953. "The Quest for Universals in Sociological Research." *American Sociological Review* 24(June):605-611.

Wallace, Anthony F. C. 1972. *The Death and Rebirth of the Seneca.* New York: Vintage Books.

Weber, Max. 1964. *The Theory of Social and Economic Organization.* New York: Free Press.

Weiland, Marion W. 1975. "Forms of Social Relations." In Carl J. Couch and Robert A. Hintz, Jr., eds., *Constructing Social Life,* 80-98. Champaign, IL: Stipes.

Weiland, Marion W., and Carl J. Couch. 1986. "The Disintegration and Solidification of Newly Formed Partisan Groups." In Carl J. Couch, Stanley L. Saxton, and Michael A. Katovich, eds., *Studies in Symbolic Interaction: The Iowa School,* 309-21. Greenwich, CT: JAI Press.

Weiland, Marion W., and Carl J. Couch. 1975. "Representative-Constituent Relationships and Their Consequences." In Carl J. Couch and Robert A. Hintz, Jr., eds., *Constructing Social Life,* 208-35. Champaign, IL: Stipes.

Wilson, E. O. 1975. *Sociobiology: The New Synthesis.* Cambridge, MA: Belknap Press of Harvard University Press.

_____ 1978. *On Human Nature.* Cambridge, MA: Harvard University Press.

Wright, Henry T. 1977. "Toward an Explanation of the Origin of the State." In Ronald Cohen and Elman R. Service, eds., *Origins of the State: The Anthropology of Political Evolution,* 49-68. Philadelphia: Institute for the Study of Human Issues.

Wright, Henry T., and Gregory A. Johnson. 1975. "Population, Exchange and Early State Formation in Southwestern Iran." *American Anthropologist* (June): 267-89.

Author Index

268

Subject Index